Spirited Women

Spirited Women

A History of Catholic Sisters in British Columbia

DEBORAH RINK

Published by the Sisters' Association Archdiocese of Vancouver
749 West 33rd Avenue, Vancouver, BC V5Z 2K4

Produced by Harbour Publishing

Page design and layout, cover design by Martin Nichols, Lionheart Graphics
Editing by Rick Dykun
Cover photograph courtesy Archives, Sisters of Providence of St. Vincent de Paul
Backcover photographs courtesy Sisters of the Child Jesus Archives, North Vancouver
(top) and Immaculate Heart Community Archives, Los Angeles

Printed in Canada

Canadian Cataloguing in Publication Data

Rink, Deborah, 1954–
    Spirited women

    ISBN 0-9687804-0-7

    1. Monastic and religious life of women—British Columbia—History. 2. Nuns—British Columbia—History. 3. Nuns—British Columbia—Biography. 4. Catholic Church—British Columbia—Biography. I. Catholic Church. Archdiocese of Vancouver. Sisters Association. II. Title.

BX4220.C2R56 2000   271'.900711   C00-911087-9

To all those spirited women whose legacy has provided us with role models for the future.

CONTENTS

Chapter Three—The Turn of the Century

PART II—COMMUNITY BUILDING 1913–1945

Chapter Four—Education and Health

Chapter Five-Growing Needs

PART III—CONTEMPORARY TIMES
1946 TO THE PRESENT

Chapter Six—Changing Habits

ACKNOWLEDGEMENTS

Thank you to the Archdiocese of Vancouver Sisters' Association for supporting this history project and especially to the following members:

Sister Helen Boyle
Sister Therese Carignan
Sister Loretta Ehman
Sister Jessie Gillis
Sister Agnes Herzog
Sister Cecilia Hudec
Sister Rita Kehoe
Sister Thérèse Kergoat
Sister Kathleen Murphy
Sister Katherine Nickerson
Sister Rita Tellier
Sister Margaret Vickers
Sister Patricia Wallace

A special thank you to Mae Waldron for her friendship and her editorial role and all the archivists who assisted in the research of this book. Grateful acknowledgement is due to the numerous individuals and organizations that provided moral and financial support.

PART 1

Settlement

1858–1912

CHAPTER ONE

The First Mission

The spread of nunneries is a rough indicator of the spread of learning among women.[1]

Vision of a Mystic
Saint Marguerite Bourgeoys (1620–1700)

Empowered by a spiritual vision, Marguerite Bourgeoys established the first school in the colony of Ville-Marie on the Isle de Montreal. Her courage and determination encouraged communities of women religious worldwide to follow in her footsteps. Two hundred years later the spiritual charism of Marguerite Bourgeoys would inspire Esther Blondin to guide a community of women religious on their journey to the new colony of British Columbia.

Marguerite Bourgeoys's legacy began when the Sisters of the Congregation of Notre Dame invited her to become a member of their extern congregation.[2] The sisters' cloistered community in Troyes, France, was dedicated to the education of girls. Although grammar schools had existed for poor urban children since the fifteenth century, by the seventeenth century

Marguerite Bourgeoys 1620–1700.
Marguerite Bourgeoys Museum

the "educational disadvantaging" of girls was standard: girls learned only rudimentary skills and were denied access to higher education.[3] To help realize their educational mission, the cloistered sisters trained externs such as Marguerite Bourgeoys to teach both girls and boys in poor urban neighbourhoods.

Convinced of the importance of their work and its success in Troyes, the sisters wanted to help children in the growing communities in New France. They discussed their intentions with Paul de Chomedey, who had founded the colony of Ville Marie on the Isle de Montreal in 1642. Although the colony was ten years old when the sisters approached de Chomedey, he believed the frontier conditions not only made it "impossible to have cloistered religious in such an outpost," but that only one teacher would be required in such a small colony.[4] The sisters were determined to expand their mission with de Chomodey's permission and assured him that one of their extern members would accompany them. However, he insisted that only one teacher was needed in the small colony. Marguerite volunteered to go despite the fact that she would have to travel alone.

The decision to leave was difficult. Daunted by the prospect of travelling on her own to a distant frontier and torn by her recent long-awaited acceptance into the much-cherished Carmelite community, Marguerite faced a challenge and a choice. Like the mystics who preceded her, Marguerite was inspired by a vision. A tall woman clad in a white robe spoke words of encouragement, instilling her with immense power and strength: "This gave me confidence for the voyage, and gave me great courage, and after that I found nothing difficult...I left Troyes without a stitch, without a penny, with only a little package that I could carry under my arm."[5]

Marguerite set out from Troyes and travelled west to Paris, an exhausting experience of endless jostling over rutted country roads. She found little relief at the inns along the stagecoach route, where her physical discomfort was replaced by fear for her personal safety: "I could not leave the coach...all these men said many insulting things to me...I closed the door and barricaded it with everything I could find."[6]

Marguerite risked her reputation by disregarding the social standards of the day, which cast serious doubt on the character of a single woman travelling alone. Even Mme Le Coq, with whom she had made previous arrangements for an overnight stay in Nantes, delayed Marguerite's arrival until her husband returned home. This married woman of some social standing believed her own reputation would be tarnished if she admitted to her home a young woman travelling without a companion.

Neither Marguerite's appearance nor her actions provoked the attitudes she encountered. Although not a religious, her modest attire reflected her association with women religious and her vow to live in perpetual celibacy and poverty. She was referred to as Sister Bourgeoys. The reproaches she endured reflected the subjugation of women of her day, which relegated them to the private sphere and afforded them few opportunities in the public realm, including the freedom to travel.

Travel, a means of exploring and learning, potentially created peril for women. In accomplishing her mission, Marguerite took a bold step forward that flew in the face of the patriarchal norm. Not only did Marguerite travel alone, but she did so as part of her goal to expand the intellectual sphere of women. She accomplished this at great risk.

After arriving in New France in 1653, Marguerite tended to the needs of the poor and the sick in Ville Marie as there were not yet enough students to establish a school. At that time the colony consisted of only a few cabins. Within five years the community's population increased and Marguerite began teaching in a humble stone stable donated to her by the colony's governor. Soon the increased responsibilities and activities of educating the children combined with caring for the poor in the growing community became too much for one woman. Marguerite journeyed to France for help and returned with three women from the extern congregation.

These women lived together, dedicated to their mission of education. The community's respect for Marguerite earned her the title Mother Bourgeoys, and the externs, that of her "daughters." Bishop Laval permitted them to teach in his Diocese of Montreal only because they were not officially sanctioned as a religious community. The bishop believed it unacceptable for professed women religious actively to participate in secular society, in keeping with a centuries old tradition of the Church.

The Law of Enclosure, which saw all professed sisters as cloistered "contemplatives," was in place from the fourteenth to the seventeenth century. In the early seventeenth century, Saint Francis de Sales attempted to reverse the Law of Enclosure by establishing the Visitation Nuns as "contemplatives-in-action."

However, it was not until the middle of the century that Saint Vincent de Paul officially succeeded in securing active work for professed religious by founding the Daughters of Charity. Established to care for the poor, the Daughters of Charity expanded their sphere of influence by considering "their monasteries, the houses of the sick and their cloister, the streets of the city." Expanding the limits of acceptability, women religious successfully reached beyond the private sphere into public life.

The colonists of New France were supportive of Mother Bourgeoys and her companions, and in 1671 successfully petitioned King Louis XIV of France to allow the sisters to establish a religious community called the Sisters of the Congregation of Notre Dame on the Isle de Montreal. The next year, Mother Bourgeoys brought six more women from France to assist with the ever-increasing work. Bishop Laval, however, was not pleased. He found it difficult to accept the idea of a religious community of non-cloistered women in his diocese. Mother Bourgeoys and her daughters persevered. Five years later, Bishop Laval officially approved the foundation of the non-cloistered community of the Sisters of the Congregation of Notre Dame on the Isle de Montreal. This gave them freedom to practise religious life while actively contributing to secular society. Their courageous achievements paved the way for Esther Blondin two hundred years later.

The Sisters of Saint Ann
Foundation

Esther Blondin—the venerable Mother Marie Anne 1809–1890. Archives Sisters of St. Ann, Victoria, BC

Marguerite Bourgeoys and the Sisters of the Congregation of Notre Dame inspired countless women to expand their intellectual life through the pursuit of education and the tradition of their religious vocation. Two centuries later, Esther Blondin (1809–1890), motivated by the enduring spirit of Marguerite Bourgeoys, aspired to become a member of the Sisters of the Congregation of Notre Dame in Montreal. Esther first encountered the religious community in her hometown of Terrebonne, Quebec, in 1831. Here, enrolled as a resident student at the age of twenty-two, Esther Blondin learned how to read. The next year she joined the Sisters of the Congregation of Notre Dame, but her delicate health necessitated withdrawal from the religious community.

Esther accepted a position as teaching assistant at the village school in Vaudreuil, Quebec, a few years later. She excelled as an educator and within eight years was the director of Blondin Academy, a reputable boarding school for young country girls.[7] Confident of herself and her mission, she approached the powerful bishop of Montreal, Ignace Bourget, to ask permission to form a community of religious in rural Quebec who would dedicate their lives to educating girls and boys. With the increasing population of Montreal and its surrounding countryside, Bishop Bourget welcomed the formation of a new community of women religious. In 1850 the bishop granted permission for Esther to found the Daughters of Saint Ann.[8] Despite the tradition of gender segregation, the sisters intended to teach boys and girls, but were compelled by circumstances to focus on the education of girls.

At the time of the daughters' formation, eight women assisted Esther Blondin, now called Mother Marie Anne, in the mission of education. When Bishop Modeste Demers arrived at their motherhouse in 1858, their community numbered forty. The bishop hoped the growing community could spare a few members to teach in the frontier mission of Fort Victoria, the fur-trading post from which he had recently arrived. Bishop Demers requested the Sisters of Saint Ann to teach the "children of the forest," and the children of the local employees of the Hudson's Bay Company.[9]

Although under financial strain, the young community of the Sisters of Saint Ann agreed to extend their mission of education beyond the rural communities of Quebec to the colony of Vancouver Island. Saddened at the

The first missionary Sisters of Saint Ann.
Archives Sisters of St. Ann, Victoria, BC

thought of leaving home forever but stirred by the excitement of adventure and the plea of Bishop Demers, many stepped forward to volunteer for the journey ahead. The religious community could spare only four women to accompany Bishop Demers to Fort Victoria. Courageous in their commitment, Sister Mary of the Sacred Heart (Salome Valois), Sister Mary Angèle (Angèle Gauthier), Sister Mary Lumena (Virginia Brasseur) and Sister Mary of the Conception (Mary Lane) departed Quebec for the distant island. In a letter to her family, Sister Mary Lumena reflected on her mission to the "foreign land":

> You know the words which Our Lord addresses to his followers: "To those who for the love of me have left father, mother, sisters, brothers, friends and possessions, I will give a hundred-fold in this life and life everlasting, that is, the happiness of Heaven, in the next."

Having understood these words, can one resist them? Can any sacrifice be too great? No it is not too much; it is not enough for one who has understood the false maxims of the world, and who follows in the footprints of Christ. For my part, dear Parents, what have I done? You knew already I have left the world. I have gone from a good father, a tender mother, from brothers and sisters who were very dear to me, and by whom I was tenderly loved. I have gone from the house in which I was born, to go and live with strangers whom I have adopted as my own kindred. My first sacrifice was followed by another—that of leaving my community in which I had thought of remaining forever, to go to a distant land. Need I describe what my heart went through in this separation? To this community, to these companions I said farewell, but I shall live its life.[10]

The Journey West

Bishop Demers considered both the overland expedition and the route around Cape Horn to be too hazardous. The latter had already claimed a missionary group of Sisters of Providence, who were lost to pirates and rerouted to South America. Instead, Bishop Demers decided that the safest route for the missionary group would be to arrive in Fort Victoria by way of Panama.

The sisters left their motherhouse in Saint-Jacques, Quebec, and set off in a carriage for the island of Montreal. They unloaded their baggage from the carriage into rowboats and manoeuvred across the icy Saint Lawrence, dodging the spring floes. After arriving safely on the other side, they trudged through fifteen acres of muddy fallow where their "feet became as large as their heads."[11] Another carriage took them to Montreal, where they joined the bishop and his religious companions. For the long trip ahead the clergy discreetly camouflaged themselves as seculars. Following the bishop's example, the sisters concealed their crosses and rosary beads during the journey to avoid any disrespectful comments from strangers.

On April 14 the religious entourage boarded the train for New York. They arrived at 7:00 p.m. on April 16 and stayed with the Sisters of Charity, whose hospitality allowed them a good night's rest before they left the next day on the SS *Philadelphia*. Throughout the voyage the captain requested their presence at his table, where they were served "the best of everything."[12] Accustomed to pumpkin sauce rather than butter, and all too familiar with meat porridge, molasses bread and tea, the sisters relished the delightful feast at the captain's table, where real butter, chicken, turkey and the "choicest desserts," as well as wine and champagne were served.[13]

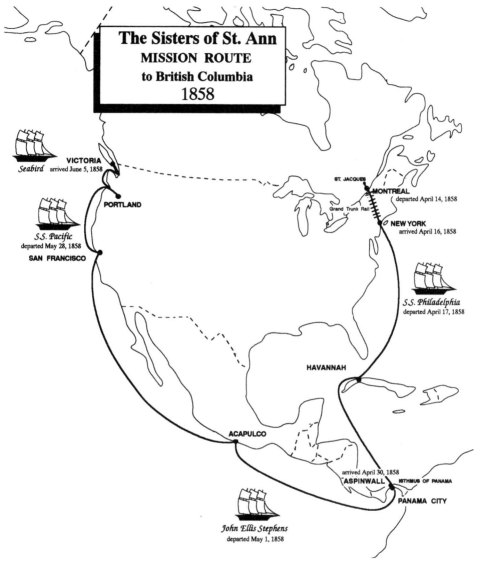

Mission route to British Columbia. Deborah Rink

During the voyage, some of the passengers queried the destination of the group—California or the Cariboo—assuming that all aboard were bound to seek their fortune in gold. Sister Lumena recounted the incident in a letter to her parents: "…we told them we did not seek gold, but the betterment of society through education. We could not say the word religion for those who addressed us were not of our belief…"[14]

On April 30 they arrived at Aspinwall, where they took the three-hour train ride across the Isthmus of Panama: "The ride through a country of fruit trees and palms is very interesting. The trees are tall and slender—very different from those of our Laurentides. The bananas which line the route has [sic] immense leaves, ten to twelve feet long and from three to four feet wide. They bear great bunches of fruit called by the same name."[15]

On the Pacific side, anchored six miles offshore at Panama City, the *John E. Stephens* prepared to take them to San Francisco. In black robes that felt heavier by the moment, the sisters languished on the dock under the hot tropical sun. Low tide prevented them from reaching the ship by rowboat. Instead, the sisters were carried to the waiting boat by men, a situation they found most distressing: "…What, we exclaimed, must those negroes pack us over? No, never. But dire necessity compelled us to yield. As for myself, I refused the services of the first one who presented himself, because I considered him too small; the second could not move me; the third, who was taller than the other two, but not much stronger, bore me over with all the trouble in the world…It is more pleasant to tell you this than to have gone through it. This bareback trip of some ninety feet cost a dollar a piece, but my carrier clamoured for more pay, since, he said, I weighed more than the others."[16]

Sister Lumena described it like this:"I who had never seen colored people was reluctant to be hoisted on one of them. I screamed twice when the carrier tried to lift me. But it had to be. My hold on him was very light…We took the precaution of hiring those who wore shirts…"[17]

The next day they cast off for San Francisco and noted once again the differences between themselves and the other passengers:"After supper we went on deck to get fresh air, and in payment had to witness the dancing which invariably took place. How much variety there was in dress and manners among this gay throng!…Accustomed as we are to live in seclusion, we find ourselves sadly out of place in these worldly amusements. In spirit, we transport ourselves to our dear community where silence reigns almost continually."[18]

In San Francisco they stayed for two weeks with the Sisters of Saint Vincent de Paul and then departed on May 28 aboard the SS *Pacific* for the last leg of their journey. After safely crossing the treacherous Columbia Bar, they arrived in Portland, Oregon, where the citizens and clergy of the town urged them to remain and teach. However tempted by this generous offer of a comfortable convent, the sisters' commitment to Bishop Demers prevailed and they continued on to their destination of Fort Victoria.

Island Mission

On June 5, 1858, more than six weeks after the sisters had left their Quebec motherhouse, the SS *Seabird* carried the missionary group into Victoria harbour: "How beautiful it looked to us, with its forest of green trees, grassy slopes and the picturesque rocky coast. The steamer rounded a headland, we entered the bay and there Victoria lay before us."[19]

To the surprise of the sisters and the astonishment of the bishop, the settlement did not appear as Bishop Demers had described it. During his absence, gold seekers destined for the Cariboo had poured in and the small fort, once surrounded by only a few cabins, had grown into a town teeming with two hundred newly constructed houses and an endless array of tents. The population had grown from three hundred to six thousand in a matter of a few months.

The missionary group rowed to shore, where a small crowd of the Catholic faith greeted them. Later, two prominent citizens who would become patrons, Dr. John Sebastian Helmcken and Mrs. Helmcken, served them a meal of venison. When evening fell, the bishop escorted the sisters to their new convent dwelling at the base of Beacon Hill, below the bishop's residence. Brother F.G. Thibodeau, one of the missionaries who had accompanied them during the voyage, described this first convent as "…a little house made of tree trunks, thirty feet by eighteen feet, quite isolated, no fence, no outhouses, not even a woodshed, no well and for exterior embellishment, nothing but brush and tall grass…This house was separated in two with rough boards and a chimney…The walls were not plastered and there was no floor upstairs. The furniture consisted of a broken chair and a table of raw wood."[20]

The bishop apologized for the state of their new home, which was situated in the swamp at the end of James Bay. Although the broken windows and unlocked doors would not keep them safe, he prayed that the "Blessed Virgin, Saint Joseph and the Holy Angels" would provide them with protection.[21] The sisters unpacked their few belongings and settled in for the night.

Two days later they began their mission. The mattresses they slept on at night were piled into a corner during the day to make space for themselves and a few students. On one side of the chimney they taught and on the other side they cooked. The bishop sent a daily pail of beef, cornflour, salted salmon and molasses, providing them with sustenance until they could fend for themselves.

In October, just four months after their arrival, the bishop made over the title deed of the land to the Sisters of Saint Ann. By mid-November, Brother Thibodeau and Brother Joseph Michaud, who had voyaged with them from Montreal, constructed a small addition to their cabin, which was by now operating as a convent, school and orphanage. The addition included a chapel with a twelve-foot belfry and a new bell. The brothers built tables, chairs, desks, washstands and beds to ready the convent for classes to start in the new addition on November 15. The bishop assisted by printing a brochure to advertise their teaching venture.

Convent school and orphanage with Beacon Hill in the background.
Archives Sisters of St. Ann, Victoria, BC

The first students who attended the school varied in age and nationality, and in social and economic status. Sister Lumena remarked, "Our boarders are English, American and German. The day scholars, with the exception of three who are sisters, are half-breeds and coloured children."[22]

Three daughters of Sir James Douglas, governor of the colony of Vancouver Island, attended the school. One of the "mixed race" students was a little orphan girl, Emilia Morrell, whose Native mother had died recently in the log cabin before the sisters arrived and whose French father had subsequently left her in the care of the sisters. The black students were the progeny of African-American parents who had come as free persons from the United States or had escaped there from slavery. When a new staff member, Sister Mary Providence Tucker, arrived from Quebec the following year, the total enrolment reached fifty-six. The first item on her agenda was to deal with the problem of overcrowding in the little log convent school.

Sister Mary Providence claimed ancestry from a privileged background in Ireland, where she had been taught by governesses and tutors and had benefited from a refined education in poetry, rhetoric, logic, philosophy, literature, mathematics, history and French. After a downturn in her family's fortune, she moved with them to Montreal. Sister Mary Providence and her companion, Sister Mary Bonsecours, followed the same travelling route as the first missionaries. Along the way they took the opportunity to visit schools in New York and San Francisco, arriving at Fort Victoria in September 1859. At the age of twenty-two, Sister Mary Providence was named superior of the Victoria community, relieving Sister Mary of the Sacred Heart of this duty. The latter welcomed the replacement, being content to contribute to the community as cook and housekeeper.

Sister Mary Providence alleviated the problem of overcrowding at the log cabin school by opening a school on Broad Street in downtown Victoria. She rented a one-storey building for twenty-five dollars a month and set up two classrooms. The first classroom, known as the free school, operated much like

Sister Mary Providence Tucker 1853–1904.

the log cabin school. The second room, known as the select school, admitted only white students. The free school charged a fee of one dollar per month and admitted non-white students, while the select school charged two dollars and fifty cents and admitted white students only.

The free school welcomed children of any denomination, race or ethnic background, whereas the select school denied most of these children admittance. According to Sister Mary Theodore, the parents of "coloured" children complained that their children were not admitted to the select school. Having so recently gained their freedom, and "imbued with a spirit of equality," [23] they subsequently complained to the bishop, who decided to let their children enrol in the select school. Complaints from the parents of white children followed and the bishop reversed his decision. The result was withdrawal of the "coloured" children from the school.

Racial segregation and discrimination permeated mid-nineteenth century Victoria and all of British Columbia. It was reflected in the separation of "officers" and "servants" of the Hudson's Bay Company and was perpetuated by the social elite through marriage.[24] Where marriage between social classes occurred, tolerance prevailed only because of the few women available for marriage. Where interracial marriage occurred, tolerance waned.

As the Hudson's Bay Company lost its power in colonial society, the British landowner elites replaced them and also snubbed the merchant class of the gold rush, whose growing numbers included Americans, Europeans, Jews, Chinese and African-Americans. Prejudice and discrimination existed in rural areas also, as exemplified in the ever-increasing marginalization of Native people. Generally, racial segregation structured the society, manifesting itself in the division of labour and the subsequent inability of the disadvantaged groups to gain wealth or power.

Educational segregation also existed in the form of gender bias. In Reverend Cridge's "Report of District Schools" in 1856, he commented on the need for a girls' school: "It seems greatly to be lamented that those who are likely hereafter to perform so important a part in the community in the capacity of wives and mothers, should be suffered to grow up without Education."[25] The social norm was the centuries-old tradition of gender-defined roles rooted in the sexual division of labour. Although a few co-educational schools existed in Victoria at the time, boys typically learned separately from girls, the latter attending school only if parents could afford to send children of both sexes to school.[26] Society upheld these conventions, perpetuating the concept of separate spheres of influence for men and women, limiting the latter's opportunities for financial autonomy and limiting their power to make decisions in the public realm.

Mother Mary Providence, undaunted by imposed limitations, was known to repeat on many occasions, "A woman's influence is not limited; life will be mostly what women truly wish it to be."[27]

During the leadership of Mother Mary Providence (1859–1881), the Sisters of Saint Ann would expand their sphere of influence through the construction of seven more institutions. These would provide educational opportunities for girls and other disadvantaged groups, including Native people, and would provide health care for minorities and the poor. Although they were humble at first, over time the institutions developed into large and extremely reputable facilities.

The Broad Street School in downtown Victoria was staffed by Sister Mary Lumena and Sister Mary Providence. Every Monday morning the sisters left their log cabin convent to spend the week teaching at the new school. At times the inclement weather nearly overpowered them, with winds almost blowing them to the ground or leaving them covered in mud by the time they arrived at school. Despite few provisions for teaching, they managed to hold classes every day. The sisters retired very early at night, covering the school windows to ensure that not even a small candle was seen burning. This prevented the intrusion of unruly passersby, who occasionally chose to extend their evening's festivities into the early hours of the morning just outside the sisters' doorstep. The two sisters returned every Friday evening to the comfort and security of the little log cabin, where they resumed their community life with the others.

In September 1860, just a year after the sisters established the Broad Street School, they were given another facility to manage. Bishop Modeste Demers presented a title deed to the sisters for a piece of land where he had built, for five thousand dollars, a fifteen-by-eleven-metre brick building. The View Street Convent, as it came to be known, also functioned as a school and orphanage. The sisters initially registered thirty-six pupils, but by the end of the year, enrolment had doubled.

Sisters and children at the View Street Convent. Archives Sisters of St. Ann, Victoria, BC

The sisters' workload increased as they expanded to house more students. Apart from operating the View Street and Broad Street schools, the six sisters still operated the log cabin (sometimes referred to as the country school), tended to the upkeep of the cathedral, cooked, mended and washed for fifteen priests and maintained the bishop's house. Maintaining the bishop's house had been added to their list of obligations only recently, as it had been the duty of Miss Marie Mainville, a layperson who had accompanied the sisters on their initial voyage from Quebec: "[It] was thought that, in a pioneer country such as Vancouver Island, the Sisters should have with them a discreet lay person to fill errands. Volunteer and free service for such a mission required a heroic, semi-religious vocation...."[28]

When Marie became ill the sisters relieved her of her duties at the bishop's house and cared for her while she recovered. Marie remained active with the sisters until the age of fifty-eight, when she returned to Montreal to enter the convent of the Sisters of Saint Ann.[29]

When the four sisters first arrived in Victoria, Marie had assisted them in domestic affairs. Whenever she went out in public as part of her work for the sisters, proposals of marriage often followed: "[Miss Mainville] was asked in marriage as much as three times in one day. She was given gifts and great promises were made to her, and among the numerous offers she received, some were sincere and favourable. Her piety and her innocence saved her in some instances, and her faithfulness to the Sisters made her refuse in other instances."[30]

Not surprisingly, in a gold-rush town populated by men, Marie was not the only woman of this first group of missionaries who received marriage proposals. Sister Mary Angèle was dismayed by an offer of marriage from a Frenchman. Despite the black habit she wore and the ring on her finger, he appeared unaware that she had committed herself to God. Her indignant reply to his offer prompted him to make a scandalous remark about her and the bishop. The chaste young woman was relieved when the Frenchman took the rumour no further.

The growing needs of the expanding population in Victoria demanded more help than the limited number of sisters could give. In 1863 eight Sisters of Saint Ann left their motherhouse in Lachine, Quebec, to assist in Victoria. Along with four priests, sixteen Sisters of the Holy Names and eight Sisters of Providence, the Sisters of Saint Ann formed part of a large group of missionaries that left Quebec for Oregon, Washington and British Columbia. Now totalling fourteen, the sisters could more adequately serve the needs of the western mission.

All too soon, however, fourteen became thirteen. Six months after her arrival in Victoria at the age of twenty-four, Sister Mary Emmerentienne died. This self-sacrificing missionary sister never recovered from the arduous journey to the western frontier. Like many others, the hardships of religious life deprived Sister Mary Emmerentienne of old age. Although the average lifespan of a Sister of Saint Ann in the nineteenth century was thirty-four, fifty percent died in their twenties. To mark Sister Mary Emmerentienne's passing, the remaining sisters planted a white hawthorn tree at her gravesite to commemorate the first death of a missionary sister in British Columbia.

Cowichan

Even with the setback of Sister Mary Emmerentienne's death, the new reinforcements from the motherhouse allowed the sisters to accept preschool boy boarders in the log cabin, to embellish the burgeoning music department with three new and talented sisters and to reorganize the View Street Convent. They also enabled the Sisters of Saint Ann to fulfil a request from Bishop Demers to open a boarding school for Native girls near the Quamichan tribal camp in the Cowichan area.

One hundred acres had been set aside for the mission in 1862. The Sisters of Saint Ann could not purchase the land under their name because successful legislation for the incorporation of the religious community of the Sisters of Saint Ann did not occur until 1892. Out of necessity, Mother Mary Providence solved the problem by purchasing the land under her maiden name, Mary Ellen Tucker. The purchase required Sister Mary Providence and Sister Mary Bonsecours to travel sixty-five kilometres by canoe to choose a location for the new convent boarding school. Upon their arrival they chose a building site about one-and-a-half kilometres from a trail leading to the Quamichan tribal camp.

Later, with only a few personal effects and a cow given to them by an ex-miner, Sister Mary of the Sacred Heart and Sister Mary of the Conception left Victoria on the SS *Fideliter* bound for Cowichan. They arrived at Maple Bay on October 10, 1864, where a team of oxen pulling a cart met them for the five-kilometre journey to their new mission on Vancouver Island.

In a clearing where giant trees once grew stood a rough nine-by-fifteen-metre log convent school built by the pioneers. They had volunteered to fell the trees and set the logs, thus enabling the sisters to fulfil their mission. The sisters put the finishing touches on their new building, chinking the logs with moss and preparing it for the little girls who would arrive from the nearby tribal camps: "[There were] no beds to be made as each boarder brought a mat to sleep upon, and a blanket to roll herself in. These she spread on the floor. There was little cooking to be done, as each was provided with smoked fish. There was no table to be set as the Indian girls squatted on the floor and ate with their fingers. By degrees they were taught the use of dishes, knives, forks and spoons."[31]

Twenty-two girls registered the first day, and school began. Registered names reflected the cultural diversity of the students: Natalie, Emilie, Catherine, Kwoentenath, Chilocet and Naksat. They included French and English children, as well as those from six Native tribes. Bishop Demers saw these children as "future mothers," young girls whom he believed "were being raised without any religious, moral or domestic training."[32] Cultural differences appeared to affect the students, resulting in irregular attendance and many children leaving before the school year had ended. They received "clothing, lodging, food and education free of charge [and] they were taught how to sew and to knit; they were washed, combed etc. [and] just when they were cleaned up and looking nice, they were not seen again."[33]

After twelve years, a day school replaced the boarding school. This allowed twenty-four "orphan boarders" in Victoria to be transferred to Cowichan. Sister Mary Theodore described how the orphans came to their care: "The word orphan is used as a kindly substitute for outcast, that is, children who were imposed upon the Sisters. The usual method employed was that of a parent, generally the father, making arrangements for his child as a boarder, and sometimes paying a sum in advance. That was the end of it so far as parental obligations went. Often these deserted children would be left many years to be cared for by the Sisters."[34]

The Cowichan mission received no government assistance and relied on school fees collected from those who attended day school. The sisters augmented the income for the orphans by teaching music lessons and holding bazaars. The Victoria sisters assisted by sending student fees received from boarders at the View Street Convent, and by sending provisions such as flour and sugar to Cowichan. This provided the sisters with supplies for a baking day, when they would fill a large stone oven with three-foot lengths of cedar and, after a couple of hours, rake out the coals and shut in the pans of dough until the air filled with the aroma of home-baked bread.

The sisters increased their self-sustenance at the mission by clearing a little land each year. By 1890, the log convent school, which had begun with a lone cow grazing humbly among the tree stumps, expanded into a productive farm with a vegetable garden and cows, horses, chickens, sheep and ducks. Eventually the Cowichan mission sisters reciprocated the generous donations of the Victoria sisters by sending them butter and meat.

Mainland Mission

In 1865, one year after the foundation of the Cowichan mission, Bishop D'Herbomez of the colony of British Columbia asked the Sisters of Saint Ann to help on the mainland in the "direction of a girls' school, as well as orphanages and hospitals."[35] Waiting for confirmation from their motherhouse in Lachine, the sisters in Victoria temporarily sent Sister Mary of the Conception from the Cowichan mission, and Sister Mary des Sept Douleurs from Victoria, to assist in operating a girls' school in New Westminster. This was the second Catholic school to open on the mainland of British Columbia, the first being a boys' school in Mission that was opened in 1863 and operated by the Oblate fathers. Three non-Catholic schools had opened earlier, one in 1859 in Sapperton, and two others in 1860 and 1862, both in New Westminster.

What began as "temporary assistance" by the Sisters of Saint Ann would last for more than one hundred years. A few years after the New Westminster convent and girls' school opened, Sister Mary Praxedes was named superior of the institution. Sister Mary Praxedes had professed her allegiance to the Sisters of Saint Ann at the age of seventeen and within five years began her twenty-two-year career in New Westminster. She raised the school from its "pioneer stage to the golden era of culture," introducing the students to music, art and "fancy work," subjects that passed from her to the girls like a "natural inheritance."[36]

The convent school, which would eventually be called Saint Ann's Academy, followed a program of studies and activities similar to those of the girls' school in Victoria. It opened the same year as its contemporary, Saint Louis College for boys, which was run by the Oblate fathers. The academy registered boarders as well as day students. The first registered day students included Mary, Elizabeth and Nellie Irving, daughters of the renowned Captain William Irving. The majority of boarders consisted of children of the "overlanders," wealthy ranchers and landowners from the interior who either hired governesses to educate their children or sent them to boarding schools such as the academy.

Not all of the students claimed high socio-economic standing. The school "harboured two distinct groups, the white children and the Indians and half-breeds."[37] The aboriginal children were taught in the kitchen, which doubled as their schoolroom:

> The three R's were taught until 10:30, when the Religion class began...Indian and half-breed pupils [at] attention [with their] arms crossed, sitting on benches; Sister Mary of the Conception, tall, grave, with the whole text of the Catechism in her memory, feeding the stove with food, attending to the kettle, pots, and pans,—questioning the class and imparting moral advice. At 11:00 o'clock dismissal; school room converted into a dining room for two nuns and eleven boarders. By one o'clock everything was restored to schoolroom order for the afternoon session. At three, visit to the Blessed Sacrament, and the school day was over, but many pupils preferred to stay and help the Sisters with the garden. [38]

The garden grew along with the academy. Apple, cherry and plum trees provided an abundance of fruit for the household supply. The vegetable garden produced many necessary food crops and the grounds flourished with lilacs, roses, lilies, gladioli, dahlias and its incomparable hedges. These hedges "grew from three different kinds of twigs, and rose from the crescent entrance on each side of the walk. They made an angle at the corners of the building, cutting off in this artistic fashion the front lawn from the playground and the vegetable garden. These well trimmed hedges were unsurpassed in both New Westminster and Victoria."[39]

Situated on Albert Crescent, Saint Ann's Academy became a landmark in New Westminster. In 1877, a two-storey brick-and-stone edifice replaced the original structure of 1865. When the sisters first purchased the property they felt compelled to yield to the grandiose scheme of the Oblate fathers of Saint Louis College, who involved themselves in plans for the new construction. The sisters decided, however, that the opulent display of two castle-like towers flanking the entry and parlours should be reduced to a single tower. Sister Mary Theodore provided a vivid description of the academy: "There is no doubt that with its ornamented dormer windows and gallery on the second storey, it was the most imposing as well as the most attractive feature along the length of the Fraser River. In the tower was a sweet-toned bell and a clock on whose dial time could be read at a considerable distance. The regular chiming of the hours and the half hours, and the ringing of the Angelus three times a day, with school calls between, was music to the citizens."[40]

St. Ann's Academy, New Westminster, 1878. Archives Sisters of St. Ann, Victoria, BC

Superior General Visits the West

In 1866 the missions of the Sisters of Saint Ann in British Columbia acquired vicariate status, with Sister Mary Providence appointed as the first sister vicar. The vicariate later developed into Saint Joseph's Province, whose religious territory coincided with the geographical boundaries of British Columbia. Along with this new provincial status, a new political framework ensued. Victoria became administrative centre of the new provincial jurisdiction, with Sister Mary Providence becoming Mother Mary Providence, the provincial superior, a position she held for twenty-two consecutive years.

Superiors were also appointed as administrative heads of smaller institutions, following the precedented framework of the larger institution. These local superiors, also addressed as "mother," took responsibility for the general operation of the institution they represented. Sister Mary Praxedes, for instance, became Mother Mary Praxedes when she took charge of Saint Ann's Academy in New Westminster. A hierarchy structured the responsibility given to each type of superior. The provincial superior oversaw the local superiors and the superior general presided over the entire community.

At the time of the installation of the Western Vicariate, the sister vicar, Mother Mary Jeanne de Chantal, was elected Superior General and was responsible for the entire community of the Sisters of Saint Ann. Because the Congregation of the Sisters of Saint Ann originated in Quebec, their motherhouse was located there also.

In 1866 Mother Mary Jeanne de Chantal left the motherhouse in Quebec to visit the mission sisters in Victoria. She brought with her five sisters who would remain with the growing mission colony. During her visit, Mother Mary Jeanne witnessed the first two religious professions in the West: Annie Farmer and Sarah Tucker became Sister Mary Patrick and Sister Catherine of Siena respectively.

Mother Mary Jeanne de Chantal returned to Quebec with the first two British Columbians to seek membership in the Congregation of the Sisters of Saint Ann, Cecilia and Anna McQuade. These two sisters encountered the Sisters of Saint Ann while students in the View Street Convent in Victoria and were inspired to enter religious life, as were many young women, by the exemplary life of the missionary sisters. Until the opening of the Western Novitiate in 1889, postulants were required to travel to the East to complete their preparation.

The notion of a marriageable young woman leaving Victoria perplexed the area's mostly non-Catholic male population. Negative attitudes toward women entering the convent prevailed in western literature during the mid-nineteenth century.[41] Paintings that appeared during this period portrayed women in convents as the victims of unhappy confinement or lost love, or as objects of desire that were inaccessible to men. Such ideas embodied narrow patriarchal views of women as objects seen strictly as wives and mothers, and perhaps this mindset explained the attitude of Cecilia McQuade's suitor. The story of Cecilia McQuade relates her bidding goodbye to her family and friends at the Victoria harbour. An assertive young suitor interrupted their parting farewells when he begged her to live with him, rather than choose to live in seclusion. Unmoved by his demonstrative offer of a rich social life, Cecilia enthusiastically went on to become Mother Mary Charles and was named the provincial superior in Victoria in 1914.

Mission Along the Fraser

With their ever-increasing numbers, the Sisters of Saint Ann were able to answer the ongoing requests for help from Bishop D'Herbomez. In 1868 Sister Mary Lumena and Sister Mary Bonsecours opened a school for girls at Saint Mary's Mission, where the Oblate fathers had established a school for Native boys five years earlier. Mother Mary Providence and Mother Mary Praxedes accompanied the two sisters up the Fraser River on a steamer. Bishop D'Herbomez, two priests and the first students of the mission, "mixed race" and Native girls from New Westminster, also travelled with them. Mother Mary Praxedes, recently appointed superior of the convent in New Westminster, was to ensure that the academy in New Westminster supplied provisions for the ongoing support of the neighbouring mission.

The entourage arrived on November 25, 1868, at a whitewashed building on the edge of the Fraser River with a majestic view of Mount Baker in the background. Amidst the three hundred acres of land purchased by the Oblate fathers of Mary Immaculate in an area known as the Matsqui Prairie, the sisters began their mission of educating Native girls, teaching in the rough lumber building that was five by fifteen metres in size. A supplemental lean-to provided space for cooking and dining. The main building served as the general living quarters and its upstairs dormitory accommodated up to thirty-six girls ranging from "baby-hood to marriageable age."[42] The school's first year was difficult: "... the novelty of civilized life did not appeal to the Indian boarders. Learning to sit on chairs, to eat at tables, to sweep and dust, to read and count, to sew and knit did not ward off their homesickness. They were sad, sullen and moody; they cried, they wept bitterly and loudly. They hid under tables or any secret place."[43]

Poverty exacerbated the situation. The sisters had to ration potatoes and when they could and bought a few pounds of pork to enhance the otherwise unpalatable soup pot. By Christmas the sisters had the means to cook a rice treat sweetened with molasses. At New Year's they baked a tiny loaf of bread for each student, and all of them found the unfamiliar food a novelty.

The following year, two sisters arrived from Victoria with fourteen aboriginal girls from New Westminster, who paddled up the river in a canoe led by the Mission chief. The sisters taught reading, writing and counting in addition to housekeeping, gardening and sewing. The girls excelled at sewing. Their skills created a demand for articles that sustained a twenty-five-year enterprise catering to Native people in the area. The skillful students enabled the sisters to operate a supply store of dry goods that stocked "bolts of prints, a quantity of yarn, needles, thread, shoes, etc."[44] The flannel and cotton shirts the girls made proved so popular that orders for the shirts were requested from the local store.

As the mission school developed, the sisters cleared land to grow vegetables and hay, and to provide room for cattle to pasture. The older girls learned how to milk the cows and make butter, but their skills were not limited to the traditional domestic realm: "In August 1889, twelve of the older girls set to build a twenty foot extension to the shed. They went to the woods where they cut the pillars and rafters, then they dragged them in place and fitted them in proper position. They also shingled the roof. This done, they levelled the kitchen yard, removed the brush, and filled ruts and holes. Their finishing touch to this outdoor work was digging up the potatoes and storing the vegetables for the winter. Then off they went to the classroom."[45]

Finally, in 1885, after enduring crowded conditions since their arrival almost twenty years previous, the sisters moved to a new convent on the picturesque plateau above the river. With its three storeys and floor-to-ceiling windows, it seemed like a mansion. The cost of furnishing the large new space, however, posed some concern, and rather than pay twelve dollars each for forty-two bedsteads, Sister Mary Lumena took up her hammer and saw. She built wood stands and laid mattresses across them, then made benches and cupboards for the school. To conserve materials she constructed washstands out of discarded beehives.

Expansion of the Sisters Educational Mission

The year after Saint Mary's Mission school opened, Mother Mary Providence left Victoria for Quebec to participate in the general elections of the Sisters of Saint Ann, which re-elected Mother Mary Jeanne de Chantal as superior general. Mary McEntee accompanied Mother Mary Providence because she wished to study in the Eastern Novitiate. They took the new Southern Pacific Railway, which had replaced the previous Panama route, reducing it to a much-preferred, eight-day overland journey. Upon her return to Victoria, Mother Mary Providence brought with her Sister Mary Beatrice, Sister Mary Winifred and Sister Mary Victor. These three professed sisters had come from Ireland, had entered the Quebec novitiate, and now wished to work in the expanding western missions of British Columbia.

During the year prior to their arrival, a devastating smallpox epidemic broke out in Victoria and the log convent school was turned into an isolation hospital under the direction of Sister Mary Virginia and Dr. J.S. Helmcken. The year the

St. Ann's Academy and grounds, 1871. BC Archives A-03432

Classroom at St. Ann's Academy, 1895. Archives Sisters of St. Ann, Victoria, BC

new sisters arrived, the log convent school was returned to classrooms to accommodate the huge increase in student enrolment. Additional classroom space became a dire necessity and at the sisters' request, a new convent school was erected across the street from the original building.

Mother Mary Providence again purchased land for the new Saint Ann's Convent on Humboldt Street. This purchase along with donations helped the sisters acquire the twenty-two lots (approximately seven acres) of the present-day grounds, an acquisition that took ten years to complete.

In 1871 British Columbia, which had included both the mainland and Vancouver Island since 1866, joined Confederation. The first lieutenant governor of the province officiated at the traditional cornerstone ceremony for the newly constructed Saint Ann's Academy. The architect presented the lieutenant governor with an inscribed silver trowel, and a succession of dignitaries including the federal minister of public works, the Honourable H.L. Langevin; Sir James Douglas; and Dr. J.S. Helmcken, proceeded to ritually strike the cornerstone with a mallet. A tin box under the cornerstone contained "a daily and weekly *British Colonist*, a daily *Standard* paper, some coins of 1871, relics given by Father Seghers and Mother Mary Providence, and the minutes of the ceremony on parchment."[46]

When British Columbia joined Confederation, the agreement included the completion of a transcontinental railroad to link eastern with western Canada. However, until 1885, when the last spike was driven into the rails at Craigellachie, travellers wishing to voyage across the newly formed country still travelled through the United States. In 1875, when eight missionary Sisters of Saint Ann departed from Quebec to assist the sisters in Victoria, they boarded the Central Pacific Railway at Montreal, travelled through Chicago and Omaha and completed the overland portion of their trip in San Francisco.

Railways represented the height of technological ingenuity during this era and allowed travellers to journey across land previously known only to its indigenous inhabitants and explorers. Sister Mary Emmanuel, one of the eight sisters who left for Victoria in 1875, described her first impressions of the people and the land she saw in a letter to her parents:

> A negro beautifully black, prepares our berths. We throw ourselves on our beds, but the incessant balancing of the train and its deafening noise defy all sleep…We take our meals at a small table in our section…The tenderest of mothers,—even a mother like mine,— could not have better provided for the needs of a dear daughter off on a long trip: good fresh bread, excellent butter, ham, chicken, eggs, sardines, tea, coffee, jam, fruit, etc…. After breakfast we pray for half an hour, and then walk up and down the aisle while the passengers are away…we roll by a number of small towns which all look alike; finally, each one takes a book and becomes absorbed in reading. After two days of this program, we arrive in Chicago…From there the train moves to Omaha with unabated hurry.

...We arrive in Omaha, Sept. 9 at eleven in the forenoon...We go to the ticket office to buy our tickets to San Francisco. We are objects of curiosity for the crowd looks at us with stupefaction as if we were beings from another planet. To be this gazed upon was intimidating, especially for our young Sisters aged eighteen and twenty.

... Here we are in California,—It is like a dream to me. I look with the keenest interest on this uneven country, every stone of which was eagerly coveted by gold-seekers. Ah! What toil has not this famous mineral caused to poor human beings! If half of this effort was spent in acquiring heavenly treasures, earth would be much happier, and heaven much fuller...[47]

Sister Emmanuel's letter reflected the exciting and sometimes intimidating experience of travelling to a foreign land. While her religious zeal motivated her to journey across the country to search out "heavenly treasures," others were equally moved to seek "earthly rewards." These cultural clashes reflected the reality of life in the western frontier.

Upon arriving in San Francisco, the Sisters of Saint Ann made the short journey across the bay to Oakland, where they stayed with the Holy Names Sisters. Eight days later they boarded a steamer for Victoria, and after enduring three days of seasickness, arrived at their destination.

The Sisters' Medical Mission: A New Hospital

The assistance of eight new sisters enabled the religious community to continue to meet the needs of the Victoria area, which had a population that now approached six thousand. A year after the new sisters arrived, the Sisters of Saint Ann opened Saint Joseph's Hospital in Victoria to help with the health care of the developing community.

The Sisters of Saint Ann's primary mission was education, but pioneer missions required a broad response by the sisters to meet the diverse needs of the community that they served. Even before their departure for the western mission in 1858, the sisters addressed the need to be trained in fields other than education. Two sisters had been sent to the Hotel Dieu Hospital in Montreal to gain experience for their "future duties of nursing and caring for the needy."[48]

In 1858 Sister Mary of the Conception began the nursing legacy in Victoria when she cared for the sick in their homes after school hours. Although the community welcomed this help, on at least one occasion her successful home remedies landed her in trouble with some of the local medical professionals. After doctors could no longer help an ailing child, the distraught mother called for Sister Mary of the Conception, who concocted a medicine she had seen her mother make. When Sister Mary administered her concoction, the baby appeared to be near death but within a few days regained its health.

One of the doctors did not share in the mother's gratitude and, perceiving Sister Mary of the Conception to be a threat to his business, requested that she be arrested for illegally practising medicine. Dr. J.S. Helmcken, who had befriended the sisters upon their arrival, came to Sister Mary's aid and had the threat of imprisonment dismissed.

In 1875 the Sisters of Saint Ann assisted in the successful recovery of Father Brabant, who had been shot. Father Brabant ministered to the aboriginal people in the vicinity of Clayoquot Sound on the northwest coast of the Island and recorded the incident in his memoirs: "Just then he shot again, this time hitting me in the right shoulder and all over my back.... Meanwhile I had been divested by some savages of my coat and underclothing. The Indians, upon noticing the blood, lost courage and one after the other walking out of the room, announced to their friends that I was dying. This was also my opinion...thinking that the best thing I could do was to pray and prepare myself to die." [49]

The bullet-riddled Father Brabant arrived in Victoria harbour from Hesquiat on HMS *Rocket* and sailors carried him from the ship up to the bishop's residence. After being placed on the dining-room table, Father Brabant recalled "warm water, towels, linen and other necessary articles" being brought for him by the sisters. [50] Five months later he was strong enough to return to Clayoquot Sound, where his amazing recovery profoundly affected those who witnessed it.

After almost two decades (1858–1876) of informal nursing, the Sisters of Saint Ann officially acknowledged their health-care ministry with the opening of Saint Joseph's Hospital. They also established a health insurance plan known as Saint Joseph's Hospital Society, offering membership to "all persons in good health, without distinction of age, sex, creed or color." [51] Memberships could be bought for one dollar a month, or one hundred dollars for a lifetime. These and other donations given to the sisters financed the thirty-five-bed red brick hospital.

In 1875, Archbishop Seghers spoke of the vital role the new hospital would play in the community: "Irrespective of creed or nationality, Saint Joseph's Hospital will open its doors to such as are afflicted with sickness; it will afford relief and comfort to persons of every condition and standing in society; it will give shelter within its walls to the poor, the needy, the friendless, and the houseless. [52]

On June 27, 1876, the building's official opening began with a procession and the blessing of a statue of Saint Joseph, patron saint of the hospital. During the festivities, an unscheduled admittance of the first patient occurred when attendants rushed a seriously injured Chinese worker into the facility.

St. Joseph's Hospital, Victoria, BC. Archives Sisters of St. Ann, Victoria, BC

The Education Mission at Williams Lake

The year Saint Joseph's Hospital opened, Sister Mary Clement, Sister Mary Joachim and Sister Mary Octavia departed for Saint Joseph's Mission at Williams Lake, where Bishop D'Herbomez had asked the sisters to staff a school for Native girls. Mother Eulalie, the visiting superior general from Quebec, and her travelling companion, Sister Mary Helen, accompanied them. After crossing the Gulf of Georgia to the mainland, the group travelled up the mouth of the Fraser River and arrived at the New Westminster convent. Here they spent a few days drawing up the terms for the Williams Lake mission with Bishop D'Herbomez. On September 16, 1876, the five sisters boarded a riverboat for Yale, where they would begin a perilous overland journey. In a letter to her sibling in Victoria, who was also a member of the religious community, one of the travelling sisters remarked, "I hope I shall not see you for a long time. I love you too much to have you undertake this terrible journey for my sake, and I do not love you enough to undertake it for yours."[53]

The women travelled to Williams Lake following the original route of the Cariboo Trail, a mule path of the gold-rush days that, since its improvements, was referred to as the Cariboo Road. The Cariboo Road began at Yale and was opened to stagecoach traffic in 1865. It extended for four hundred miles, with occasional roadhouses along the way providing lodging for travellers. Sister Mary Theodore described the treacherous journey:

> At one o'clock the Sisters took seats in the stage. Its six horses...[were] changed every twenty miles, sometimes less along the highway...It may have been exhilarating for the galloping horses, but it was terrifying for the travelling Sisters. From the road, so narrow at times as not to allow two coaches to meet, the Sisters saw precipices reaching down, down, to vociferous water; looking on the opposite side, they saw mountains which rose from the very wheels of their conveyance, barring the sky and all means of escape. These Sisters had already travelled long distances—some had come west by the Isthmus of Panama, and others by the Central Pacific, but never had they seen such angry canyons, such appalling heights.[54]

At one point the sisters' stagecoach met an oxen freight wagon. Although the trail had been widened to five-and-a-half metres, it allowed no room for carriages to pass. Perched high on a precipice, with swirling waters below, they deliberated. The men detached the horses from the stagecoach, giving Mother Mary Eulalie control of the reins. While she steadied the frightened animals, they unloaded the stagecoach and carefully lifted it over the top of the freight wagon and continued on their journey.

Trepidation diminished as the formidable canyons of the Fraser rolled into rugged ranchland. After three days, the stagecoach approached the San Jose Valley, where three rustic buildings comprising Williams Lake appeared faintly in the distance. Reverend Father James McGuckin greeted the sisters, along with Father Charles Francois Jayol and Brother Philippe Surel. The building that they called home measured twenty-four by six metres, "...with a lean-to kitchen and a room for a helper at the back. The main building was divided by a corridor; to the left was a chapel and a small office, to the right was a classroom and a dining room."[55]

Again terror crept into the women's hearts when they spent the first night listening to a large pack of what they believed to be howling wolves surrounding their building. Only later did they realize that the coyotes would do them no harm.

Mother Mary Eulalie, foreseeing the hardships of the isolated mission where temperatures would drop to minus fifty degrees Celsius and supplies would be scarce, gave the sisters the option to come back with her to Victoria. Like the hardy souls who remained after the gold rush to take up land in the Williams Lake area, the sisters unanimously chose to remain.

Many of the French settlers in the area married Native women, who were unfamiliar with European culture and customs. Native mothers taught their children wilderness skills, while fathers often encouraged their daughters to become more European in their behaviour.[56] The Oblate fathers provided education for the boys in Williams Lake and the sisters, who remained in the area for over a decade, answered the educational needs of girls.

Similar to their experience at other missions, the sisters found the girls unaccustomed to using furniture and regarded their preference to squat on the floor rather than sit on chairs as a curious cultural distinction. The sisters may have also held the girls' traditional Native skills in some esteem. While walking in the woods one day, the children detected sounds the sisters didn't notice. The older girls quickly gathered branches from nearby trees and formed a circle around the sisters and younger girls. When the sisters could finally see wolves approaching, the older girls began waving their arms and shouting, intimidating the animals into retreat. The frightened group went on, unharmed.

Education at Williams Lake paralleled other mission schools such as Cowichan and Saint Mary's Mission. The girls learned how to cook and sew and performed household duties in the kitchen, and in the dining and laundry rooms. The Oblate fathers maintained a large farm at the mission that provided meat, eggs and vegetables. The winter food supply included salmon caught during the year, and local berries such as Oregon grape, blueberries, salmonberries, cranberries and blackberries picked during the spring, fall and summer months.

Sisters in Nanaimo

When Nanaimo became a city in 1875, it required both educational and health-care facilities to serve its population. As the recently opened Saint Joseph's Hospital in Victoria engaged all available sister nurses, the sisters at Nanaimo turned their energies to education. Sister Mary de la Croix and Sister Mary Eleanor arrived in Nanaimo in April 1877 to open the first Catholic school. With no other building available, Father Lemmens moved out of his home to a nearby cabin and gave his house to the sisters for their convent and school.

The next month twenty-nine pupils enrolled in the school, fifteen of them non-Catholic. The sisters instructed the students in English, French, arithmetic, music, drawing and needlework. The lower floor of the eleven-by-six-metre structure housed a chapel, two classrooms, a music room and an adjoining kitchen. The upper storey provided sleeping quarters for the sisters and space for two additional classrooms.

Two years later the congregation built a three-storey wood-frame school, which was later destroyed by fire. Through the savings of the sisters, another school was constructed in 1911. The sisters continued to provide educational services and responded to emergency health-care needs when epidemics such as measles, smallpox, diphtheria and scarlet fever threatened the lives of Nanaimo's citizens.

In 1937 the mayor honoured sixty years of service of the Sisters of Saint Ann in Nanaimo: "They always came to the help of the people, often in spite of their own acute needs. The presence of the Sisters in Nanaimo has had a cultural and moral influence not only on the pupils who went to school, but also on the citizens."[57]

Sisters in Kamloops

At the request of the Oblate fathers, Sister Mary Infant Jesus Lavigne, Sister Mary Catherine of Sienna McEntee and Sister Mary Celestine Fontaine left for Kamloops in the fall of 1880 to open a girls' school. They took the stagecoach along the Cariboo Road, veering west at Cache Creek for the forty-mile trip to Kamloops. Along the way they stopped at a hotel. One sister recalled the following:

> It was 11 o'clock when they arrived at the Cosmopolitan Hotel. They felt quite at home with Mrs. Spellman, a former Saint Ann's student, who was delighted to receive the Sisters. An hour after their arrival they had occasion to exercise their charity. A young man in the billiard room was stabbed by his unsuccessful opponent. The Sisters thought they might be helpful. And they were, for the victim's wound had not been properly dressed. They made lint from an article of their coif, and gave, not only first aid, but permanent aid, as there was no doctor in the vicinity. The man proved his gratitude by a donation of $260.00 and becoming a constant benefactor.[58]

St. Ann's Convent in Kamloops, built 1900. Archives Sisters of St. Ann, Victoria, BC

They arrived the next day at a building that Father Grandidier had erected outside of town for the sisters and their students. Compared to the small cabins in nearby Kamloops, the two-storey building seemed like a veritable mansion. Its twelve rooms housed only ten students.

The provincial superior, Mother Mary Providence, had predicted low student enrolment would result from the sparse population of ranchers in the area. She believed the new school to be twenty years premature. However, the Oblate fathers disagreed and, when in the planning stages of the Kamloops school, appealed to her superiors at the motherhouse in Quebec. The general council in the East advised Mother Mary Providence to send sisters to open the school.

At first, blame for low registration focused on location rather than population. In 1888 the convent school was floated on a raft down the river three miles to town and repositioned in the centre of Kamloops. This increased attendance slightly. Only in 1913, three years after completion of a new four-storey brick school, did student enrolment begin to noticeably increase. Up until this time "cattle kings," such as the one described here, kept the convent from financial disaster: "Leaping from the finest of horses, and dismounting his girls from the saddle, this giant in physique, entered the small parlour, threw his saddle bags on the floor, and grasping the hand of the Superior, introduced himself in a hearty, informal way. This social part over, the big pioneer went to his bags, drew out his purse and handed over payment in gold coin for several months' tuition."[59]

Saint Ann's Academy, as it had been known since 1920, taught young boys and girls and also functioned as a boarding school for girls. In 1910 a commercial class had been added to a list of subjects that already included religion, writing, geography, composition, arithmetic, grammar and history. The students enjoyed extracurricular activities such as baseball, "rounders" and music.

A Question of Language

In 1885 the superior general, Mother Mary Anastasia, came to visit the western missions. She arrived from Quebec via the Northern Pacific Railway and brought with her the two McQuade sisters and Sister Mary Joseph Calasanctias, who had come to Quebec from her native Belgium to become a missionary among the Natives in America.

About this time in British Columbia, approximately half of the ethnic population were Natives, while about one third were British born and the remainder came from continental Europe or Asia. The majority of sisters spoke French, being of French-Canadian heritage. When the superior general arrived she discussed the use of the French language in a "strictly English country." Although the sisters spoke English while teaching, French dominated their conversations and community prayers. They spoke English when teaching classes. The clergy, and even the retreat priests from San Francisco, spoke French fluently. The use of French seemed only natural given their heritage, but the superior general asked that although the sisters were not obliged to speak English, every time they did, they would be practising this virtue.

With Mother Mary Anastasia's influence, English became the common language. The use of "Ma Tante" (aunt) to address the sisters also disappeared. This French custom had been practised since the mid-seventeenth century during Marguerite Bourgeoys's era and was passed on to Esther Blondin and her daughters. Other changes also occurred. In 1884 all the Daughters of Saint Anne officially became Sisters of Saint Anne. In the West, to accommodate the English, the Sisters of Saint Anne dropped the "e."

Continued Expansion

A few years after the mother general's departure, the Sisters of Saint Ann opened a kindergarten and primary school in the vacated View Street Convent in Victoria. In the same year they responded to Bishop d'Herbomez's request to open the first Catholic school in Vancouver. The sisters borrowed the money for the purchase of three lots as the bishop could offer no financial support for their services, the land purchase or construction of the building. The Sisters of Saint Ann opened Sacred Heart Academy at 406 Dunsmuir Street in 1888. Two years later the name was changed to Saint Mary's Academy. In 1904 the sisters enlarged the school to accept boarders, stuccoed it and changed its name again, this time to Saint Ann's Academy. The school flourished, and within six years enrolment of day students reached 270 while the boarders numbered 63. However, to comply with the bishop's new plans the sisters closed the boarding school and turned it into a parochial school called Holy Rosary Parish Elementary School.

From the academy's early days the sisters in Vancouver offered hospitality to many visitors. Sisters who arrived from Quebec received comfort at "The Rosary" before venturing north to Alaska and the Yukon. Also, those coming from the motherhouse in Victoria to take the train east to Quebec also rested with the sisters in Vancouver. The school, which included commercial, music and art departments, finally closed in 1946. The surrounding area had grown into a busy business district and the city required the land for a civic centre.

As population increased, the request for sisters to work in new missions throughout British Columbia intensified. This prompted Mother Mary Anastasia Lesage to hold a profession ceremony in Victoria to motivate local young aspirants to enter religious life. Bishop Lemmens offered Saint Andrew's Cathedral in Victoria for the ceremony and two novices came from Quebec to profess vows in Victoria. Impressed with the affair, the bishop requested that the superior general apply to Rome for permission to open a western novitiate in Victoria. Up until 1889, anyone wishing to enter convent life with the Congregation of the Sisters of Saint Ann travelled to Lachine, Quebec, to spend two years preparing for religious life.

Two Native residential schools opened in the 1890s, one in Kamloops in 1890 and one on Kuper Island the following year. The Kamloops school became the largest Native residential school in Canada. The sisters were asked to teach at both schools. To reach the Kamloops School, the sisters took the Canadian Pacific Railway from Vancouver. At the end of the first year, the sisters realized their spiritual needs could not be met under the direction of a lay principal and they withdrew from teaching at the school. In 1893, with a Catholic priest as principal, three sisters returned to Kamloops to teach. The Sisters of Saint Ann continued educating Native students at Kamloops for eight decades.

At the end of 1890, Sister Mary Joachim Archambeault and Sister Mary Celestine Fontaine accepted a teaching mission on Kuper Island. They travelled from Victoria by canoe 113 kilometres north along the eastern shore of Vancouver Island, where they met the principal of the school, a Belgian missionary priest. The sisters took charge of the priest's domestic duties in addition to teaching and supervising the girls. The Montfortian fathers replaced the Belgian priest in 1906, and from then until 1957, the sisters worked alongside the fathers. The sisters continued teaching on Kuper Island until 1974.

The Boys Protectorate

Saint Aloysius' Boys' Protectorate was the final institution opened by the sisters before the turn of the century. With Sister Mary Zephyrin as superior and Sister Mary Zoe as maintenance manager, the boys' orphanage opened in a vacant wooden church on Mason Street in Victoria in 1899. Initially the facility housed thirty-five boys. A laywoman attended to those under school age as the sisters judged this work unsuitable for religious.

In 1904 circumstances dictated that the orphanage relocate to Duncan. The Duncan mission first operated as a boarding school for young Native girls beginning in 1864. In 1876 it expanded with an additional floor and annex to accommodate twenty-four orphan girls from Victoria. The orphan girls utilized only half the space and were moved to the sisters' facility in Nanaimo. This made room for twenty-six orphan boys transferred from Victoria. The sisters believed the boys would benefit from farm life and a spacious grounds.

The construction of a new building in 1921 allowed the orphanage to operate as a convent and boarding school for boys. In 1925 the Saint Ann's Boys' School prospectus stated:

Picturesque, Modern and Healthy

THIS WELL-EQUIPPED BOARDING ESTABLISHMENT
TEACHES EVERYTHING IN THE ORDINARY
CURRICULUM, IS SITUATED ON A FARM OF 400 ACRES
AND IS CONDUCTED BY THE PIONEER TEACHING ORDER
OF BRITISH COLUMBIA

Instructors Strive to Build Strong Foundations for
Good Citizenship[60]

Girls were allowed as externs (day students) from 1956 until 1964, when the school closed.

Turn of the Century—The Sisters Combine Education and Nursing

In preparation for the initial mission to Victoria in 1858, two missionary sisters had travelled to Montreal to be trained by the nursing Sisters of Providence. Although the Sisters of Saint Ann were committed to education, they also recognized the potential demands of a frontier mission and prepared themselves accordingly. Almost twenty years later, in preparation for the opening of Saint Joseph's Hospital, they again sought training from the nursing Sisters of Providence. This time two sisters headed south to Saint Vincent's Hospital in Portland, Oregon.

When Saint Joseph's Hospital opened in 1876, Dr. J.S. Helmcken gave this address: ". . . it (is) a great point in favor of this particular institution that it would be under the care of the Sisters of Saint Ann, as this would guarantee good nursing which is more important than medicine, and it would be valuable if only for a school of nursing."[61]

Dr. J.S. Helmcken, considered one of the founders of the hospital's future school of nursing, had forseen the importance of Saint Joseph's Hospital as a training ground for nurses. At that time nursing education focused on experiential training in a hospital rather than formal classroom studies.

Like most nursing schools of the late nineteenth century and early twentieth century, Saint Joseph's School of Nursing followed the Nightingale system of nursing, that is, of providing education through ward practise. Although the Nightingale school did not associate itself with a hospital, most nursing schools did and student nurses were an indispensable labour force for the hospital. Upon graduation, the majority of nurses left for private practice, reinforcing the need to continue using student nurses as the mainstay of the hospital labour force.

The Sisters of Saint Ann founded Saint Joseph's School of Nursing in 1900. Sister Mary Gertrude of Jesus became its founder and director. The German-born "Miss Weimer" was living in Holland when she heard Bishop Lemmens of Victoria on his European tour. The bishop spoke with great zeal about missionary life in the frontier West, and Miss Weimer soon left for Quebec, motivated by Bishop Lemmens to join the Canadian missionaries. She became a member of the Sisters of Saint Ann and arrived in Victoria as Sister Mary Gertrude in 1894. Her first assignment in surgical service led to her eventual appointment as the first superintendent of nurses and the school's first instructor.

In the mid-nineteenth century nursing was not considered a suitable vocation for "any cultured woman." However, Sister Mary Gertrude supported the profession of nursing and the importance of education:

> How can a nurse learn by practice alone all that is to be known to fearlessly and confidently meet an emergency...I am not trying to make the nurse a close competitor of the doctor. On the other hand, I find it unjust to find fault with the nurse because she knows somewhat of the doctor's business...It is the duty of the physicians and teachers to fortify the nurse with knowledge of all those things which will serve her. This we must do faithfully, even at a terrible risk of teaching her a few facts more than is absolutely necessary...Today, our first meeting in class, is, or should be to each of you, a serious day...nursing is a noble work but let me add it is done not merely through desire of remuneration, but through a more supernatural motive...with your whole heart and soul, learn how to practice your noble profession well...[62]

Thus began eighty-one years of Catholic nursing education in Victoria. On the closing of Saint Joseph's School of Nursing in 1981, an elderly woman who had nursed during Sister Mary Gertrude's era recalled the early days: "...we lived in a room near the Chapel on the main floor. We had straw ticks in the beginning but, I can remember Sister Mary Gertrude asking me if I would like a woollen mattress...Sister Mary Gertrude gave me an apron pattern so I could make my own aprons. In those days some of the nurses were wearing black ties but I never liked them so I made myself an Eaton collar...Our class did not wear caps. We wore soft black kid high boots..."[63]

At night the nurses carried small coal-oil lanterns rather than using the gas lamps provided in patients' rooms. Economical measures such as this helped the sisters stay within tight hospital budgets, as did the use of student nurses. Students typically acted as ward nurses, chambermaids and kitchen attendants, providing inexpensive labour for both nursing and non-nursing activities. They worked long and hard, rising at 5:00 a.m. to begin twelve-hour shifts at 7:00 a.m.,

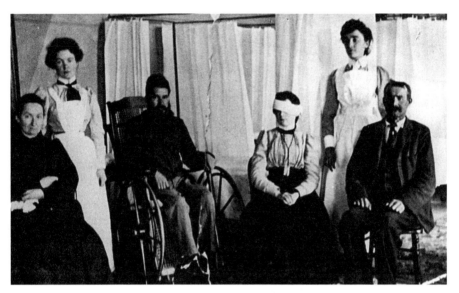

Two early student nurses pose with patients at the St Joseph's School of Nursing.
Archives Sisters of St. Ann, Victoria, BC

with one hour off during the day and one afternoon off during the week. Classes usually began at 1:00 p.m. but hospital work always took precedent. Typical of the era, nurses' training focused on patient care and housekeeping duties.

The trainees' non-nursing work eventually decreased in favour of patient care, and gradually formal education took precedence over experiential training. In the 1920s, Saint Joseph's schedules recorded less than four hundred academic hours in the year, whereas over four thousand hours were recorded in 1981. Five years after its opening, the school graduated the first "sister nurse," Sister Mary Peter, S.S.A., who later became head nurse and kept a tight rein on the comings and goings of her proteges. Throughout the school's operation, over two thousand students graduated from Saint Joseph's School of Nursing, while forty-five graduated as "sister nurses."

Sisters of Saint Ann in the West

The year 1900 marked the opening of Saint Joseph's School of Nursing, and fifty years of service for the Sisters of Saint Ann as a religious congregation. By this time, they had established missions throughout Quebec, British Columbia, the eastern United States, Alaska and the Yukon. Over the fifty years (1850–1900), eight hundred women had devoted their lives to the religious community of the Sisters of Saint Ann for the purpose of "the instruction and Christian education of young girls and, in certain cases ... the works of charity, care of the poor and the sick."[64]

St. Ann's Academy, Novitiate & Administration. Archives Sisters of St. Ann, Victoria, BC

The increasing numbers of sisters and the expansion of their work to fifty-four missions throughout North America required an effective means of administration. In 1896 the Sisters of Saint Ann grouped themselves into four religious provinces. Within the geographic boundary of Quebec, two of the provinces were formed, one called Sacre-Coeur Province and the other, Notre-Dame-du-Bon-Conseil Province. A third, Saint Marie Province, encompassed all the missions in the United States. The fourth province, established within the boundaries of British Columbia, was called Saint Joseph's Province.

By 1900 almost one hundred of the eight hundred sisters in the Congregation of the Sisters of Saint Ann had left Quebec to serve in Saint Joseph's Province in British Columbia, sixty-five percent heralding French-Canadian ancestry. At this time, the sisters served in eleven locations throughout the religious province, from the southern tip of Vancouver Island and the mainland, as far north as Williams Lake, and to Kamloops in the eastern interior. After fifty years of work, the sisters operated two orphanages and five boarding/day schools, had opened a hospital and school of nursing, and taught at two Native residential schools.

By 1958, the centennial anniversary of the sisters' arrival in British Columbia, the number of entrants to the British Columbian novitiate was almost three times the number of arrivals to the province during the previous fifty years. Two hundred and ninety-two women had entered the Western Novitiate and professed their vows, but now only thirty-seven percent of the sisters in the West claimed French-Canadian heritage. Two hundred and two of these women were born in British Columbia. Others came from various parts of Canada, and throughout the United States, England, Ireland, Germany, Belgium, France and a number of other European countries.

Although the sisters served the immediate needs of the western frontier by opening two orphanages and the congregation's first hospital, with the opening of numerous educational facilities they followed the intentions of Mother Marie

Anne. With perseverance and devotion, the sisters transformed the first of these institutions from a little log cabin in a swamp to the stately Saint Ann's Academy. In her address to the graduating students of Saint Ann's Academy in Victoria (1947), Sister Mary Ludovic reiterated the intentions of those sisters who had gone before them and those who would follow in years to come: "My dear girls, you are the women of tomorrow. I pray that you may realize two things and accepting the challenge of the times, put these into action in your life: first ... be conscious of the power you can wield for good in whatever sphere you may find yourself; and second ... accept the responsibility that goes with the opportunity to use this influence as a part of your Christian heritage."[65]

CHAPTER ONE NOTES

1. Gerda Lerner, *The Creation of Feminist Consciousness* (New York: Oxford University Press, 1993), 24.
2. "Extern" refers to a member of a contemplative or cloistered community who performs duties outside of the convent or monastery.
3. Lerner, 21–45.
4. Simone Poissant, *Marguerite Bourgeoys 1620–1700*, trans. Frances Kirwan,. 2d ed. (Bellarmin, 1993), 24.
5. Ibid., 25.
6. Ibid., 26.
7. Bishop André-M. Cimichella, *Mother Marie Anne Esther Blondin: Woman of Hope* (1988), 16.
8. With the approval of Pope Leo XIII, the Daughters of Saint Anne become the Sister of Saint Anne in 1884. The "e" was dropped when the sisters in the West officially adopted the English spelling. For consistency, the English spelling is used throughout the text, and the daughters are referred to as "the sisters."
9. Marie Mainville (Sister Marie des Sept Douleurs,), *The Ten First Years of the Sisters of Saint Ann 1858–1868* (no.92, Archives of the Sisters of Saint Ann, Victoria, BC), 1.
10. Virginia Brasseur (Sister Mary Lumena), (letter to her parents, December 8,1858, from Archives of the Sisters of Saint Ann, Victoria, BC).
11. Mainville, 14.
12. Brasseur.
13. Ibid.
14. Ibid.
15. Ibid.
16. Angèle Gauthier (Sister Mary Angèle,), "Travel Journal, 1858," (Archives of the Sisters of Saint Ann, Victoria, BC), 8.
17. Brasseur.
18. Brasseur.
19. Gauthier, 12.
20. V. Pinneault (Sister Mary Theodore), *The Sisters of Saint Ann on the North Pacific Shores* (Archives of the Sisters of Saint Ann, Victoria, BC), 30–31.
21. Gauthier, 13.
22. Brasseur.
23. Pinneault, 72.

24. Sharon Meen, "Colonial Society and Economy," in *The Pacific Province*, edited by Hugh J.M. Johnston (Vancouver: Douglas & McIntyre, 1996), 123.

25. Francis Johnson, *A History of Public Education in BC* (Vancouver: University of British Columbia Publications Centre, 1964), 20.

26. Johnston, 125.

27. Edith Down, (Sister Mary Margaret) *A Century of Service* (Victoria: Morriss Printing Co. Ltd., 1966), 46.

28. Pinneault, 12.

29. Down, 32.

30. Mainville, 44.

31. Ibid., 123

32. Down, 54.

33. Mainville, 99–100.

34. Pinneault, 248–249.

35. Bishop L.J. D'Herbomez, letter to Sister Mary Providence, August 16, 1865 (Archives of the Sisters of Saint Ann, Victoria, BC).

36. Pinneault, 142.

37. Ibid., 141.

38. Ibid., 141.

39. Pinneault 148.

40. Pinneault, 143.

41. Susan Czsterzs, *Images of Victorian Womanhood in English Art* (Farleigh Dickenson University Press, 1987), 74–84.

42. Down, 63.

43. Pinneault, 161.

44. Ibid., 164.

45. Ibid., 175.

46. Down, 69.

47. Pinneault, 203–208 (excerpt from letter of Sister Mary Emmanuel to her parents).

48. Chronicles of the Sisters of Saint Ann, (Archives of the Sisters of Saint Ann, Victoria, BC), 44.

49. A.J. Brabant, *Vancouver Island and Its Missions* (1899), 27.

50. Ibid., 29.

51. Louise Roy, *The Sisters of Saint Anne: A century of History, Volume II, 1900–1950* (Lachine: Les Editions Sainte-Anne, 1994), 330.

52. *Daily British Colonist*, August 22, 1875.

53. Pinneault, 224.

54. Ibid., 224.

55. Down, 78.

56. M. Conrad, A Finkel, and C. Jaenen, *Volume I, History of the Canadian Peoples: Beginnings to 1867* (Toronto: Copp Clark Pittman Ltd., 1993), 478.

57. Roy, 11.

58. Pinneault, 273.

59. Ibid., 274.

60. Saint Ann's Boys' Protectorate Prospectus, 1925 (Archives of the Sisters of Saint Ann, Victoria, BC).

61. Reminiscing: St. Joseph's School of Nursing Commemorative Yearbook 1900–1981, p.75.

62. Ibid., 76.

63. Ibid., 78.

64. Roy, 500.

65. Flora Dozios, (Sister Mary Ludovic), Aquinian Yearbook (June 1947, Victoria, BC).

CHAPTER TWO

Help Arrives on the Mainland

The Sisters of Providence

T he Sisters of Providence, founded as the Daughters of Charity, Servants of the Poor, were established in Montreal in 1843. They built on the inspiring and charitable works of their foundress, Emilie Gamelin (Emilie Tavernier, 1800–1851). The Sisters of Providence originated through the influence of the magnanimous accomplishments of Emilie Gamelin, an active and motivating member of the Ladies of Charity. This secular group of women, organized in 1827, undertook various activities to help the poor. Their support of Emilie enabled her to open the first shelter for neglected elderly women in Montreal.

An orphan, Emilie Tavernier was raised by an aunt who sent her to be educated by the Sisters of the Congregation of Notre-Dame. As a young girl Emilie gave some thought to joining the Grey Nuns but, at

The Venerable Emilie Gamelin 1800–1851.
Providence Archives, Edmonton, Alberta

the age of twenty-three, she married Jean-Baptiste Gamelin. Within five years her three children and husband had died. During this time of nearly insurmountable

41

grief, a friend gave her a picture of Our Mother of Sorrows. This memorable gift instilled within her a source of comfort and inspiration that persisted throughout her life, allowing her to overcome great pain and to achieve exceptional acts of generosity and love.

Although comfortably prosperous during their marriage, both Emilie and her husband had concerned themselves with the poor. Upon her husband's death, Emilie inherited the prestigious property in Montreal where she had lived with her husband and children, and where she cared for a mentally handicapped boy and his mother. With the selling off of these resources and help from others who witnessed her exemplary efforts, Emilie established Providence House, an institution housing elderly and disabled women.

Under her direction the charitable works of Providence House flourished, growing to include the care of orphan girls and visits to prisoners, the poor and the sick. Emilie Gamelin had an ability to clearly identify the most urgent needs of the time and quickly respond to them, and she expanded the services of Providence House to respond to many charitable requests.

Bishop Bourget recognized Emilie's gift and, like so many others in the community, wanted to see her work continue. He hoped the Daughters of Charity of Saint Vincent de Paul would operate the institution Emilie Gamelin had established, but the Daughters of Charity felt compelled to respond to another mission. The bishop organized a new religious community instead. He intended the new community to follow the spirit of Saint Vincent de Paul and hoped they would be associated with the Daughters of Charity of Saint Vincent de Paul.

Although Emilie Gamelin had earlier been told she was not called to religious life, her situation led her to enter as a novice in the newly formed Daughters of Charity. She was elected their first superior and, following the rules of Saint Vincent de Paul, led her community in the example of charity and humility that she had demonstrated for so many years.

Ten years after the inception of the Daughters of Charity, Servants of the Poor, Bishop Magloire Blanchet of Washington Territory requested sisters from their community to assist with missions in the Pacific Northwest. The sisters agreed and departed for Washington Territory, where they stayed only a short time. Their return voyage to Montreal included a disastrous sea voyage and an encounter with pirates, and ended in a detour to Chile. The women diverged from their original plan and formed a new mission in a Chilean community, where they continue to serve the poor today.

Mother Joseph Arrives in Washington Territory
This first attempt to recruit missionaries for the Pacific Northwest did not deter Bishop Blanchet from asking for a second group of missionary sisters in

Mother Joseph 1823–1902.
Providence Archives, Edmonton, Alberta

1856. Sister Joseph of the Sacred Heart (Esther Pariseau, 1823–1902) agreed to lead four of her missionary sisters on the long journey to the West, this time accompanied by Bishop Blanchet and Father Rossi. Sister Joseph had been directly influenced by Mother Gamelin, who accepted her as the thirteenth member of the Daughters of Charity, Servants of the Poor, in 1843.

The sisters left for Washington Territory on November 3, 1856. They took the train from Montreal to New York, sailed to Kingston, Jamaica, and by November 17, began their trek across the Isthmus of Panama. Unlike the first missionary sisters who travelled by mule across the Isthmus in 1852, these sisters had the luxury of making the journey by rail, as did the Sisters of Saint Ann, who would follow the same route two years later.

On December 7, after a stop in Acapulco and a two-day stay in San Francisco with the Sisters of Mercy, the travellers reached the treacherous Columbia River bar. Although many ships had gone down at the mouth of this notable river, the group passed safely across and rested overnight in Astoria. On December 8, the Feast of the Immaculate Conception, they arrived at Fort Vancouver, Washington. The bishop had assured the sisters that convent quarters would be available but in fact there were none. Mother Joseph and her four sister companions spent their first night in Washington Territory in the bishop's empty attic.

Although the Daughters of Charity, Servants of the Poor, began their mission in dire poverty, they went on to create a viable life, not only for themselves, but also for those who they came to serve. Although they were commonly known as the Sisters of Providence, officially changing their name in 1970, no title could more aptly describe these self-sacrificing women than "Servants of the Poor." Their determination and courage, motivated by their love of God, would build a haven for the destitute, the needy and the forgotten.

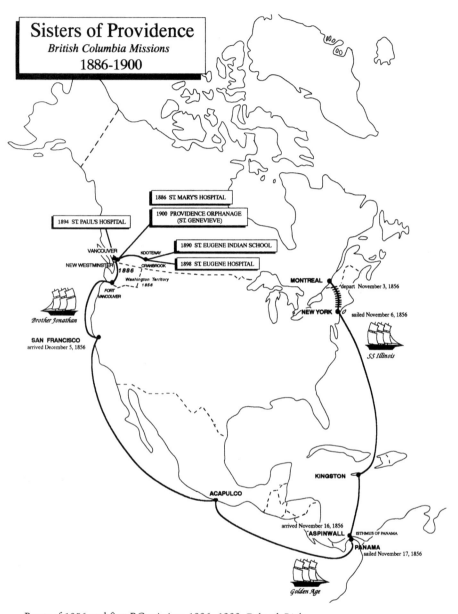

Route of 1856 and first BC missions 1886–1900. Deborah Rink

North to New Westminster—Saint Mary's Hospital

The Oblate fathers from British Columbia hoped the reputable works of the Sisters of Providence would expand beyond Washington to their communities in the north. But given the demand for services in the south, the sisters could respond to the fathers' request only three decades later, in 1886. By this time the sisters had constructed a total of seventeen institutions throughout

Washington, Oregon, Idaho and Montana, with seven providing hospital care for the indigent.

Mother Joseph's leadership and personal involvement in the planning, designing and building of these facilities led to the completion of sixteen more institutions in the Pacific Northwest by the end of the century. Of these thirty-three institutions, sixteen were health-care facilities, three of them in British Columbia.

On July 4, 1886, Mother Joseph accompanied the mother provincial to choose a location for a hospital in New Westminster. The bishop gave them a lot valued at fifteen hundred dollars. With foresight based on experience, the women purchased an adjacent lot for future expansion.

Sister John of Calvary and Sister Paul of the Sacred Heart left their provincial house in Vancouver, Washington, for British Columbia, where they would collect funds for the hospital venture. They followed in the famous footsteps of Mother Joseph, who had made many successful begging tours over the previous decade. They first solicited funds from the citizens of New Westminster, where they enjoyed the gracious hospitality of the Sisters of Saint Ann, the only other community of women religious in the province. By the end of August the sisters had collected three thousand dollars.

On September 1, 1886, Sister Ethelbert accompanied Sister John to collect funds from the Canadian Pacific Railway employees working in the interior. An Oblate father escorted them for protection, as they wanted to avoid Mother Joseph's memorable but treacherous experiences of outwitting thieves. By the end of October the sisters had collected an additional two thousand dollars.

Six months after the purchase of the hospital lot, and with the building under construction, the contractor lost his life in a hotel fire. Plans were destroyed in the disastrous incident and Mother Joseph stepped in to act as contractor. Rarely seen without a hammer and saw in her rosary belt, this skilled carpenter, designer and determined project manager completed construction of the fifteen-bed hospital. Saint Mary's Hospital received the blessing of Bishop Durieu on May 24, 1887.

Many patients who came to the hospital could not pay for the sisters' services. In fact, many showed no signs of physical ailment but came simply for the meals, for which they often could not pay. The records in June 1890 show that nineteen hundred meals had been given out to the poor over one year. Apart from their charitable work in the hospital, the five sisters who staffed it also visited the sick in their homes.

In July 1891 an epidemic of typhoid fever ravaged New Westminster. During this time a number of indigents came to the hospital for treatment, and their successful recovery brought in the previously skeptical upper-class citizens.

St. Mary's Hospital, New Westminster. Sisters of Providence Archives, Seattle, WA

"They were cured of typhoid and their prejudices against the hospital and in gratitude, donations poured in."[1]

However, as time progressed the number of non-paying patients exceeded those able to pay. These included Natives during the fishing season, who came to the hospital for medication and surgery. To assist with the operating costs of the hospital, the city provided free water, a fish cannery provided all the fish they could use and a sawmill supported them with the majority of wood required for heat.

To help mitigate the financial burden, the sisters resumed a series of begging tours. In addition, they brought in money by charging construction workers one dollar a month for health insurance during the building of the Fraser River Bridge in 1902. The bridge was just a short distance away from the hospital, which received one third of these insurance funds while the doctors received the remainder. Not until 1923 did the hospital receive its first government grant to assist the facility's operating costs.

Toward the end of 1910 the number of patients diminished to the point where closing the hospital seemed imminent. The sisters continued to accept the patients who came and to receive the poor, but they also lived from day to day on the verge of destitution. Within two years the population of New

Westminster increased so significantly that the sisters could not accept all the admission requests. The construction of a three-storey annex provided for the continued expansion of the hospital.

Begging tour, 1896. Sisters of Providence Archives, Seattle, WA

Saint Paul's Hospital and School of Nursing, Vancouver

The second hospital initiated by the Sisters of Providence in British Columbia also began at the request of the Oblate bishop. On March 20, 1894, Mother Therese and Sister Rodrigue came from Portland, Oregon, to purchase seven lots of land in Vancouver, British Columbia, at a cost of nine thousand dollars. Construction on the four-storey hospital began under the direction of Sister Frederic, who commuted between the hospital site in Vancouver and her temporary residence at Saint Mary's Hospital in New Westminster.

Five Sisters of Providence from Montreal arrived to operate Saint Paul's Hospital, named in honour of Bishop Paul Durieu. The first patient was admitted on November 21, 1894. Like Saint Mary's Hospital in New Westminster, Saint Paul's Hospital also accepted patients who could not pay and gave out meals to the poor. To ease their financial burden, in 1900, sisters went to nearby mining and logging camps to raise funds. They sold ten-dollar tickets that guaranteed the purchaser hospital care for the year as well as the freedom to choose their own doctor. The following year, the hospital received its first government grant of eight hundred dollars, but the sisters continued their fundraising.

St. Paul's Hospital 1907, with 1904 addition. Saint Paul's Hospital Archives

From 1898 to 1910 the population of Vancouver increased from 24,000 to 110,000. This growth resulted in increased admissions and initiated the planning of a new wing. The sisters purchased land for expansion in 1899, and by 1904 completed a 38-by-138-foot building that housed an additional seventy-five beds.

The sisters provided the hospital's patient care from the beginning, and staffing the expanded hospital required even more nursing personnel. Some of the sisters had trained at nursing schools in Montreal, while others had little or no training at all. In 1899 Sister Praxedes began a training program for the untrained staff. When it became clear that the sisters alone could not meet the demands of the health-care facility, the hospital took steps to resolve the problem by establishing a school for laypersons.

On September 1, 1907, the School of Nursing at Saint Paul's Hospital opened its doors to fourteen young women, eleven of who graduated three years later. The nurses-in-training resided on the top floor of a new two-storey outbuilding adjacent to the hospital. On the lower floor were a carpentry shop and a fully equipped laundry with a mattress sterilizer and washing and ironing machines.

Apart from the necessity of nurses, the hospital relied on the assistance of outside support. An auxiliary organized itself within the first year of the hospital's

St. Paul's Hospital Graduation class with Sister Hermyle, 1912. Saint Paul's Hospital Archives

The Ladies of Charity, fundraising for St. Pauls' Hospital. Saint Paul's Hospital Archives

opening. The auxiliary emulated Mother Gamelin's Ladies of Charity in Montreal by generously contributing to the health-care facility through organized activities such as tag days, garden parties, bazaars and other fundraising ventures. They approached businesses throughout the city and received cash during their solicitations as well as groceries and gifts-in-kind donated to the hospital. The Ladies of Charity also provided visitation services to patients and, in their first year, presented Christmas presents to each patient.

When Mrs. Martin, a Lady of Charity from Montreal, arrived in Vancouver, she imbued the auxiliary with new spirit and influenced the purchase of the first ambulance brought duty free from Philadelphia. Later, the Ladies raised several hundred dollars toward the purchase of the hospital's first X-ray machine. Well on its way to embracing technological advancements, the X-ray department opened in 1913 with machines "... imported from Paris ... practically unique in this country."[2]

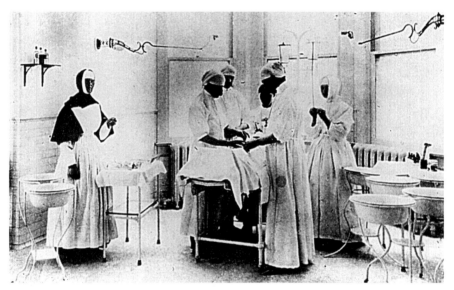

Operating room at St. Paul's Hospital. Saint Paul's Hospital Archives

The notable Sister Charles Spinola, who worked at Saint Paul's from 1910 to 1963, saw many technological innovations in her lifetime, among them the "Saint Charles Ether Machine." Although only one of many innovations, her 1918 invention gained wide acclaim. The ether vaporizer was used extensively around the country and heralded a technological development that advanced the anaesthesiology field.

While technology progressed, the urban population grew and soon its demands required additional expansion of the hospital. In 1913 the sisters opened a reinforced concrete structure called the Burrard Building. Near its completion the sisters endured financial hardships, not the least being a world-wide depression. However, the Knights of Columbus came to their rescue with a forty thousand-dollar donation and the hospital continued in its progressive improvements and expansions.

A School and Hospital in the Kootenays

Between 1879 and 1890, Bishop d'Herbomez persisted in asking the Sisters of Providence to open a school for the Kootenay Natives at Saint Eugene Mission. In 1890 they could finally accept the invitation. The Sisters of Providence had already established Native schools throughout Washington, Idaho and Montana. Sister Pacifique appeared most suitable for the position of director because by this time she had nineteen years of experience among Natives in Washington.

Sister Adrien (niece of Mother Joseph), Sister Rita from Walla Walla, Washington, and Sister Mary of Nazareth from Limerick, Ireland, accompanied Sister Pacifique to the Kootenays. They journeyed by train from Vancouver, Washington, to just north of Golden, British Columbia, where they headed south by wagon to Saint Eugene Mission over the treacherous mountain trails. The reputation of the Sisters of Providence hospitals, which served the logging, mining and railroad industries, earned the sisters free passes on the train.

They arrived at Saint Eugene Mission on August 15, 1890, and were welcomed by church bells and Native handshakes. Three wooden buildings constituted the residential school complex and their lodgings. Their experience suggested some necessary alterations, which were soon underway. They had a well dug and a laundry and root cellar added, and erected a fence around the complex. Within two months the school was ready. They accepted boys and, due to the sisters' presence, they also accepted girls.

The residential school opened on October 16, 1890. It took some time before the children became accustomed to the indoors. The girls were taught cooking, sewing, washing, ironing and mending, and seemed particularly interested in learning about baking bread. The boys learned carpentry and farming. The sisters taught all day and tended to the children at night. Many children suffered from tuberculosis, and the sisters realized there was a pressing need for a hospital to separate the healthy children from the sick, who needed nursing care.

The first summer, the children accompanied the sisters during their visit to the sick in the Native community in Columbia Lake. The sisters adapted to the children's custom of sleeping outdoors on beds made of pine branches, spending almost two weeks in this environment. The trip became an annual event.

To the dismay of both the children and the sisters, Sister Mary of Nazareth and Sister Adrien were called back to Oregon, and the poor health of Sister

Pacifique resulted in her replacement by Sister Mary Conrad. Although these changes of personnel meant difficult adjustments for all, at least one replacement was a happy one. The boys could not contain their thrill when the new Sister Cassilda took them horseback riding on holidays and weekends.

After serving for six years at the mission Sister Cassilda took an opportunity for a three-week retreat in Portland. When she returned, the excited boys insisted on riding out to meet her and brought her horse with them. The boys felt a great loss when Sister Cassilda left for the Blackfoot reserve at Cluny. They saw her off in Cranbrook, where she boarded the train to the sad serenade of their brass band bidding her goodbye.

By 1905, some fifteen years after it had opened, seventy students lived at the residential school. The superintendent of Indian affairs, the Honourable Duncan Campbell Scott, promised a new building to replace the old dilapidated structures still being occupied. The new building provided more space, running water and a central heating system.

Although Sister Marie du Cenacle acted as principal, the Honourable Duncan Campbell Scott suggested she allow the Oblates to take this position in hopes of alleviating some discipline problems beginning to arise with the older boys. Within five years, however, six priests had come and gone with disastrous results. Compounding this was the lack of cooperation developing between the younger Oblate priests and the older Providence sisters. Conflicting directions given to employees, who maintained loyalty to the sisters, added to the difficulties. Thirty-nine years of service ended when the sisters felt compelled to withdraw their services due to the deteriorating circumstances at the residential school.

Saint Eugene Hospital

The compassionate care of the Sisters of Providence continued with the opening of Saint Eugene Hospital. Aware of the sisters' abilities, the superintendent of the Canadian Pacific Railway requested that Sister Mary Conrad, former director of Saint Eugene School, travel to the provincial house in Portland to ask permission to establish a hospital in the vicinity of Saint Eugene Mission. He contributed one hundred dollars for Sister Mary Conrad's trip and included a further offer of five thousand dollars toward construction of the hospital.

The sisters had previously received a request to build a hospital in the area, but they had declined at the time due to the lack of sisters who could help. Now the provincial superior in Portland and the superior general in Montreal believed a hospital project merited consideration. Mother Joseph travelled to British Columbia to consider a location for the new hospital. It would soon stand on the banks of Saint Mary's River, near the residential school at Saint Eugene Mission.

During hospital construction the old residence of the Oblate fathers housed patients, allowing admittance of the first patient in December 1897. The temporary hospital was staffed by a Native girl, an orderly and two sisters. These four lovingly provided nursing care, performed all laundry services and managed to cook for up to twenty patients. Finally, on March 18, 1898, four sisters arrived to assist the overburdened sisters and staff.

The reinforcements left their motherhouse in Montreal and travelled for a week by train to Golden. From there they travelled by wagon, and it is the wagon portion of the trip that left a lasting memory on Sister Melitine. A few days after their arrival, she wrote to Mother John of the Cross in Montreal, describing the experience of leaving:

> ... by wagon on Tuesday morning on ground frozen so hard it was like rock. We found it difficult to get in and out of that high wagon ... We did not get to bed until midnight when we slept in the attic of a small house, separated only by a blanket from the ten men travelling with us. The next day, we continued our journey through mountain roads of snow, ice, and mud. At times, there was barely room for the wagon, with a precipice so dangerously close that we were filled with terror. It did not help to be shown the exact place where last week, a stage coach fell off this mountain!
>
> At a very dangerous point, we all had to get off the wagon and climb for a mile up a mountain so steep it made one dizzy. We took off our heaviest wraps and, with a stick in hand, began to climb. A large rock rolled from the top of the mountain and just missed one of the travellers ... [3]

Despite the harrowing journey, the sisters arrived at the Saint Eugene Mission and stepped in as much-needed staff when Saint Eugene Hospital opened in May 1898. The new two-storey, forty-bed hospital measured sixty feet by forty-five feet. The new building's location relieved the first two sisters of their daily trek between the convent and the temporary hospital, some distance away. This facility continued under the sisters' care for seventy years.

Although principally established to serve the CPR employees, the hospital extended care equally to the Native population and settlers. In the first year of the hospital's operation, a typhoid epidemic broke out in the railway camps. To accommodate the overflow of typhoid victims, the sisters erected a tent and sent requests for assistance to all who could help. The superior general, along with three sisters, came directly from Montreal to assist, as did Mother Marie and one other sister from Portland. Although Sister Mary Conrad contracted

First St. Eugene's Hospital, Cranbrook. Providence Archives, Edmonton, Alberta

the disease, she made a surprising recovery toward the end of the exhausting situation.

Within three years, in 1901, replacement of Saint Eugene Hospital, which was located along the banks of Saint Mary's River, began with new construction in Cranbrook, a few miles away. This more suitable location accommodated the extension of the railroad further into the West. As the local population increased, so did the need for hospital services requiring additional space. In 1905 the sisters constructed an addition to Saint Eugene Hospital in Cranbrook and hired twelve girls to help in the hospital. In 1911 a second addition coincided with the opening of the Saint Eugene Hospital School of Nursing, which provided career training and contributed to patient care and other hospital needs such as cooking and laundry.

Sister John Gabriel, who was appointed director of the Sisters of Providence School of Nursing in the West, instituted a training school for nurses. Following her curriculum, the doctors and sisters graduated five nurses from the program at Cranbrook in 1914. A separate building for the school was opened in 1928 and the last students left in 1949, finishing their course at Saint Paul's Hospital in Vancouver.

A New Province and Mission—Providence Orphanage

As with the Sisters of Saint Ann, the increased numbers of the Sisters of Providence in Canada and their expanding missions required a new organizational plan of their community in the Pacific Northwest. The Province of Saint Vincent de Paul, established in 1891, had its provincial house in Vancouver, Washington, and covered the territory of the northwestern United States as well as British Columbia. On August 28, 1912, however, the Sisters of Providence in the Canadian West formed a new province called Holy Angels Province. Saint Paul's Hospital in Vancouver became its headquarters.

The indelible impression the Sisters of Providence would leave on British Columbia began with four missionary sisters, led by the determined Mother Joseph. They settled in Washington Territory, two years before the Sisters of Saint Ann established themselves in British Columbia. After serving south of British Columbia in Washington, Idaho, Montana and Oregon for thirty years, the Sisters of Providence became the second community of Catholic women religious to enter British Columbia. By the turn of the century, they had begun the fifth of their charitable institutions in British Columbia.

Sincerely devoted to the cause and memory of Emilie Gamelin, and with the loving support of her religious sisters, the aging but undaunted Mother Joseph undertook her last mission. When a fire in New Westminster (Sapperton) left numerous orphans homeless at the Sisters of the Good Shepherd Orphanage, an urgent call went out to the Sisters of Providence. At the age of seventy-eight Mother Joseph planned and supervised the construction of Providence Orphanage in New Westminster.

Begun in 1899 and completed in 1900, the four-storey brick building provided fifty children with a new home on an expansive twelve-acre plot. After overseeing its construction, Mother Joseph made one last

Providence Orphanage and School.
Sisters of Providence Archives, Seattle, WA

request of the superior general in Montreal: "I will be the godmother ... grant me the favor of this beautiful name, Providence Orphanage. It is probably the last child I will have the honor of holding over the baptismal fount...to honor the memory of our venerable Mother Gamelin, in her splendid example of devotion to Divine Providence."[4]

Providence Orphanage operated for fifty-nine years. During these years the Sisters of Providence continued to operate the two hospitals and schools of nursing in the lower mainland of British Columbia. They went north to open three more hospitals in Fort Saint John, Vanderhoof and Dawson Creek. They also taught at the first Catholic School in Dawson Creek and opened a business college there.

The Religious of the Good Shepherd

Saint Mary Euphrasia Pelletier 1796–1868.
Sisters of the Good Shepherd, Canada

In 1641, in Caen, France, Saint John Eudes (1601–1680) founded the Order of Our Lady of Charity to care for women and girls "endangered by immoral circumstances." Over the next two centuries eleven houses were established. In 1829 Sister Mary Euphrasia Pelletier (1796–1868), superior of the house of Our Lady of Charity at Tours, founded a house at Angers, calling it Good Shepherd, in memory of a work that had existed under that name before the French Revolution. Two years later she was appointed superior of this house and subsequently witnessed an influx of vocations and numerous requests to found more houses. By 1835 Sister Mary Euphrasia received permission from Pope Gregory XVI for the foundation of the Religious of the Good Shepherd.

The first attempt by Canadians to obtain help from the Good Shepherd Sisters was in 1841, when Bishop Bourget of Montreal went to the Monastery of the Good Shepherd in Angers, France. He met Mother Euphrasia and her religious companions and spoke to the sisters about the missions in Canada, telling them of his desire to open a house of refuge in his Diocese of Montreal. Although they generously volunteered to depart on the mission, the bishop of Angers, to whom they deferred, would not allow them to proceed.

In 1844 there was a new bishop in Angers and Bishop Bourget again approached the Sisters of the Good Shepherd, hopeful that the new bishop would agree to the mission. Four sisters were allowed to depart in June, initiating the legacy of the Good Shepherd in Canada.

The Orphanage in New Westminster

The first Good Shepherd Sisters of Our Lady of Charity who arrived in British Columbia came from Ottawa and were referred to as Good Shepherd Sisters. This house had been founded in 1866 by sisters arriving from Buffalo. Almost twenty-five years later Reverend Louis-Joseph d'Herbomez and Reverend Paul Durieu invited these Ottawa sisters to serve in the Diocese of New Westminster. Father McGuckin, who had recently worked in New Westminster but now resided in Ottawa, approached the superior of the Good Shepherd Sisters to assist with the request to start an orphanage in New Westminster (Sapperton). Father Fayard, who had assumed the duties of Father McGuckin in New Westminster, also supported the plans for an orphanage.

The "energetic and most capable" Sister Mary of the Good Shepherd Bingham was designated as superior and left the Order of Our Lady of Charity in Toronto to join Sister Marie de Saint Paul Montrose and Sister Marie de Saint Norbert Tierney in Ottawa. The three sisters departed from Ottawa by train on May 14, 1890, intending to acquire land for the new orphanage. They arrived in New Westminster nine days later and were welcomed by the Sisters of Providence into their home at Saint Mary's Hospital. These three sisters eagerly prepared the way for the sisters who would soon follow.

The sisters hoped their acceptance of the orphanage operation would eventually allow them to open a refuge, the focus of their intended apostolic mission. In the interim the sisters rallied to the needs of the children, in the spirit of Saint Mary Euphrasia: "A cup of sugared milk, given opportunely to one of our dear children will be more effective in bringing back right sentiments, than acts of severity… The children should find in you, comfort in their trials and help in their troubles… Let kindness be the rule of our conduct, of our language, of our manner; thus the children may render testimony that we are as we ought to be."[5]

To support the mission the sisters undertook gruelling collection trips that sometimes lasted for months. Apart from donations gathered in rural and urban communities, contributions also came from bishops, priests and businesses. Their own community in Ottawa assisted by financing the new orphanage and by sending additional sisters.

Within three months of the first sisters' arrival, seven more sisters came from Ottawa to assist in the mission.[6] Now all ten sisters lived in an old church near Saint Peter's Cathedral until November, when they purchased two acres of property along the Fraser River. There they established themselves in the extant cottage and started construction of a residence for orphan children.

In January 1892 the sisters founded "a house for orphans and a home and protectory for penitent women."[7] The latter were trained in laundry work and sewing as much to support themselves as well as prepare them for the future.

Some of these women wished to dedicate their lives to God in the service of the Good Shepherd. While they did not take vows, they did wear a simple black dress.

Within two years the sisters were caring for twelve boys and twenty-six girls. To meet the growing needs of the New Westminster mission, the original residence was expanded, and in September 1893, sixty children lived at the Good Shepherd Orphanage.

To sustain themselves, the community opened a laundry and a sewing service. The mission also relied on cash donations and fundraising ventures conducted by the lay community, such as bazaars. People in the area offered what they could to help the sisters in their venture, including donations of farm produce.

Although the women were experienced in laundry work, in 1899 one of the presses caught fire. The small children were outside playing when the tragedy struck, but the older ones and the sisters were still in the building. They quickly vacated the building and fortunately no loss of life occurred, but the fire completely destroyed the place, causing considerable upheaval in the lives of the children and the sisters.

The Sisters of Saint Ann and the Sisters of Providence gave assistance to the homeless sisters and the children, while the Oblate fathers quickly transformed the old Saint Mary's Church into a temporary accommodation for them. Although grateful for their new residence, they thought it less than adequate:

> The interior of the Church was about twenty-five feet high with a gallery half way up. The gallery served as classroom, refectory and dormitory for the Preservation and Angel Guardian classes, while the lower part was converted into a community room, refectory, sewing room, etc. The basement served as a dormitory, the sheets and counterpanes used being sent from our Monasteries of Ottawa and Portland. Although all had warm covering, still they suffered considerably from the cold, the Church being old and the keen autumn winds penetrating freely through large crevices in floor and walls ... One wash basin served for half of the community and soap was considered quite a luxury.[8]

Relocating to Vancouver

For almost a year they endured these conditions, until the Sisters of Providence accepted the financial responsibility of constructing a new orphanage. Funds from the fire insurance allowed the Sisters of the Good Shepherd an opportunity to begin again. In the fall of 1900 they moved to 562 West Fourteenth Avenue in Vancouver, where they also operated a laundry and sewing service.

Their new lodgings had room for improvements: "They were without bedsteads, chairs, stoves and lamps. The neighbors kindly supplied the lamps. In lieu of a stove they placed stones so that a fire might be made in the center and a good-sized oil can served as a tea kettle. For tables, boards were placed on trestles. The Monastery was right in the bush, a distance of five blocks from street cars."[9]

The new community in Vancouver began with twelve professed sisters and three novices. Of the twenty children under their care, over half were of the "preservation class." The term "preservation class" referred to orphans, destitute girls or those suffering from neglect or abuse. The sisters educated them in employable skills. The girls enjoyed regular classes and ballet, drama, religion, piano and recreation. The sisters kept these preservation class girls separate from the "penitent class."

The term "penitent class" originated during the sisters' early history, when these girls or women were described as seeking refuge in their convents through a spiritual desire to change their manner of living. Although some residents came voluntarily, others were sent by some authority such as a parent, guardian, social worker or law officer. The aspiration of spiritual renewal did not apply to all the women in this class: "The Sisters of the Good Shepherd were sometimes a target for slander because of their ministry to delinquent young women. The courts often sent them to the sisters instead of prison. This apostolate exposed the sisters to false testimony from some of their charges, making them vulnerable to vicious rumors. Some bishops even found their ministry an embarrassment. Sisters sometimes found it necessary to invite civic authorities to inspect the convents in order to allay their suspicions and disprove false charges."[10]

The call to serve God in religious life was inclusive as there were various ways of serving as a member of the Religious of the Good Shepherd, depending on one's preparation or desire. One could be a choir, lay or touriere sister. In 1900 there were nine professed choir sisters and one novice. Two lay sisters also resided in the community with two novices of the same rank. Only one touriere sister lived in the Vancouver monastery.

The uncloistered touriere sisters went out into the community to shop, accompanied children to appointments and completed various tasks that required venturing outside the monastery. Their involvement in the community allowed the cloistered choir and lay sisters to remain within the monastery and keep their commitment to enclosure. The lay sister status was discontinued in 1946.

The sisters and children constituted a diverse community living together in the new Vancouver monastery. The sisters and children always had separate living arrangements, except where the sister in charge had her bedroom near the children. In the early days, they worked amidst humble and difficult conditions:

The first laundry in Vancouver was a little shed put up by the Sisters who used for the purpose the pieces of lumber left from the building. This shed served for some weeks, until one night during a severe storm it was blown down. The good neighbours seeing the difficulty in which the community found themselves, gathered together, and by working evenings and week-ends put up a laundry and a barn. This last was quite necessary to house horse and van for laundry delivery... The years following were spent in such works as are necessary in a new foundation—finishing the building which was incomplete, clearing the land, building fences, putting in an orchard and a garden... [11]

Backyard of the Vancouver monastery. Sisters of the Good Shepherd, Canada

When the 1918 flu epidemic struck the community, everyone fell ill and one sister died. Five years later, smallpox infested the community. Although some of the children who contracted the disease were moved to the isolation hospital, they all recovered.

After residing in Vancouver for almost thirty years, the sisters decided to purchase adjoining property on Sixteenth Avenue to initiate construction of a new laundry. They used borrowed money to build the new building. In addition to providing income for the foundation, the laundry existed to "teach the women a trade and help them establish good work habits."

In 1938 the Sisters of Our Lady of Charity voted unanimously to affiliate themselves with the Sisters of the Good Shepherd, an international congregation founded by Mary Euphrasia Pelletier, herself a Sister of Our Lady of

Charity. Her vision included a general administration designed to provide strength through mutual support.

A contemplative group called the Magdalens, now known as the Contemplative Sisters of the Good Shepherd, formed in Vancouver in 1943. Following the Carmelite tradition, they engaged in prayer as their main activity, with specific intentions for the apostolic work of the Sisters of the Good Shepherd and those they served. As a separate community, these women took a vow to pray for the salvation of souls. By 1962 these sisters left Vancouver to join a community of their sisters in Windsor, Ontario.

In 1955 the sisters began a new program for troubled girls aged eleven to fifteen years. The organization was structured so that "in many ways the Sisters of the Good Shepherd anticipated modern professional counselling and psychological therapy."[12]

On site for new facility, White Rock, 1961. Sisters of the Good Shepherd, Canada

In 1960 the sisters sold their monastery in Vancouver, but occupied it for a year-and-a-half until the completion of a new convent and school in White Rock in 1962. Set on thirty acres of land, the new facility was called Saint Euphrasia's School after the order's saintly foundress, Mother Mary Euphrasia Pelletier. The school focussed on developing a program of specialized treatment whereby the sisters helped troubled young girls to become valuable contributing members of society.

Sister Mary Francis Feener and Mother Mary Margaret Thompson—recreation at Alice Lake, 1958. Sisters of the Good Shepherd, Canada

The name of Saint Euphrasia was changed to Rosemary Heights in 1973, reflecting Saint Mary Euphrasia's baptismal name, Rose Virginie. In March 1973 the sisters opened a group home in Vancouver, Rosemary Residence, where young women prepared to live independently. Two years later, in 1975, Rosemary Heights became a retreat and renewal centre. While responding to the needs of the outside community, the sisters' manifested the charism of their own community by welcoming individual women who needed a quiet place of rest, reflection and prayer.

In 1995 the sisters sadly returned east, ending over one hundred years of devoted service to British Columbians and leaving behind a legacy of love and devotion to the many young women entrusted to their care. The Archdiocese of Vancouver, recognizing the value of their work, was determined to carry it on. They purchased the retreat centre from the sisters and employed lay personnel to continue its operation.

Sisters of Saint Joseph of Peace

Margaret Anna Cusack (1829–1899) converted to Catholicism after being a member of the Anglican Sellonite Sisterhood. She joined the Irish Poor Clares in Kenmare, Ireland, and became Sister Mary Francis Clare. For twenty-five years her work as a spiritual writer and religious historian with the Poor Clares earned her international acclaim as the "Nun of Kenmare." Her writings became increasingly political shortly before she left the Poor Clares to found the Order of the

Margaret Anna Cusack, the "Nun of Kenmare"1829–1899. Sisters of Saint Joseph of Peace Archives, Bellevue, WA

Sisters of Saint Joseph of Peace in Nottingham, England, in 1884. The mission of the community promoted "the peace of the church by both word and work."

In 1872 she completed the first volume of *The Spouse of Christ*, stating, "We are privileged to use our speech for the benefit of others—to console the afflicted, to teach the ignorant, to give counsel to the troubled, and above all to praise and glorify him who has given us the power of utterance."[13]

She wrote eloquently of the "unjust structures" of the church and state, which she believed contributed to the institutionalization of the poverty of the Irish people. In her writings she also advocated that Irish women be given equal access to education, equal pay for equal work, control of their own property and a voice in political affairs: "Give women their rights, then, for these rights are justice—justice to men as well as to women, for the interests of men and women cannot be separated."[14]

When Mother Francis Clare attempted to expand her work in England to the Irish-American emigrants in New York and New Jersey, she met with opposition. The following words express most clearly the wrath of the American hierarchy that resulted in her leaving the congregation in 1888, four years after she founded it: "As long as your Christianity is merely theoretical they are all very well pleased with you, but once they find you are practical in carrying it out, they part company from you, angrily or scornfully, as their dispositions incline them."[15]

Mother Evangelista Gaffney.
Sisters of Saint Joseph of Peace Archives, Bellevue, WA

To ensure the continuation of the work in which she so strongly believed, Mother Frances Clare quietly withdrew her leadership and resigned from the community. Her lifelong friend, Sister Evangelista Gaffney, was elected superior and continued to direct the community in England. As Mother Francis Clare departed from the community she founded, she bid her friend farewell with these words of encouragement: "With you at the helm, nothing can go wrong."[16]

In 1888 the Sisters of Saint Joseph of Peace proceeded forward under new leadership and established themselves in the eastern United States. Two years later they boldly began their first mission in the Pacific Northwest, and it is from there that the Sisters of Saint Joseph of Peace first came to British Columbia.

Mater Misericordiae, A Hospital for Miners

The reputation of the sisters' first mission in the Pacific Northwest, Saint Joseph's Hospital in Fairhaven, Washington, spread from there to Rossland, British Columbia by 1896. Saint Joseph's Hospital provided medical care for the men engaged in the hazardous logging industry. A request for similar assistance came from the mining industry in the districts surrounding Rossland.

Collecting donations for a hospital had already begun in the mining town of Rossland. Reverend Lemay invited the Sisters of Saint Joseph of Peace to visit, hoping to interest them in starting the health-care facility. In April 1896 Sister Teresa Moran and Sister Stanislaus Tighe left Fairhaven on the arduous two-day journey to Rossland. They intended to stay a few days and assess the situation, but remained for two months, collecting money from miners in the area with the intention of starting the new hospital.

A temporary hospital opened in a rented building on November 4, 1896. The two-storey building accommodated thirty patients and quickly filled to capacity. A week later, four Sisters of Saint Joseph of Peace arrived from the eastern United States to staff the hospital. Sister Teresa, Sister Ursula, Sister Carmelita and Sister Joseph Marie arrived at midnight, having been "lost, stumbling through the deep snow."[17] They were guided back to the frontier town of Rossland, where they endured further trauma when they learned their trunks had fallen into the Columbia River. All their belongings were damaged, including their new habits.

By March 15, 1897, four more sisters arrived in Rossland from Jersey City in the eastern United States. At the time, the sisters paid $100 dollars a month rent for the temporary hospital building, to be increased to $250 a month in April when their six-month lease expired. Although the hospital collected fees through a payroll deduction of $1 a month from each miner, payment for the physician's services reduced the institution's operating income. Rent was the largest expenditure by the hospital and became the limiting factor. It prompted them to look for a new location where they could construct their own hospital.

The sisters purchased three lots at a cost of $477.50. Then they employed the services of a local resident to design and build a three-storey frame structure. The thirty-five bed hospital cost $3,971.00 but did not include a heating system. On June 4, 1897, the hospital opened and patients were transferred from the temporary building to the new hospital. The following day Monsignor Eumelen blessed Mater Misericordiae Hospital.

Soon after the hospital opened, a strike by the mine workers ensued and the numbers at the hospital diminished substantially. By the end of the first year the sisters had treated 206 patients, incurring a debt of $4,245. Just as had been done at their convent schools in England, Mother Teresa (Kiernan) applied for a grant

Mater Miscericordae Hospital, 1896. Sisters of Saint Joseph of Peace Archives, Bellevue, WA

from the government. Her successful application added $3,000 to their coffers. This first grant awarded to a denominational hospital in British Columbia initiated annual grants to hospitals across Canada.

Funds came through various means, including a fair in November 1899 that raised $2,168 for the hospital. Contributions to Mater Misericordiae were also received from an Irish Church of England minister, Reverend Henry Irwin, who befriended the sisters and praised their work to his congregation.

The sisters became directly involved in fundraising when, clad in their long dark robes, they travelled throughout the region on horseback. They became expert riders, traversing terrifying trails where one wrong step could plunge them into raging rivers below treacherous precipices. By completing these dangerous and exhausting treks, they reduced their debt and collected enough to purchase more land and expand the hospital.

In Rossland, Mater Misericordiae continued to thrive, with major growth spurts in 1938, 1953 and 1962. The sisters built up this institution until 1969, when they relinquished its administration to the Regional Hospital District. Seventy-three years of medical care to the miners and residents of the area left many memories for those who had worked with the sisters and had been recipients of their kindness and care.

Sacred Heart Hospital, Greenwood
With the development of copper mines in the Kootenays, the need for another hospital arose in the area. An Oblate, Father Bedard, asked the sisters in

Rossland to start a hospital in the town of Greenwood. Mother Teresa Moran, provincial superior, and Sister Teresa Kiernan, superior of Mater Misericordiae, met with the mayor and council, who provided them with a loan of thirty-five hundred dollars to begin the project. They agreed to pay back the money with interest over a period of three years.

The sisters purchased a vacant schoolhouse on land adjoining Sacred Heart Church in Greenwood. The building required a number of alterations before it could be used as a hospital, but in May 1901 it opened under the name Sacred Heart Hospital. The following year, additions costing two thousand dollars included an entire new ward, as well as a sun parlour and operating room.

The mining industry declined over the years, resulting in a reduced need for hospital services. One by one the mines of the district closed due to low copper prices. The last one closed in 1918. With few residents left in Greenwood and its surrounding area, there were few patients to serve. The sisters closed the Sacred Heart Hospital in 1918 and moved to back to Washington State, while some relocated to Rossland.

Although the sisters had hoped mining conditions would improve so they could return to their hospital in Rossland, by 1921 it became clear the mines would not reopen. In 1921 the sisters had Sacred Heart Hospital dismantled. They saved two thousand dollars by using salvaged materials from the hospital to build an addition to a school in Nelson.

Saint Joseph's School, Nelson

Before the turn of the century, no Catholic schools had been established in the vicinity of Nelson. Bishop Dotenwill requested that Mother Evangelista Gaffney meet with him during her visit to British Columbia in order that they might discuss the opening of a new school in his Nelson parish. This encounter in September 1899 resulted in Mother Evangelista sending three sisters to begin the foundation for the first Catholic school in Nelson. Sister Joseph Marie and Sister Stanislaus, who happened to be Mother Evangelista's nieces, left with Sister Teresa for Nelson, arriving in December.

Upon their arrival they began soliciting "subscriptions" for the purchase of five lots Father Ferland had secured from the Canadian Pacific Railway Company. They later acquired two more lots with the intention of expanding.

The sisters offered classes in their convent until the new school could be built next door on the corner of Josephine and Mill streets. On February 5, 1900, Saint Joseph's Academy opened its doors to eighty-four students, including both day students and boarders.

Three weeks after the academy opened, Sister Cecilia and Sister De Pazzi arrived from Jersey City to assist in teaching. Three months later Sister

Sister Winefrid (l) and Sister Francis with students at St. Joseph's Academy circa 1900. Sisters of Saint Joseph of Peace Archives, Bellevue, WA

Hieronyme and Sister Winefride came from England, increasing the total number of sisters to seven. Sister Winefride became both superior of the new community and principal of the school.

The thirty-by-fifty-foot one-storey school cost two thousand dollars. One of its rooms incorporated a movable partition, which could be used to divide the room in two, as the occasion required. The school also included two music rooms for lessons taught after school. Other after-hours classes included a program of bookkeeping, stenography and typewriting taught by Sister Stanislaus. In addition, plain and art needlework augmented the school's curriculum along with special studies for young children.

By August of that year, just six months after opening Saint Joseph's Academy, the sisters undertook construction of a more permanent facility for a school and convent, which would also house boarders. Although it opened March 1901, only half of the plans had been completed due to lack of funds. Parishioners sponsored bazaars and other events to raise more money for the new school, and Sister Joseph Marie and Sister Hieronyme set out on a collection tour to the mining camps.

As always, soliciting donations required interacting directly with miners at their work site. While speaking with the miners, the sisters often took the oppor-

St. Joseph's Academy, Nelson, 1935.
Sisters of Saint Joseph of Peace Archives, Bellevue, WA

tunity to bring words of "cheer and consolation" to these hard-working men. On this particular tour, Sister Joseph Marie and Sister Hieronyme visited the Ymir Mine.

Limited access to the Ymir mine meant the sisters had to ride up the face of the mountain in an ore bucket. The mechanically operated bucket lifted them perpendicularly into the air, filling the white-knuckled Sister Hieronyme with great fear. Sister Joseph Marie, on the other hand, found the trip exhilarating, as if ascending into heaven. As the panoramic view unfolded before them, Sister Joseph praised the glories of God while Sister Hieronyme, eyes closed tight, stood rigidly praying that they would not descend to the depths of hell below.

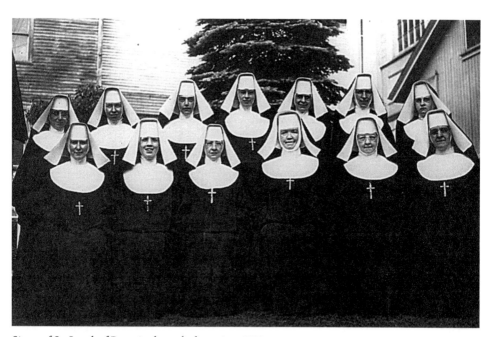

Sisters of St. Joseph of Peace in the early days, circa 1920.
Sisters of Saint Joseph of Peace Archives, Bellevue, WA

They returned safely home to Nelson. Like many sisters, their home, however, was not originally in the West. Until this time, all the sisters serving in the northwest missions came from either the eastern United States or from England. Imbued with missionary zeal, sisters left home with some trepidation and sorrow, aware of the impending hardships of the foreign missions. Not all sisters experienced an enthusiasm for missionary life, and the reality of being sent far away from home began to take its toll on aspiring postulants in the East. The resulting inexpediency of sisters coming west contributed to the inauguration of a western novitiate.

In 1902 Miss Alice O'Reilly of Nelson, British Columbia, became the first to seek admission at the provisional Western Novitiate, located at Saint Joseph's Hospital in the Fairhaven district of Bellingham. Miss O'Reilly eventually became Sister Mary Agnes, one of the many aspiring and increasing numbers of young women who came from the West to enter the new novitiate in Washington. The Eastern Novitiate, located in Englewood, New Jersey, continued to receive postulants, and in 1907 Sister Winefride went east to become its mistress of novices.

The final plans for Saint Joseph's Academy reached completion by 1922. A few years previous, four classrooms were added at the back of the parish hall. Now with the new construction, the convent and school had greatly improved facilities for both sisters and students.

As time progressed, community needs changed and the boarding school closed in 1948. It became a parochial school and ten years later, in 1958, the first lay teacher arrived to teach at what was now called Saint Joseph's School. As the number of sisters diminished, the number of lay teachers increased until finally only Sister Emilia Sosnowski, the principal, remained. In 1979 the old Saint Joseph's school was demolished and a new one built to replace it. Sister Emilia continued to devote herself to the children. With her retirement in 1989, she ended the legacy of the Sisters of Saint Joseph of Peace at Saint Joseph School in Nelson, which had begun with the support and encouragement of Mother Evangelista Gaffney.

Mother Evangelista Gaffney died in 1920. She had initiated the Nelson mission the year of the death of her friend and foundress of the community, Mother Frances Clare. Successfully, Mother Evangelista transformed the vision of Mother Francis Clare into reality. Her faith in the congregation's future in the Northwest motivated the women religious of her community to accomplish numerous missions throughout the United States and Canada. In 1929 the community changed its name to the Sisters of Saint Joseph of Newark. After Vatican II in 1970, the community returned to its original name of the Sisters of Saint Joseph of Peace, honouring the spirit and charism of their first foundress, the Nun of Kenmare.

Sisters of the Child Jesus

Anne-Marie Martel 1644–1673.
Sisters of the Child Jesus Archives, North Vancouver

Anne-Marie Martel spent the last six years of her short life (1644–1673) laying the charismatic groundwork for the Congregation of the Sisters of the Child Jesus. For more than three centuries countless women would continue to emulate her response to divine influence. Anne-Marie's work began with a request by her spiritual advisor, Father Tronson, to educate the poor in the Christian faith.

In 1667, in a small hospital near Le Puy, France, she started instructing women in Christian doctrine. The following year, she went with her friend, Catherine Felix, to do the same for young peasant women who sought employment in the city, where the burgeoning lace-making industry offered rural women an opportunity to eke out a living.

Anne-Marie called the groups of women who worked in the lace-making industry "assemblies." She took the opportunity to instruct them in religious doctrine while they worked, but she did not limit her efforts to teaching them about Christianity. The lace merchants did not pay their workers a fair price for their work, and this exploitation motivated Anne-Marie to assist the lace makers by selling their lace at a fair price and by improving their physical situation and their self esteem.

Anne-Marie Martel was eventually called to teach Christian doctrine in the surrounding villages. She realized that providing religious instruction throughout the countryside would require assistance by more women, and many were attracted to her way of life. The first community of the Ladies of Instruction consisting of nine Ladies, representing the nine choirs of angels, organized itself by adhering to the vision of Anne-Marie Martel.

Anne-Marie Martel also trained single young women to live among the villagers. Known as "Beates" or "Daughters of Instruction," the young women took no vow but committed themselves to the ideals and values of the Anne-Marie Martel foundation. As Beates increased in number, the mission of evangelization flourished throughout the area surrounding Le Puy.

When Anne-Marie Martel died in 1673, her goal was realized. She had left her foundation with two kinds of members, the Ladies of the Instruction and the Daughters of the Instruction. The Ladies of the Instruction obtained the official approbation of the church in 1676, and in 1678 the nine Ladies in charge of the congregation made a public vow of chastity in the bishop's chapel.

By 1708 the Ladies of Instruction had joined with the Ladies of the Child Jesus to become the Ladies of Instruction of the Child Jesus, later to be called the Sisters of Instruction of the Child Jesus. Before their descendants reached British Columbia they endured the many hardships typical of a newly founded society. The first hurdle to overcome involved being born a woman. According to the annals about the time the two organizations merged, some deemed it inappropriate that women teach Christian doctrine.

The women exacerbated the problem by teaching in barns and other seemingly irreverent places. Their spiritual director, M. De Lantages, took up their cause. He tirelessly preached of the many examples of women teaching catechism throughout history, as far back as ancient times. His efforts fostered the continuation of the apostolic mission of these women, which continued to expand until the onset of the French Revolution in 1789.

During the French Revolution the guillotine was a threat to anyone who practised or taught religion, and therefore religion was not allowed in the school curricula. The basis of the Anne-Marie Martel foundation lay in teaching the poor to read for the purpose of studying catechism.

The tumultuous years following the Revolution saw the disbanding of the community. But a few remaining women from the community survived the almost insurmountable odds of the French Revolution and courageously picked up the cause of the Anne-Marie Martel foundation. They reclaimed their house, which had been turned into a cotton-weaving factory, and opened a school for poor children, expanding their mission from catechism to the regular curriculum.

Their apostolic mission continued into the twentieth century, but not without enduring another major persecution. In 1904 the government of France initiated a law that disallowed the involvement of any religious communities in schools, thereby cutting off the influence of the Catholic Church throughout France and demanding the secularization of religious communities. The sisters' schools and colleges became the property of private individuals or the property of the French government through sales or confiscation. The religious communities no longer controlled the institutions they worked so hard to build. It was at this time that some sisters, rather than disband, chose to emigrate to Canada, thus strengthening the first party of four sisters who arrived in British Columbia in 1896.

Voyage to the New World

Bishop Durieu became acquainted with the Sisters of the Child Jesus when his niece joined as a member of their congregation. She lived in Le Puy, France, the city of his birth, and he would often visit her there. On one of several occasions, he requested the sisters to consider assisting in missionary work in British Columbia, where he maintained jurisdiction. Their eventual positive reply resulted in four members leaving for British Columbia in April 1896. Sister Aimée de Marie, Sister Félicien, Sister Saint-Fabien and Sister Euphrasia left for the Cariboo region of British Columbia to teach Native people.

First Missionary Sisters of the Child Jesus, 1896.
From top left: Sisters Felicien, Fabian and Euphrasia.
Seated: Mother Aimée de Marie.
Sisters of the Child Jesus Archives, North Vancouver

Sister Félicien's journal recollects their sorrow and strength on leaving France. Sadness surrounded them as they bid goodbye to friends and family, whose faces they would likely never see again. The pain of leaving their country and religious community touched them deeply, but the joy of spreading the spirit of their community gave them strength to journey to the New World.

At four in the morning on April 28, they left Le Puy for Paris by train. At station stops all along the way, members from their community greeted the zealous adventurers with goodwill and gifts for their long journey. On May 1 they left Paris, again by train, to catch a boat to Southampton, where they boarded the *Paris*. En route to New York, Mother Aimée and Sister Félicien suffered seasickness for nine days on what they called the "tiny floating city." Finally, on May 9, "thousands of hankies" waved them ashore and they found themselves "transplanted in a crowd speaking Milton's language."[18]

They left New York by train for Montreal, where the Sisters of Providence, who ran the Saint Vincent de Paul Shelter, offered them a short but restful night and the warm comfort of French-speaking sisters. The next day they began their seemingly endless trip across a vast territory more expansive then they had ever imagined, through the Canadian Shield, across the Prairies and into the mountains of British Columbia.

At 5:00 a.m. on May 16 they arrived at a dilapidated little station in Ashcroft, believing their journey had ended. However, Bishop Durieu met the four sisters there to guide them along the last leg of their historic journey. They boarded a shabby stagecoach pulled by six horses and judged it a rather undignified mode of transport for the distinguished bishop.

The group spent the next two days bumping about on a beaten path riddled with holes. Each bump initiated a burst of laughter from Sister Félicien and cries of "Mercy!" from Mother Aimée de Marie. In prayer-like fashion, Sister Fabien methodically repeated, "These American miles are certainly long." Lizze, a young Native girl from the Sta:los tribe, squatted in the corner of the coach, seeming to hardly notice any hardships of the ride. The bishop brought her along believing she had a religious vocation.

On May 16, the first day of their two-day journey to Saint Joseph's Mission, the snow fell all afternoon. By 9:30 p.m. they reached the top of a mountain where the custodians of Eighty-three Mile House awaited their arrival. Dizzy from the day's ride, they stretched out onto the much-appreciated beds. Sister Félicien recalled: "I felt as seasick as if I were still rocking on the waves. This rocking seemed to put me to sleep, for I fell into a deep sleep, neither knowing where I was, nor what time it was, until four o'clock the next morning. After a hurried breakfast, we climbed back into the heavy wagon…The only thing that I remember on this last stage was that large numbers of bluebirds blue as the sky played about in leaves, green as the ocean! Nature with its savage beauty, unknown in France, delighted me during my short stay in the Cariboo!"[19]

Williams Lake

A group of white people announced with gunshots the arrival of the sisters and bishop to Saint Joseph's Mission. The Natives formed a semicircle, welcoming the sisters with traditional handshakes and a song. Although neither knew the other's language, they all understood that the sisters had come a long way to assist at the mission.

The Sisters of Saint Ann had arrived in 1878 to teach girls at the mission, but circumstances forced them to leave in 1890. The mission school then became a Native residential school where the Oblate fathers educated the boys and a laywoman taught the girls. When the Sisters of the Child Jesus took over from the lay teacher, thirty girls came into their care. The attire and manner of these girls appeared quite foreign to the sisters, who spent the first night "with heavy hearts" longing for their native France.

Williams Lake Mission. Sisters of the Child Jesus Archives, North Vancouver

The sisters found familiar comfort in the chapel of their small convent, located at the base of gentle mountain slopes. They had difficulty maintaining physical comfort, as horrible swarms of mosquitoes descended upon them. These incessant insects relentlessly assaulted them. The sisters covered themselves with transparent gauze veils while they crocheted after supper, and the girls assisted their work by shaking aspen branches to help keep away the annoying insects. The next summer, screens helped to alleviate the invasion of insects. The arrival of the cool autumn rescued them from the insufferable scourge, which was only to be replaced by the unbearable cold of winter: "Despite well-filled, swelling stoves, we could hardly protect ourselves from the excessive cold! Especially in the morning, if we stood with our backs to the fire, our noses or our shoulders would freeze. In vain we jumped and ran back and forth to warm up, we still shivered and our teeth chattered, without our being able to stop them! In the refectory, it was even worse. The stove made so much noise, we could almost think there was a fire in the chimney, yet the whole room was icy! Meat, milk, coffee, all was frozen … Sister Fabien needed a lot of strength and courage to cut beefsteak as hard as a stone."[20]

Since coming to Canada the sisters had learned a good deal, including a new language taught to them by Father Dottenwil. Sister Félicien tried to control her laughter when she heard her companions attempt to pronounce the harsh English consonants. When Bishop Durieu returned to visit the mission in August, he tested Mother Aimée de Marie by immediately addressing her in

Camping at the Williams Lake Mission. Sisters of the Child Jesus Archives, North Vancouver

English and asking a number of questions in the same tongue. Pleased with her response, the bishop finally broke the formality with "Now, let's talk French."[21]

The bishop spent some time at the mission before he left. At the end of January he wrote to them, announcing his intent to leave again for France, promising to bring back some of their sisters from Le Puy. They found consola-

Sisters with girls doing needlework circa 1910. Sisters of the Child Jesus Archives, North Vancouver

Sisters and children canoeing on Yellow Lake. Sisters of the Child Jesus Archives, North Vancouver

tion in the possibility that their isolated community might increase in numbers, but they also felt grateful for their small family and noted that "our days, weeks, and months were blessed in a thousand ways in our intimate family life. Our mutual love made us forget many a worry, pass over many a trouble. When we love each other, nothing is hard."[22]

However, life for the sisters was very hard and it took incredible courage and strength to overcome the many difficulties they endured in those early years. Work at Williams Lake was long and hard, lasting twenty-four hours a day. Although the sisters taught classes during the day, they were also responsible for the supervision of the children, including their recreation and study. Also, they had dormitory night duty. In the early days they slept in the same dormitory as the children who had tuberculosis, and some of the sisters succumbed to this disease. They took no holidays and during the summer they did the canning for the entire year.

Word of help from Le Puy was joyful news. A letter arrived from the mother general in France, advising them that on August 27, 1899, the bishop departed from Le Puy with four sisters from their community. The arrival of Sister Joannes, Sister Laurentie, Sister Cecilien and Sister Hieronymie resulted in some changes. Sister Euphrasia replaced Mother Aimée as superior of Saint Joseph's Mission, allowing Mother Aimée to become principal of a new Native school near the city of Vancouver.

A New Mission on the West Coast

The four new sisters from France stayed only a few days at Saint Joseph's Mission before two left with Sister Félicien to begin a new mission on the West Coast. Sister Félicien had become attached to Saint Joseph's Mission and when she left, her heart filled with sorrow. The hospitality of the Sisters of Saint Ann in New Westminster helped Sister Félicien's sorrow fade.

The three sisters went on to stay briefly with the Sisters of Providence at Saint Mary's Hospital in New Westminster before leaving for their final destination. Although inundated with the casualties of a recent fire that had devastated two thirds of New Westminster, the Sisters of Providence welcomed the Sisters of the Child Jesus with "boundless charity." They offered them a spacious private room and, in their precious hours of recreation, companionship. Although the situation began with something of a tense atmosphere because of the fire, the consideration shown by the Sisters of Providence resulted in the development of a supportive friendship: "The Superior had been so motherly to us! The sisters so affectionate, so self-forgetful!...the memory of the gracious hospitality received at the St. Mary's Hospital will always remain graven in our hearts! The blessed name of the Sisters of Providence will be mingled in the history of the foundation of the Sisters of the Child Jesus in British Columbia!"[23]

Finally, accompanied by the bishop, the sisters left for their new mission on the north shore of Burrard Inlet. From across the inlet, they saw "a lovely little village of white houses dotting, in the distance and in front of a cloudy sky, the opposite side of the water, facing the young, growing city of Vancouver...The Church with its pointed bell-tower dominated the homes of the Squamish tribe Indians. After a detour, the tramway stopped at the BC Electric Station where we got off...and there we were on the way to the dock..."[24]

On the shores of Vancouver they met the Squamish people, who took the sisters and the bishop across the inlet to the other side. Terrified, Sister Félicien hesitated to get into their "delicate" birchbark canoes, but she was determined to complete this last leg of her journey and finally climbed in. The Natives hoisted the sails and they arrived safely on the north shore. With trunks in tow they traversed a narrow footbridge to reach the group of little white houses that sheltered the inhabitants of the area.

For the next three months, while members of the Squamish Nation built a convent school for them, the sisters occupied one of the little white houses along the shore. The men first cleared the land of enormous stumps and the women extracted roots and gathered stones. By January 22, 1899, under the direction of Father De Vrienldt, this building was completed. A ceremonial procession welcomed them into their new home and launched the legacy of Saint Paul's School, named after Bishop Paul Durieu.

St. Paul's School, North Vancouver. Sisters of the Child Jesus Archives, North Vancouver

Sister Joannes took on kitchen duty and Sisters Hieronymie and Félicien taught the children the basics of reading, writing and arithmetic. At the end of their lessons the sisters and students went outside to help remove the gigantic stumps that surrounded the convent in preparation for a garden that would eventually support cabbage, potatoes, lettuce and flowers: "His Excellency had already lighted the fire; and we raced to see who was the fastest worker for supplying it, bringing twigs from the area we proudly called 'the garden'; brambles, ferns, and bushes of every kind had grown there freely since Creation...For the moment we had to clean up the thick mass,—converted now to a little garden, with several flower-beds to brighten it up! We rivalled in finding dead branches, throwing them around the colossal trunk where they soon burst out in yellow flames, acclaimed by joyous, prolonged yells."[25]

The inhabitants of the new mission continued on as usual,

In the garden of St. Paul's School, circa 1910.
Sisters of the Child Jesus Archives, North Vancouver

Picking raspberries at St. Paul's School. Sisters of the Child Jesus Archives, North Vancouver

clearing the land and teaching the children. In mid-February, much to the excitement of the sisters, Mother Aimée de Marie finally arrived from the Cariboo to take charge. The sisters spoke French amongst themselves, but once a week a young woman would come to assist them in their English. For their hard work, Bishop Durieu promised them a boat trip and picnic in May. This outing held a special memory for them, as Bishop Durieu died in June, causing much grief throughout the community. He provided them with much-needed strength and direction during the establishment of this new mission.

Bishop Dotenwill replaced Bishop Durieu. A short time later the new bishop came to the Squamish village, where the people welcomed him: "...the Indians had decorated the pavilion beside the river bank...several old multi-colored rags were the only expense...all the villages came around: men standing, women hunched on their heels...children ran to-and-fro without paying any attention to the ceremony. Chief Harry, in the name of the people, addressed a speech to His Excellency in the Squamish language; Chief Joe translated into Chinook and His Excellency answered in that dialect, which Chief Joe retranslated into Squamish for the audience!"[26]

By September 1899 the sisters accepted boys at their school, as directed by the bishop. They constructed an addition to their building to accommodate the new students, who were taught by Sister Hieronymie. The boys and girls totalled eighteen.

Just as Bishop Durieu had done before him, Bishop Dotenwill journeyed to France and brought back five more sisters from Le Puy. Two left for Saint Joseph's Mission in the Cariboo, two went to work in the Seminary in New Westminster and one assisted at Saint Paul's School. By 1902 the increased enrolment of Saint Paul's to fifty-two led to a request from Mother Aimée for more sisters from France. On October 25 of that same year, five more sisters arrived to help. The following year they enlarged the convent school.

Sechelt

The Laws of Association and Separation, which were in effect in France from 1901 to 1905, caused the secularization of religious congregations, the closure of their schools and the confiscation of their property. The Sisters of the Child Jesus endured the closure of sixty-seven of their houses in France and made a mass exodus to missions in Argentina and Canada.

In 1903 the mother general from France announced that in October, ten sisters would be leaving Le Puy to assist the missions in British Columbia. This news filled the mission sisters with joy. When the new recruits arrived as scheduled, all remained to help with the Squamish mission. There, the new sisters

At the Thitaker House, Sechelt, circa 1905. Sisters of the Child Jesus Archives, North Vancouver

learned the customs of the Natives and the English language, which they would soon teach. The following June they left for Saint Augustine's School in Sechelt.

The convent school had just been built by the Sechelt people, who two years previously had urged the sisters to come and teach their children. With an increased workforce, the sisters could meet their request. The Sechelt Native settlement resembled that of Squamish, with little white houses built around a church and set in the forest, which opened up to the ocean. As Sister Félicien later described it on one of her summer visits, "... every year we roamed along its incomparable banks, bathed in sunshine and rested in the fresh breeze from the water. It was a happiness without clouds...sprayed by the sea...long walks among the beautiful pine and spruce...It was nature as the Creator had made it; man had not yet ruined it by his modern inventions, and had not yet troubled the restful solitude."[27]

The life of the sisters in Sechelt remained full, teaching the children and carrying out the many daily tasks required to maintain their survival. The sisters depended on fish—fresh or dry, salted or smoked—and deer meat that the Native people brought to them. They supplemented this diet by growing vegetables in a garden on land they cleared, and by keeping cows. The sisters were very poor and at one time used felt hats to make themselves shoes. This life differed substantially from the life they had left behind in France, where fine boarding schools afforded them a more comfortable existence.

Maillardville

Five years after the Sechelt school opened, a small group of French Canadians, recruited from eastern Canada by Father O'Boyle, established themselves on the north shore of the Fraser River near New Westminster. They worked at Fraser Mills, a sawmill company that offered them "miserable huts where there were no comforts or commodities."[28] They eventually built permanent homes on a piece of wooded property granted to them by the company. In honour of the first parish priest, Father Maillard, the settlement became known as Maillardville.

The community, composed almost entirely of Catholics, wanted the amenities of a Catholic church and school. A young Catholic girl taught classes until Mother Aimée sent Sisters Amelie and Alix to relieve her. These two sisters lodged at Saint Louis College in New Westminster until they could be accommodated in Maillardville. Other sisters also resided and worked at the college, which was run by the Oblate fathers. The fathers paid the sisters' daily train fare to Maillardville, where the sisters taught French-Canadian children, providing lessons in both French and English at Our Lady of Lourdes School. The settlers paid for the sisters' room and board, but could not offer to pay them a salary.

Corpus Christie procession in Maillardville. Sisters of the Child Jesus Archives, North Vancouver

Expansion and Change

While French-speaking Maillardville established its settlement, Saint Edmund's School began offering an education to English-speaking children in a settlement located near the Squamish reserve on the north shore of Burrard Inlet. The French-speaking Sisters of the Child Jesus had taught in the English language for over a decade and agreed to teach these children as well. There were now sisters living in the Squamish and Sechelt reserves, New Westminster, Maillardville and North Vancouver, and teaching at Native, French and English schools.

The growing missions in British Columbia required more sisters. New vocations often came from schools where the sisters taught, where young girls influenced by their example would enter the novitiate. Although the sisters considered their schools fertile ground for new entrants, they deemed their present student population too young for convent life and looked elsewhere to increase their numbers.

Bishop McNeil gave the sisters some hope that new recruits could be coming from France and perhaps even Ireland. The bishop knew of an institution in Callan, Ireland, called the Sisters of Mercy, which prepared young women for lives as foreign missionaries. The regional superior, Mother Aimée and Mother Thérèsine left for Ireland, where they met Miss Josephine Tuite. She accepted

Sister Henrietta with her family on her profession day, 1911.
Sisters of the Child Jesus Archives, North Vancouver

Rosy Louis, (Sister Henrietta) became the province's first Native Catholic sister. Sisters of the Child Jesus Archives, North Vancouver

their offer to return with them to British Columbia and enter the Novitiate of the Sisters of the Child Jesus. During their overseas excursion they also visited their motherhouse in LePuy, where two young French girls answered their request for assistance in Canada. On August 24, 1911, all three recruits accompanied Mother Aimée and Sister Thérèsine back to the Squamish mission.

Sister Euphrasia had prepared a little cottage in North Vancouver to be used as a novitiate. It was decided, however, that because of the solitude and beautiful ambiance at Sechelt, the novitiate should be located there. The three postulants began their training, joined by a fourth, Rosy Louis, a Shushwap Native who took the name of Sister Henrietta. Thus the Novitiate of the Sisters of the Child Jesus began training postulants in the West, solidly establishing themselves on Canadian ground.

Original fluted bonnet worn with ankle-length black dress, 1896 (top) and updated 1911 version (bottom). Sisters of the Child Jesus Archives, North Vancouver

At the time of the formation of the novitiate in 1911, the sisters who resided in Canada collectively became known as a Region of the Congregation of the Sisters of the Child Jesus. The regional superior, Mother Aimée, resided at the Squamish mission, which became the centre of administrative activity. The jurisdictional change, approved in France, included another change. When Mother Aimée and her companions returned from France, they looked noticeably different. Bishop McNeil had asked Mother Aimée and Sister Thérèsine to consider a change of habit before they left for Ireland and France. He advised them that their dress, which included the "cobra" headdress, no longer appeared suitable for Canada. This issue could not be resolved without the consent and approval of the generalate.[29]

The teaching sisters in France, who had been unable to wear the habit for a number of years, found this a grave issue. Although the change of habit would not affect them directly, the habit represented their solidarity with the women who followed the ideals of Anne-Marie Martel. After much deliberation and assurance that a change of headdress would not dissociate foreign mission sisters from their counterparts in France, it was agreed that the style of headdress would change.

When the sisters returned from France, those in British Columbia hardly recognized them. Each wore a fluted "round the face" bonnet instead of the familiar "cobra" or "sunray" bonnet. The change met with the approval of the sisters and Bishop McNeil. A few days later all the Sisters of the Child Jesus donned their new headdress. A new frame around their face, however, did not change their mission.

With the establishment of the novitiate in Sechelt, the Sisters of the Child Jesus were able to educate women interested in following in the footsteps of Anne-Marie Martel and expand her work across British Columbia and into Alberta, Saskatchewan, Manitoba and Quebec. The pioneer work of the first four sisters who ventured from their homeland had entered a new era and century. For the next hundred years they would continue to expand into the north, Vancouver Island, the lower mainland and the interior of British Columbia.

Mother Aimée de Marie, Canadian foundress, meets the Duke of Connaught in Vancouver, September 1912. Sisters of the Child Jesus Archives, North Vancouver

CHAPTER TWO NOTES

1. Hortense Quesnelle, Précis of Chronicles for Saint Mary's Hospital, New Westminster, BC, July 1891 (Sisters of Providence Archives, Edmonton, Alberta).
2. Ibid., February 1909.
3. Sister Jean LaBissoniere, *Providence Trail Blazers* (Providence Centre: Sisters of Providence, 1976), 12.
4. Sister Mary Gleason, *He has given me a flame* (Collection Providence), 89.
5. Sister Mary Euphrasia, *Practical Rules* (Religious of the Good Shepherd Archives, Ottawa, 1898).
6. Annals of the Religious of the Good Shepherd, Ottawa, July 26, 1890.
7. *The Month*, (diocesan monthly publication from 1892–1896) New Westminster, January, 1892 (from Public Library, New Westminster, BC), 115.
8. Pamphlet titled "Stand Still and Consider the Wondrous Works of God" (Religious of the Good Shepherd, Vancouver, BC).
9. Ibid.
10. George C. Stewart Jr., *Marvels of Charity: History of American Sisters and Nuns* (Huntington, Indiana: Our Sunday Visitor Publishing Division, 1994), 270.
11. Annals of the Religious of the Good Shepherd, Ottawa.
12. George C. Stewart Jr., *Marvels of Charity: History of American Sisters and Nuns* (Huntington, Indiana: Our Sunday Visitor Publishing Division, 1994), 142.
13. Eleanor Gilmore, (from executive orientation notebook, Sacred Heart Hospital, Eugene, Oregon, March 28, 1994), A-3.
14. Centenary Year of Jubilee 1884–1984 Congregation of the Sisters of St. Joseph of Peace "Quotes from Margaret Anna Cusack," (Congregation of Saint Joseph of Peace Archives, Bellevue, Washington).

15. Eleanor Gilmore, (from executive orientation notebook, Sacred Heart Hospital, Eugene, Oregon, March 28, 1994), A-3.
16. "Service Issue" (brochure, CJSP Archives, Bellevue, Washington, September 1979).
17. Reverend P.R. McCaffrey, *From Dusk to Dawn* (1932), 215.
18. *Early History of the Congregation in Canada (1896–1943)*: Notes taken from Sister Félicien's journal, (Sisters of the Child Jesus Archives, North Vancouver, BC), 3.
19. Ibid., 5.
20. Ibid., 9.
21. Ibid., 10.
22. Ibid., 11.
23. Ibid., 17.
24. Ibid., 17.
25. Ibid., 29.
26. Ibid., 36.
27. Ibid., 103.
28. Ibid., 96.
29. "Generalate" refers to the central administration office of a congregation.

CHAPTER THREE

The Turn of the Century

The Benedictine Sisters

The long history of the Benedictine sisters began in Italy in the early sixth century, when Saint Benedict and his sister, Saint Scholastica, founded the monastic Order of Saint Benedict. The first Benedictine sisters to arrive in North America came from Saint Walburga's Abbey in Eichstatt, Bavaria, Germany, in the mid-nineteenth century. By the mid-twentieth century these Benedictine sisters, who by then totalled over sixty-five hundred, had established thirty-five foundations throughout the United States, Mexico and Canada.

The first Benedictine sisters in British Columbia trace their roots to a regional settlement known as French Prairie on Oregon's Willamette Valley,

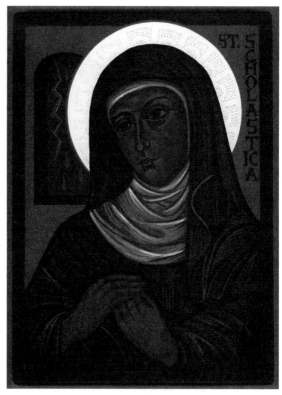

Icon of St. Scholastica by Mary Charles McGough.
O.S.B St. Scholastica Monastery, Duluth, MN

south of Portland. Archbishop Segher of the Archdiocese of Portland welcomed their influence in the small French Catholic settlement of Gervais, where the sisters started a convent and school. As was so often the case, the "fine home" promised to them did not materialize and they established a convent on the second floor of Matt's Saloon.

Although the sisters served as religious instructors to the white settlers of Gervais, they hoped to participate in the Native missions of America as well. Father Adelhelm recruited sisters for Gervais in the late nineteenth century, going directly to monasteries in Switzerland, where conversion of the Native North Americans was considered "one of the new Benedictine apostolates of the nineteenth century." The writings of contemporary authors motivated the sisters to leave their homeland for North America.[1] They were especially influenced by the writings of James Fenimore Cooper, who wrote *The Last of the Mohicans*. Karl Friedrich May, a widely read German author, promoted the evangelization of the "savages" in his books.[2] Sister Beatrice affirmed that she had come to the United States with her brother, who had read James Fenimore Cooper, in order to convert Natives[3].

En route from Switzerland to Gervais in 1882, Father Adelhelm stopped at a Benedictine monastery in Missouri. Six years earlier, Mother Bernardine Wachter had arrived there from Maria Rickenbach monastery in Switzerland. When Father Adelhelm left Missouri with his Swiss recruits, she joined them. Just two days after their arrival in Gervais, Mother Bernardine took three sisters with her to begin teaching at a boarding school for Native children on Oregon's Grande Ronde Indian Reservation.

The sisters taught there for almost two decades, until the federal government took control of all reservation schools in the US and required the withdrawal of the sisters in 1900.[4] At that time their numbers had increased with added postulants from both Switzerland and North America. To house their growing community they built the Queen of Angels Monastery, a new four-storey structure situated on the hill below Mount Angel Abbey, which was the home of the Benedictine priests and brothers. The Queen of Angels Monastery in Mount Angel, Oregon, provided a home for the sisters as well as housing and classrooms for their students.

Three sisters from the Queen of Angels Monastery were the first to arrive in British Columbia. The sisters left Oregon with two Benedictine priests and two brothers from Mount Angel Abbey in 1900. Their destination was Meares Island, west of Vancouver Island. At a place called Kakawis, they began to teach at the newly constructed Christie School, a boarding school for Native people.

Establishing a Benedictine School

Father Brabant proposed the idea of a boarding school for Native children on the West Coast:

> Our Indians all over the coast are well disposed; ... This being known seems to have excited the Presbyterian and Methodist denominations, and their efforts to invade the coast are very pronounced ... the zeal of the Protestant ministers has grown to the extent that they now have established themselves at different points on the coast. When a man's life was in danger and when the only means of travelling was an Indian canoe; when the mails reached us only once or twice a year ... we were welcome to do alone the work of converting the natives; but now with the present facilities and the absence of danger, the ministers come in sight to give us trouble and to pervert our Indian children. After mature reflection I made up my mind to propose to our Bishop a plan for his approbation. I would build in a central part of the coast an industrial school for boys and girls.[5]

Bishop Lemmens rejected Father Brabant's plan for an industrial school due to a lack of available funds. However, Bishop Lemmens died in 1897 and Bishop Christie took his place. Bishop Christie wanted Father Brabant's twenty-five years of missionary work with the Natives to continue and went to Ottawa to request help. At that time the federal Department of Indian Affairs financially supported missionaries' education and health-care programs for Natives. The bishop returned from Ottawa with an annual grant for fifty students.

In 1898 Bishop Christie became archbishop of Oregon City (Portland, Oregon). He met with some members of the Mount Angel Benedictine community in Portland and urged them to staff the school he was building at Kakawis. In August 1899 the procurator and Prior Adelhelm, who established Oregon's Benedictine community of men, went to Kakawis to determine its suitability as a Benedictine mission. Although construction of Christie School had not been completed yet, they were pleased with the facilities and agreed to be responsible for the education of the boys when the school opened the following year. The sisters agreed to be responsible for the girls. At the time of opening the school at Kakawis, about sixty percent of the Nootka accepted Christianity, at least to some extent.

Father Brabant Prepares the Way

The history of Christie School began in 1875 with Father Brabant, who spent twenty-five years as a missionary with the Natives along the West Coast. He recorded, "I have never been able to detect anything but that the Indians at the time of our arrival here were addicted almost beyond redemption to every description of pagan practices."[6]

When Father Brabant first settled in a camp of Natives, only four other white men lived along the west coast of Vancouver Island. The population of whites slowly increased, while the population of the Nootka slowly diminished. Ten years after Father Brabant's arrival, the Nootka numbered approximately thirty-five hundred. By the time the Benedictines arrived in 1900, the population of the Nootka had diminished to approximately twenty-five hundred.

During Father Brabant's missionary years he recorded the culture and behaviour of the Natives in his journal, where he described many ceremonial events and rituals. His recordings allow us some insight into his perspective of the Native people and reflect the vast differences between European and Native cultures at the time. On one occasion after a funeral procession "the Indians all rushed into the river praying and shouting; and having thrown away their blankets which were their only covering, they next came in every one of them as naked as the moment he had been born."[7]

On another occasion the Natives honoured Father Brabant with a feast where "the men were dressed up in red blankets over their red skins...their faces covered with black and red paint, and down of birds covered their heads...there were dancing and shouting and gesticulations and many other extravagant things, which no one can fancy who has not seen wild men and women, covered with feathers and with painted cheeks, giving free expression to the feelings of their savage heart and nature."[8]

Through much effort over a long period of time, Father Brabant managed to capture the interest of the Natives: "After the usual instructions, I administered baptism to one hundred and thirty-five children. The afternoon was spent in teaching songs and the Sign of the Cross. Such was the zeal of these Indians that, when we went on board of the schooner to take our meals, they would stay in the house, and hardly leave us time to finish, but wanted us to recommence our work at once."[9]

Father Brabant spent a great deal of time sparring with the medicine men and women in an attempt to convert the Natives to Christianity. He tried to expose their legends and "superstitions" as falsehoods: "The Indians tell their yarns with such conviction of truth that it is almost painful to have to contradict them."[10]

Father Brabant's life appeared to be over when he was shot repeatedly by a Native. However, as the story is told, he managed to get to Victoria, where the Sisters of Saint Ann nursed his bullet-riddled body back to health and he returned to his mission regarded as a superman. His miraculous recovery likely added to the numbers of adult conversions among the Natives.

The Benedictine Sisters Travel to Kakawis

On May 7, 1900, Sister Placide Casey, Sister Clotilde Wildhaber and Sister Frances Wildhaber left the Queen of Angels Convent in Mount Angel for their mission on Meares Island. Two brothers and two priests from Mount Angel Abbey accompanied them. The missionary party met with Archbishop Christie in Portland and received his blessing, then continued on to Victoria, where they arrived on May 10. The Benedictine sisters spent the night with the Sisters of Saint Ann, while the monks stayed at the Bishop's Palace. The following morning they left with Father Nicolaye for Kuper Island to observe the Native residential school operated by the Sisters of Saint Ann. They returned to Victoria four days later and boarded the *Willopa* headed for Clayoquot Sound.

During their voyage, the vessel, which had been converted from a sailboat to a steamer, caught fire. With some effort one of the priests and the crew members extinguished the fire and they arrived safely at Clayoquot harbour, where they were met at the wharf by Father Van Nevel, some white settlers and "all the Indians and canoes of the village."[11] The fire episode provided a memorable story for the passengers, but the crew focused on their unique cargo, as "it wasn't every day that the ship carried sisters on their passenger list."[12]

On May 16, 1900, the missionary party transferred their belongings, including sixteen trunks, to canoes, and paddled to Kakawis on Meares Island. On the island they found no village but only the school, which was located fifty feet

Christie Industrial School on Meares Island. Archives, Queen of Angels Monastery, Oregon

above the beach at the foot of Lone Cone Mountain. The frame building rose two-and-a-half storeys high and measured sixty by forty feet. A small outbuilding used for a laundry stood nearby.

Surrounding the school were remnants of the rain forest, which stood in its primal form just a short distance away, enveloping the mountainous island. The cleared land provided no garden, but the sisters harvested fresh fish and clams from the saltwater bay, and the nearby stream provided fresh water. Although the grand and rugged green exuded a calm ambiance, this remote place seemed very far from the civilized world they had left behind.

When the sisters arrived, there were no children at the school. Father Maurus set out on the *Willopa* with a priest from Clayoquot to recruit students and within a week, ten pupils enrolled. On May 29, 1900, school began at Kakawis.

The majority of students, who came from nearby tribes including the Cayoquot and Ahousat, could not speak English. The sisters themselves first had to master English and then transfer their knowledge of the language to the children. In the early years the children and sisters used sign language to communicate.

To varying degrees many Natives accepted Christianity but they were not easily convinced that their children should be entrusted to the care of the missionaries to learn the culture and language of the Europeans. In his accounts of Christie School, Father Maurus remembers, "In general Indian fathers and mothers of the West Coast were and still are very fond of children ... Such affection of parents for their children is a factor to be reckoned with. In many cases the Indians were reluctant in sending their children to school ... many were still pagan ... medicine men and Indian doctors and sorcerers spared no pains in discouraging the parents sending the children to school ... They said the boys would have to wear pants all the time. For them pants were an abomination to the blanket savage ..."[13]

Working in Kakawis

Sister Placide began teaching, Sister Frances took her position as cook and Sister Clotilde began working as seamstress and dressmaker. The sisters cared for the girls, who learned to cook, bake, wash, sew, embroider, knit and darn. The priests and brothers taught the boys carpentry, shoe repair and painting. Girls and boys took lessons in reading, writing, arithmetic and religion, generally following the curriculum of the School Branch of the Department of Indian Affairs. The curriculum had been initiated years previously, in 1895.

The children spent half their day in lessons and divided the rest of the day into work and recreation. The girls generally worked in the kitchen, sewing room and laundry, whereas the boys worked in the barns and gardens, and in the car-

Christie Schoolyard. Archives, Queen of Angels Monastery, Oregon

pentry and shoe shops. The assistance of the students in everyday tasks was crucial to the survival of students and sisters both.

The first Christmas, Father Brabant returned to teach the children catechism in their own language. He brought with him an entire set of brass band instruments he acquired in Belgium, and the children learned to play these in addition to the piano and violin. When the enrolment of children increased, the addition of a large gymnasium accommodated indoor recreational activities, including gymnastics.

Christie Industrial School Brass Band. Archives, Queen of Angels Monastery, Oregon

Sisters with students on Meares Island, 1900. Archives, Queen of Angels Monastery, Oregon

Kakawis, meaning "place of berries," reflected the children's favourite outdoor recreational activity. In the summer the sisters enjoyed berry picking with the children and made jellies from the tasty morsels they collected. Sister Justine Zollner remembered the children speaking their native language during these informal times, unlike during classes, when English was required: "Though she couldn't understand the animated stories, she got a sense of the rich oral tradition of the Northwest Coast culture."[14]

Getting acquainted with each other's language and customs required patience and flexibility. Not until 1950 could the majority of children who arrived at the school speak English. Sister Roberta Dyer relayed an early encounter with one of the new children: "She just stood there and looked at me and blinked her eyes. I asked her again and it didn't do anything. Then I said, 'Well, just say yes or no'…She still didn't say anything. Finally, one of the little boys said, 'She said yes.' I said, 'I didn't hear her say yes.' The little boy told me, 'She raised her eyebrow.' I later learned that a wrinkle of the nose meant no."[15]

Apart from berry-picking excursions, the school's immediate surroundings provided space for other outdoor recreational activities. When the tide receded, the beach below the school became a twenty-acre playground, and Sister Julia McGanty recalled "learning to pick mussels from the rocks and using the beach as the school playground, where 'long pieces of kelp became jump ropes.'"[16]

Life at Kakawis included hardships as well as joys. Rarely did the sisters have free time. From the moment they woke up until they went to bed exhausted, they worked. They operated the school, tended to the needs of the children and ensured availability of food and water. In 1912, in a letter to Father Maurus, Sister Elizabeth Treis revealed the pioneer conditions when she related how well the chickens were laying eggs: "[They are] the one[s] from the first hatch I raised in the kitchen . . . [17]" Sister Clara provided a glimpse of the many hours required in the garden, and her grasp of English: "Today I make short letter. I am very tired planting carrots nearly all day."[18]

The enrolment of the school reached fifty after a year of operation and more space for the children was needed. The school building, which included a chapel, classroom, kitchen and dormitories, was enlarged to accommodate seventy students four years later. The sisters and brothers also improved the water system by laying pipes from the creek that they had dammed as a water source. In 1905 a hot-water heating system replaced wood stoves. Two years later they installed an electric light plant and the following year added a fully equipped steam laundry. In 1914 they built a large barn for cows and a smaller one for hogs.

As the numbers of children increased, it became more difficult for the sisters to find the time to attend to their own religious needs. However, the presence of the community of priests and brothers who cared for the boys helped to support the religious environment. When Father Maurus, the first and much-loved principal, left in 1911, Sister Sophie Thibodeau lamented his separation from their small community: "Let not time or distance or sorrow + (and) trials separate us from each other but let pure brotherly and sisterly love draw us nearer to each other and bring us nearer in love to Our God and Maker . . ."[19]

The religious community at Kakawis had little contact with the outside world. What contact did occur came with the arrival of the mail boat, which would stop every ten days if the weather permitted. Some of the sisters worked for years at the school without ever leaving the island. The sisters who did take trips off the island left from the beach below the school in a dugout canoe. They then paddled out to the steamboat *Maquinna*, which took them to their destination, often south to Victoria or points beyond.[20]

The Federal Plan Underfunds the Education of Native People

The need for further financial support soon became apparent and the sisters submitted a request to Ottawa to increase their original grant for fifty students to one for seventy students. The Department of Indian Affairs received their application along with a letter of recommendation from the superintendent of

Indian affairs of British Columbia. The Indian agent applauded the work of the missionaries in his 1905 report: "The school is doing excellent work among the Indians. The principal (Maurus Snyder) and the matron (Sister Placide) being exceedingly well qualified for their respective positions, and the whole machinery of this important institution moves smoothly and without friction.[21]

Education of aboriginal peoples came under federal jurisdiction, according to Canadian law. In his essay in *The Pacific Province* Hugh Johnson states that "the Department of Indian Affairs discharged this responsibility with grants to missionary schools, but the school system so created was underfunded and inadequate."[22] When Christie School was established, the federal government allotted sixty dollars for each Aboriginal child attending a boarding or industrial school such as Christie. In reality this translated to much less because the schools so often had higher numbers of children than covered by the grants. Although in 1910 the federal government increased the grant per child, the increase did not seem to materialize in a practical sense. At the same time, the Department of Indian Affairs set higher standards for buildings and administration, which virtually used up the increase.[23]

The federal government's attempt to assimilate aboriginal people into mainstream Canadian society was executed through mandatory enrolment of Native children at boarding schools, day schools and industrial schools, sometimes interchangeably referred to as residential schools. The results and the purpose of the attempt to civilize the Native children by teaching them European ways have recently come into question. One historian discusses her perspective of the residential school system, which she believed to be based on inequality: "The reasons for the failure had to do less with the actions of individual teachers or administrators than with a federal policy that legitimized and even compelled children to be schooled, not for assimilation but for inequality. While teachers and administrators of goodwill were able to ameliorate the worst aspects of the system for their pupils, all of the individual goodwill in the world could not have rescued a system that was fundamentally flawed."[24]

Underfunding appeared to be the basic reason for inequality. Even into the late 1940s, federal funding for residential schools was one fourth that of provincial funding for public school students. From 1915 to 1950, federal funding of the residential schools remained virtually unchanged. The 1906 annual report from the Department of Indian Affairs stated that missionary societies largely supplemented the residential schools across Canada.[25] The so-called supplement to federal funding often manifested as half-day schooling at a majority of the residential schools.

The half-day program allowed both the sisters and students to work part of the day to take care of basic survival needs. Sister Amelia Heinrich recalled that even in the 1940s and 1950s when she worked as cook and baker, the female students helped out in the kitchen. She noted that without the students' help, the sisters "couldn't have made it."[26]

Tending the garden. Archives, Queen of Angels Monastery, Oregon

Requisite student labour reinforced the philosophy of the federal government, which mandated the education of Native children to follow "industrial lines." The federal government believed residential schools should become self-reliant through students "raising crops, making clothes and generally doing outside work."[27] This was the situation at Kakawis.

Unpaid student labour was the practice, together with the volunteer labour of the sisters, and the latter was not always viewed as a positive attribute. It has been purported that for the sisters, the aspect of volunteerism overrode aspirations of professionalism, and that the primary concern of Christian missionaries to save souls overrode the goal of literacy.[28] Diamond Jenness, who wrote of aboriginal education in the 1920s, noted that it was "exceedingly poor." Jenness acknowledged that missionaries "should not be blamed since they lacked the resources and the staffs to provide a proper education... It was not the missions that shirked their responsibility, but the federal government..."[29]

Certainly the new Benedictine apostolate of the nineteenth century enticed many Benedictine sisters to come to North America, and eventually to Kakawis,

Sister Placide Casey with girls. Archives, Queen of Angels Monastery, Oregon

to devote their lives to converting the Natives. But this mission did not necessarily indicate a lack of teaching ability, credentials or interest in professionalism. Quite the contrary was true. One of the first three sisters to arrive at Kakawis, Sister Placide Casey, was "a public school teacher with some formal training and held a teaching certificate she had obtained at Normal School."[30] When she arrived from Oregon in 1900, British Columbia had not yet opened a normal school to train teachers. The Benedictine community, like most other communities of women religious, carefully chose sisters who could adequately fulfil the responsibilities at the various missions to which they committed.

The sisters who came from Switzerland and Germany to Oregon in the early years were often graduates of finishing schools and could speak two or three languages, reflecting an appropriate education for teaching language to others. By the 1940s, when the concern for residential teacher qualifications arose, Father Arthur Sullivan, an Oregonian priest, insisted that all the Benedictine sisters at the Queen of Angels Monastery obtain a teaching certificate, which by this time required three years of training. All of the forty sisters who had spent time at Kakawis came from the Queen of Angels Monastery, and although not all of them taught, those who did obtained appropriate qualifications.

As for specialized training and long-term commitment, the Benedictine sisters likely attained higher professional standards than most pioneer teachers of their day, especially before the first normal school opened its doors to British

Columbians in 1901. A number of secular pioneer teachers considered their work a temporary situation to be abandoned once they attained their true goal of marriage. Others saw teaching as a means to acquire quick cash in a field that required few or no credentials.[31] The sisters, however, given their commitment to a religious career, adhered to the vow of chastity and poverty and therefore never considered goals of marriage or wealth. Their mission for Native education began in the 1870s in the United States and continued for almost a century. The Benedictines finally left Kakawis and returned to Oregon in 1960.

Christie School and Cultural Changes

The sisters had considered leaving Kakawis in 1938 when the Benedictine priests and brothers left the school to set up a priory and abbey near Vancouver. However, the Oblate fathers, who replaced the Benedictines in educating the boys, convinced the sisters to stay:"At any rate, Father Forbes tells me that he will be lost without them (the sisters) and so he has asked me to do my utmost to persuade you, Reverend Mother, to let your Sisters stay permanently. Having the interest of the school very much at heart myself, I join my personal plea to his request that the good Benedictine sisters continue to work for the honour and glory of God under the direction of the Oblates of Mary Immaculate as they have done under the Sons of St. Benedict."[32]

By the mid 1950s, however, times had begun to change, as described in a letter from Sister Loretta Bonn at Christie School to Mother Gemma Piennett in Oregon: "That committee of inspectors with Mr. Parminter and Mr. Garrard, the Indian Agent arrived Thursday evening, late for supper. They toured the whole building, finding fault everywhere, nearly. Mr. Parminter told me three times that they, the other three men, did not like the set-up here. One told Father Kearney that Christie is finished; she has had her day. They want integration. They want day schools to take care of the Indian children and the parents to take over the responsibility of caring for their own children ... This Indian education is rapidly changing."[33]

Beyond the problems at the school, the Benedictine Order experienced "increasing expansion of the work in their own diocese in Oregon, the retirement and death of several of the older sisters and the increased preparation time for the younger sisters who were unable to act as replacements."[34]

In a letter to Father Kearney, the prioress describes her viewpoint:

> Before my sisters get stretched so far some of them snap altogether, I must draw in some of the more scattered forces we have out in distant fields—and that means Kakawis. Of course, that cannot be done without the consent of the Chapter—but I am almost positive

the Chapter will vote affirmatively to give up this mission...Besides the extreme shortage of teaching Sisters we have, there is even a greater shortage of domestic help...and when these older Sisters talk about their aches and pains—and how they can hardly go anymore—it just adds up more pressure on the younger ones. I understand well that they are doing good work up there—but I have to be realistic—and conserve my "manpower" to continue the good works we are doing in our own area.[35]

She notes the need for the proper formation of new sisters: "[We are]...responsible for seeing to it that [our] young junior sisters are not sent out until well formed—professionally and spiritually, which means, in our case, keeping them at home an additional three years—where formerly we sent them out to teach."[36]

In September 1959 three sisters from the Immaculate Heart of Mary in Los Angeles arrived at Christie School for training by three Benedictine sisters. In June 1960 the Benedictine sisters said goodbye to Christie School for the last time. The Benedictine sisters devoted sixty years to educating the children at Kakawis. Counting from 1900, the students totalled eight thousand. The decision to leave was difficult for some of the sisters, who were quite attached to the children and life at Kakawis.

In 1992 the Benedictine sisters at the Queen of Angels Monastery in Oregon celebrated their 110th anniversary. They invited former students to their monastery for "Kakawis Days," remembered by Sister Damian Beyer as "a day full of love, celebration, healing, remembrance and joy!" The high point for Sister Roberta occurred when three men and one woman from Kakawis spoke spontaneously "in gratitude for what the sisters had given and what they had helped them become."[37] Sister Alberta Dieker remembers a Native man saying, "I can go to Ottawa and speak English and I can speak my native language with my mother. Our culture was not destroyed."[38] A number of the sisters' former students became "tribal leaders, teachers, counsellors, technicians and managers."[39]

The Daughters of Wisdom

Marie-Louise Trichet wanted to become a religious when by chance, she met Louis-Marie Grignion in her hometown of Poitiers, France. Louis-Marie Grignion was a priest who came from the town of Montfort, France, and was known as Father de Montfort. Through Marie-Louise Trichet and Louis-Marie Grignion, the congregation of the Daughters of Wisdom was founded on February 2, 1703. Throughout her religious life Marie-Louise exemplified the charism that she passed on to her community, which included a preference for the poor in every walk of life.

Marie-Louise Trichet, co-foundress of the Daughters of Wisdom. Daughters of Wisdom, Edmonton

Father de Montfort died in 1716 in St. Laurent-sur-Sevre, Vendee, France and there, near the founder's tomb, Marie-Louise established the motherhouse of the Daughters of Wisdom in 1722. The motherhouse remains in Saint Laurent-sur-Sevre, but the general administration was moved to Rome after World War II at the request of Pope Pius XII. Throughout her religious life Marie-Louise lived the charism that she handed down to her followers.

During the French Revolution the Montfortian fathers and sisters fled France and sought refuge in Holland. Later, in 1884, seven of these sisters left for Canada, intending to settle in Quebec because the French language was spoken there. After arriving at Notre-Dame-des-Lacs, Quebec, they assisted in the management of an orphanage that the Montfortian fathers had opened the previous year. There, in the Laurentian mountains, the sisters began their first North American mission, teaching and caring for orphans.

From Notre-Dame-des-Lacs the Daughters of Wisdom opened houses in Quebec, Ontario, New Brunswick and the United States. At the turn of the century they ventured into western Canada to serve in the province of British Columbia.

In 1904 the Daughters of Wisdom responded to Archbishop Bertrand Orth's request that they come to his newly established Diocese of Victoria "to look after his (the bishop's) residence, and to take charge of the sanctuary and the sacristy of the cathedral." The Montfortian missionaries had established themselves in Victoria in August of the previous year and had set up missions throughout the city from their residence at Saint Louis College, where they began teaching in 1904. The request for the sisters' services came through a Montfortian father working on Vancouver Island: "This offer is the key to the door of this large island where there is only one religious congregation…We Montfortians have too high hopes for the apostolate on Vancouver Island not to associate les Filles de la Sagesse with us."[40]

Four sisters were chosen for the mission in Victoria. Sister Louise de Savoie and Sister Agnes du Sacre-Coeur sailed from France, enduring the rough seas of the Atlantic and arriving in New York in October 1904. After gathering their luggage, they sent nineteen pieces ahead to Victoria while they went on to Montreal. From Montreal they travelled to Montfort, Quebec, where they expected to meet Archbishop Bertrand Orth and travel with him across the country to his diocese in Victoria. The Archbishop and sisters, however, did not meet in Montfort, and Father M. Castex, who had accompanied the two sisters across the Atlantic, continued as their travelling companion.

On October 22 they departed from Montfort for Ottawa, where Sister Suzanne de Saint Therese and Sister Olave joined them. Now finally all together, the party headed for their new mission on Vancouver Island. Archbishop Orth was concerned for the comfort and privacy of the sisters on this long train trip and had arranged for a hot meal at noon in the diner car and a separate compartment for the sisters. They arrived in Vancouver at 12:30 p.m. on October 29, 1904, and continued on to Victoria the same day. By 6:00 p.m. they had reached their destination, having crossed the Georgia Strait on the *Princess Victoria*. Two priests welcomed the weary travellers at the dock and drove them to the archbishop's residence.

When the four sisters arrived in Victoria, the archbishop met them and showed them to their rooms on the third floor. These would be their quarters until the housekeeper, whom they were replacing, left: "The sisters dormitory consisted of two communicating bedrooms, each furnished with two beds...each room had two night tables, a dresser with a large mirror, a small stove to take off the chill at night, and a fireplace surmounted by an alarm clock that called them in the morning."[41]

They joined Archbishop Orth in the dining room for a meal and felt quite humbled by the extravagant situation. A young Chinese boy came to serve them at the ring of a bell, which the archbishop controlled by pressing a button on the floor. In what must have seemed curious to these Europeans, they received no wine at the meal. They soon realized that "tea time" was an alternative tradition to which they would eventually become accustomed. The archbishop arranged for the sisters to attend Mass in his private chapel after dinner. The next day he reserved the front pew of the cathedral for the sisters, causing them some embarrassment at being so conspicuously placed.

Three days after their cross-country trip, the sisters had been briefed on the routine of the household and took charge of the archbishop's residence. The superior, Sister Louise, began the domestic duties of washing and ironing, which took up the better part of her day. Sister Suzanne oversaw all cooking duties, and since this French-speaking sister could also speak English, she answered the door and telephone. Sister Agnes, who could understand English but spoke little, served meals at the archbishop's table and assisted with the housework and cathedral duties. Among Sister Olave's duties was preparing breakfast, which included porridge, eggs, fruit and coffee, and serving it to the archbishop and Father Laterme, who said daily Mass at the cathedral.

The sisters lit the daily fire in the archbishop's private study. They also tended to the needs of priests who came to stay with the archbishop on their way to or from other missions. While the priests ate breakfast, the sisters made their beds and took their own breakfast in the kitchen. The archbishop offered his dining room to the sisters, but they preferred to eat in the kitchen. When they had time, they mended the linens, darned socks and mended the clothing of the archbishop and the Montfortian fathers, who lived at St. Louis College.

The Daughters of Wisdom were the second religious congregation to establish themselves on Vancouver Island, preceded almost half a century earlier by the Sisters of Saint Ann. The Sisters of Saint Ann visited the Daughters of Wisdom when they first arrived, and the daughters reciprocated the friendship by visiting them at their hospital and convent. However, the friendship was short-lived, as less than two years later the motherhouse recalled the daughters.

The decision to leave was partly based on the Montfortian fathers' expected departure from Vancouver Island. Although the Montfortian priests and brothers were teaching at Saint Louis College, they did not consider this their main line of work, hoping rather to participate in missionary work elsewhere. This uncertainty resulted in the departure of all four sisters. Three returned east and the fourth departed for the United States. The sisters came to the island hoping to eventually assist the Montfortian fathers in their apostolate, but saw no reason to stay, particularly given the urgent need for their work elsewhere. The daughters in Victoria felt quite isolated from their community in the East and if the fathers left, it would only exacerbate the situation.

The archbishop, who enjoyed their services, lamented their departure. In May 1907 he again requested sisters from the Daughters of Wisdom for assistance in the operation of his household. He offered them the same agreement as the previous year—board and lodging and $100 each per annum, plus $120 for the first year to help compensate for their travel expenses. He also offered to pay fares from France. The Daughters of Wisdom considered the request premature, especially given the lack of personnel available and the great distance between Victoria and other communities of their congregation.

Although the Daughters of Wisdom could be found in missions throughout western Canada, they did not return to British Columbia in significant numbers. In 1970, however, Sister Henri-Marie de la Croix was invited to Rutland, British Columbia, to begin a rural catechetical program based on the one she had helped to initiate in Alberta. She stayed for one year and worked with Father Francis Flynn and two Sisters of Saint Joseph.

The Poor Clares

Icons of St. Francis and St. Clare. St. Clare's Monastery, Mission, BC

In 1993 the Order of Saint Clare celebrated the eight hundredth anniversary of the birth of their foundress, Clare Offreduccio di Favarone (St. Clare, 1193–1253). Saint Clare, as she became known, was the first of the Poor Ladies who, under the guidance of Saint Frances of Assisi, came to dwell in the little Church of San Damiano. Within a short period of time she was joined by many other women, including her sisters and her mother, Ortulana. Although she was born to a noble family in Assisi, Italy, Clare rejected her personal wealth. She and her companions, who chose a life of radical poverty in imitation of Christ, eventually became known as the Poor Clares.

Clare's inspiration and guidance came from a man eleven years her senior, also born into wealth and prosperity in the town of Assisi. Francis Bernadone (Saint Francis of Assisi, 1182–1226), the son of a wealthy merchant, entertained himself with the riches of his father. Soon, however, Francis rebelled against the indulgences of a materialistic world and rejected this life. He began a life of poverty and prayer and followed the exemplary teachings of Christ, preaching this message to others.

Clare listened to the young Francis preach to the people of Assisi and met with him secretly to seek his advice and spiritual guidance. Inflamed with the ideals that Francis shared with her, Clare resolved to follow his example of poverty and love. At the age of eighteen she secretly left her parental home and committed herself to follow Francis and his brothers: "With all the freedom of a daughter of God she chose a form of life in which, clinging to Christ alone, she could be occupied with transcendent concerns."[42]

Francis and his brothers entrusted Clare to the Benedictines for a short time, where, until further arrangements could be made, she was guaranteed sanctuary. Clare's family had expected her to marry a wealthy nobleman or merchant and thereby increase the family wealth. They were enraged at Clare's actions and some members of her family attempted to have her physically removed from the monastery, but they could not prevail against Clare's strong determination. Francis then moved her to a monastery of recluses and then to the Church of San Damiano, which Francis himself had rebuilt. Now free, Clare chose to live the rest of her life in this little cloister, devoting herself entirely to prayer.

Clare set an example that inspired many other women of the noble class to join her. With the help of her dear friend and spiritual confident, her new community received official approval as the Poor Ladies, with Clare as their abbess: "Clare hid herself, and her life was known to all; Clare was silent, yet the fame of her was everywhere heard; she remained in her cell, yet she was preaching to the city."[43]

After Francis's death in 1226, Clare continued to nurture her own spiritual life and those of her sisters. She wrote a rule for her community, the first by a woman to be approved by the Church. On her deathbed in 1253, the Pope accepted and approved it. By this time 150 monasteries had dedicated themselves to Clare's spiritual legacy. They eventually became known as the Order of Saint Clare. Rooted in the medieval tradition of Saint Clare, contemporary Poor Clares continue their contemplative life of prayer, bringing the brilliance of Clare's light into the second millennium: "Our life, hidden within the enclosure, is a light to the Church. It must be possible to say of every sister what was said of our mother St. Clare:...such a bright and resplendent lamp could not be hidden but would spread its light and shine in all its clarity in the house of the Lord..."[44]

Poor Clares Trek to North America

Poor Clare monasteries flourished throughout Europe for six centuries and in the nineteenth century, two sisters carried Clare's torch from Italy to America. Pope Pius IX chose Magdalen and Constance Bentivoglio to venture to America from the San Lorenzo Monastery in Rome.

At the time the Bentivoglio sisters left Italy in 1875, the Italian government had begun closing convents and monasteries throughout the country. The

Mother Mary Magdalen Bentivoglio 1834–1905.
St. Clare's Monastery, Mission, BC

government's confiscation of property often left many religious homeless. The foundress of the Franciscan Sisters of the Immaculate Conception had offered them the use of some land she had in Minnesota. Magdalen Bentivoglio was appointed the foundress of the community and her sister, Constance Bentivoglio, the vicaress.

On the way to America the sisters stopped in Nice and then in Marseilles, where they spent time with the Poor Clares and learned the observance of the Primitive Rule.[45] Upon their arrival in New York they received new orders directing them to set up a cloistered monastery in that city rather than Minnesota. They requested permission from Cardinal McCloskey of New York to establish a community in his diocese, but he refused, stating that "their form of life went against the spirit of the country."[46] For the same reason, they could not obtain permission for a cloister in either Cincinnati or Philadelphia.

Finally, after many years and many trials, Mother Magdalen Bentivoglio established a monastery in Omaha, Nebraska. This first Poor Clare Monastery in America was officially recognized by Rome in 1881. Four years later Mother Bentivoglio established a second monastery in New Orleans, Louisiana. Mother Magdalen died in 1905, and six years later four Poor Clares ventured from the New Orleans monastery to British Columbia.

From New Orleans to Victoria

On February 17, 1911, Sister Mary Agnes Cahill, Sister Mary Clare Schnorrenberg, Sister Angela O'Connor and Sister Mary Bernadine Flanagan departed from New Orleans in search of a new home. These cloistered nuns[47] began their trek across the United States and by early October arrived on the West Coast. They then headed north to Canada, where Bishop Alexander McDonald accepted them into his diocese in Victoria, British Columbia.

Clare's Rule outlined directions for land acquisition as well as stewardship. Clare saw the importance of creating an appropriate spiritual ambiance for the work of prayer, laying out a procedure that would structure monasteries for more than eight hundred years: "… as much land as necessity requires for the integrity and proper seclusion of the monastery, and this land may not be cultivated except as a garden for the needs of the sisters.[48]...do not acquire or receive more land about the place than extreme necessity requires for a vegetable garden. But, if for the integrity and privacy of the monastery, it becomes necessary to have more land beyond the limits of the garden, no more should be acquired than extreme necessity demands. This land should not

Three of the first four Poor Clare Nuns to arrive in Victoria: Sister Mary Clare Schnorrenberg, Sister Mary Angela O'Connor and Sister Mary Agnes Cahills.
St. Clare's Monastery, Duncan

be cultivated or planted but remain always untouched and undeveloped."[49]

The sisters resided in a small house in a residential neighbourhood at 632 Dunedin Street and began to solicit funds for a new monastery. A prominent contractor who owned land in the Oak Bay area donated three lots to the Poor Clares for their new monastery, and a fourth lot was purchased by the sisters on the outskirts of Victoria. Construction began in a field of prairie without even a road to access the site. Only the goat building at the exhibition grounds could be seen in the far distance. Funds for the twelve-thousand-dollar enterprise came from local donations. On December 8, 1912, the first Mass was celebrated in the Church of Our Lady of Lourdes and the new monastery was dedicated.

The completed monastery included a house for the sisters and a chapel, the two joined together by a central gabled structure. The sisters divided the chapel into two parts. The main chapel served the parishioners of Our Lady of Lourdes Parish, later to become Saint Patrick's Parish, and the second adjoining chapel served the Poor Clares. The sisters celebrated Mass through a heavy black curtain that covered the grille separating them from the congregation. This arrangement gave them the privacy from the outside world that is referred to as "enclosure" or the "cloister." The intent was to create an ambiance conducive to their life of prayer.

The spatial organization of the monastery was also designed to achieve privacy. The cloistered nuns lived toward the back of the complex, separate from the extern sisters, who resided in quarters at the front. The externs acted as ambassadors for the cloistered nuns, meeting the public and visitors at the front door of the monastery and allowing the nuns to maintain complete privacy.

Although after Vatican II the physical restrictions lessened, during the early and mid-twentieth century the community permitted little access within the monastery to anyone. The Rule and General Constitutions applied to friends and family and required the presence of two additional sisters during any visit in the parlour: "The sisters may not speak in the parlor or at the grille without the permission of the Abbess or her Vicaress... in the presence and hearing of two sisters."[50]

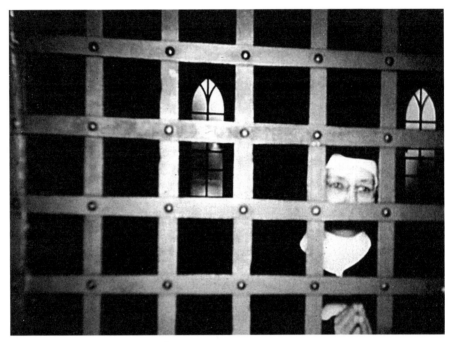

Sister Clare Lewis at the choir grille, circa 1963. St. Clare's Monastery, Duncan

The sisters lived within the walls of the monastery, each nun having her own cell (bedroom) with the remaining rooms being reserved for communal living. A garden area at the back of the monastery was enclosed by a perimeter board fence, which eventually was replaced with a nine-foot concrete wall.

Apart from adherence to traditional daily prayers, the sisters' routine included going out into the garden each day. Sister Clare Lewis observed, "Both Francis and Clare were keenly aware of the beauty of nature... [it was] a source of praising God...a part of Franciscanism [is] to be in touch with the beauty of nature...touching the earth."[51]

The nuns performed various assigned tasks of weeding, planting, picking fruit, raking leaves or whatever was required. In the early years they built a chicken house near the back of the property. As the garden was enlarged, they developed a narrow walk skirting the perimeter of the garden, similar to that in a traditional monastic enclosure.

Reminiscent of medieval days, a few feet beyond the monastery door, at the entrance to the garden, a gabled wooden structure housed a bell. Immediately inside was a small flourishing rose garden. A rose arbor shaded the narrow wooden boardwalk along the garden's east side and led to the back corner, where a shrine to Our Lady of Lourdes stood. In the opposite corner, on the west side of the garden, was a shrine dedicated to Saint Joseph. An arbor covered in a lush green canopy of table grapes paralleled the back fence and connected the two shrines. Along the west side, a second rose arbor covered a walk that passed the shrine of Saint Rita, which was situated on the lawn. Pear and apple trees dappled the central grass garden space with shade.

The nuns picked fruit and vegetables from the garden, but the harvest could not meet all their basic needs. Although they generated some revenue through typical cloister work such as the making of altar breads, candles and altar cloths, it did not sustain them as they followed Clare's Rule of adhering closely to the vow of poverty: "Let the sisters not appropriate anything...let them confidently send for alms. Nor should they be ashamed ... This is that summit of the highest poverty which has established you, my dearest sisters, heiresses and queens of the kingdom of heaven; it has made you poor in the things [of this world] but exalted you in virtue."[52]

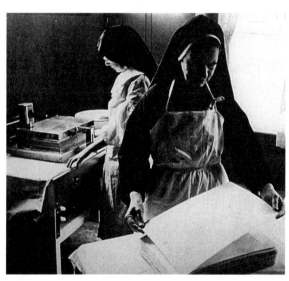

Sisters Mary Clare Francis Ellis and Mary Michael McMullon making altar breads. St. Clare's Monastery, Duncan

The externs, and the postulants who had not yet committed to the vow of enclosure, begged for alms. These sisters often boarded the trolleys and streetcars, spending the day collecting whatever they could to help sustain the monastery. They begged to ensure the cloistered nuns could expend their energies on prayer, the focus of their contemplative life: "The contemplative life is found in the very heart of the Church, the Body of Christ, whose purpose is redeeming all humanity and giving perfect glory to God. Because the sisters are wholly given to contemplation they offer to God an exceptional sacrifice of praise, they lend lustre to God's people with abundant fruits of holiness, they sway them by their example and they enlarge the Church by their hidden apostolic fruitfulness."[53]

The Poor Clares Establish a Community in Vancouver

In 1950 Archbishop Duke asked the Poor Clares to establish a monastery in the Vancouver Archdiocese. The Victoria monastery had already founded a monastery in Sauk Rapids, Minnesota, when Mother Mary Agnes MacDonald became the founding mother of a new monastery on the mainland of British Columbia. She had entered the Victoria monastery in 1927 and left there with three other nuns from Victoria, Sister M. Barbara Collins, Sister M. Pascal Sinclair and Sister M. Angela Sherrer. Their search for a new home on the mainland became a twelve-year pilgrimage.

The four sisters arrived in Burnaby on September 7, 1950, and moved into a small residence on Fourteenth Avenue, naming it Rivo Torto after the first home of Saint Francis. There they learned the limited extent of their carpentry skills by building a high fence around the property. The Fathers of Mercy and the Franciscans from Maillardville came to celebrate their Mass. They later moved to Burris Street, also in Burnaby, where priests continued to come to their residence/monastery to celebrate Mass. Mass at the Burris Street residence took place in what had previously been the living and dining room, but now served as a chapel.

After twelve years in Burnaby the sisters relocated to the outskirts of Mission and were finally separated from the dense and growing urban population of the lower mainland. On March 24, 1962, they moved into their newly constructed

Sister Clare Marie's Solemn Profession Day, Mission, August 2, 1978.
St. Clare's Monastery, Mission, BC

monastery, atop of one of the many lush rolling hills in a bucolic setting above the Fraser River, where the Benedictine monks at Westminster Abbey provided for their spiritual welfare.

They cultivated the land immediately surrounding the monastery, helping to sustain their physical and spiritual lives with a harvest of vegetables and flowers. The Mission monastery continues to thrive, and the sisters continue to realize the truth of Clare's connection between the beauty of nature and praising God as they live surrounded by a forested landscape that provides seclusion from the outside world.

The women of this community quietly enjoy the many small but significant miracles that occur in their daily lives. The living memory of Clare shines through them clearly, presenting an extremely powerful glimpse of Clare's impassioned spirit. As the sisters graciously accept visitors into their chapel and their lives, the contemporary world has an opportunity to experience the dynamic power of an exceptional human spirit.

Mother Mary Agnes MacDonald has a swing in the forest garden, Mission, 1978.
St. Clare's Monastery, Mission, BC

The Mission monastery was the physical and spiritual origin for a new community of Poor Clares. In October 1994, at the request of Bishop LaRocque, Sister Mary Clare McDonald, Sister Mary Francis Macaballug, Sister Mary Kathleen McGarry and Sister Ann Marie Moriarty left the monastery to establish a new community of Poor Clares in Alexandria, Ontario. There are now three English-speaking autonomous monasteries in Canada, two in British Columbia, one in Ontario and four French-speaking monasteries in Quebec.

Contemporary Poor Clares
The Victoria community of Poor Clares decided to leave the old monastery that they had occupied since the early decades of the twentieth century because of

extensive and costly repairs required to the old building. They searched for a suitable and affordable location elsewhere on the island and after sixty-one years in Victoria, the community relocated to the outskirts of Duncan. A country road winding through rolling hills and a lush green rain forest set a tranquil scene for the new home, which allowed them to be "apart from the world but, integrally connected to it, through a life of prayer."

Just as they had known the providence of God, which had allowed them a fruitful existence in Victoria, they now experienced the same generosity in Duncan. They bought a single-family home on Calais Road and redesigned it through additions, depending as always on "the Providence of God and the help of others" to provide for their needs. As the remodelling process neared completion, their concern grew. They realized they would not have funds to make the final payment, but the sisters' trust and confidence in God was not disappointed. At the last moment a donation arrived that miraculously answered their prayers and resulted in the payment for the completion of their new home.

Although the relocation of these nuns did not change their traditional monastic lifestyle, Vatican II did. Dedication to a life of prayer and the spirituality of Saint Clare remained constant, but in their lives, the physical expression of enclosure appeared less regimented. The grille no longer separated them from the community and externs no longer shielded them from outsiders. The sisters left the monastery to perform necessary business and found also that with the shortage of priests, they had to join the local parish for Sunday Mass when no priest was available to come to the monastery. On rare occasions the sisters attended conferences or workshops that were seen as educational and an enhancement to the contemplative life.

Vatican II encouraged the autonomous nature of each community to develop according to the spirituality of its community members. Although following the spiritual inspiration of Saint Clare remains constant today, each community interprets it according to the directives of the Church within their different cultural environment. This is expressed in the varied aspects of their communal living.

Speaking about her community members, who number nine, Sister Clare Lewis says, "It's amazing how different we are ... Our monastery has always been cosmopolitan. We have had sisters from Egypt, Ireland, Scotland, Jamaica, from the United States and recently women from Asian and African cultures are making enquiries about our community."[54] Their commitment to a life of prayer permeates their lives and unites them by its common bond.

The twenty-first century offers technology for cloistered nuns that expands opportunities for communication with the world. The community receives enquiries from women who request information about their way of life via the

Internet. The sisters continue their lives of simplicity and prayer and rejoice in the legacy of their thirteenth-century foundress, who still presents an inviting and challenging voice that is attractive to many women in this new age.

The Religious of the Sacred Heart of Jesus

A frail child, Madeleine Sophie Barat (1779–1865) was born in Joigny, a small town in Burgundy, France. It was Sophie's brother, a Jesuit Scholastic, Louis (Father Louis Barat), who first perceived the exceptional gifts of his little sister. With more zeal than compassion he undertook to teach Sophie the same subjects that he was teaching his students at the nearby Jesuit college. As Sophie struggled with an education in philosophy, Latin and the classics, the outside world was being caught up in a turmoil and violence that led to the French Revolution. Little did Sophie realize that she was being prepared to found the Society of the Sacred Heart, a teaching order foremost among those that would indeed revolutionize the education of girls all around the world.

Madeleine Sophie Barat 1779–1865. Courtesy of Archives, Society of the Sacred Heart, Montreal

At the time Father Louis Barat brought his sister to Paris to seek out her vocation, Father Joseph Varin met her and decided she was the woman to help build a new order, which had been the earlier vision of a fellow Jesuit, Father Tournely. He wished the new community to be similar in charism and mission to the Jesuit community and to be an order for women.

Father Varin dissuaded Sophie Barat from joining the contemplative Carmelites, to whom she was more attracted. With several like-minded companions, Sophie Barat formed a community of Dilette di Gesu, an Order of Italian origin, but it did not have the charism they desired. On November 21, 1800, the little group made their vows in the new Society of the Sacred Heart. Sophie Barat was chosen as superior and, with Father Varin, began writing the constitution and the plan of studies for the new Institute. The first school was opened in Amiens, France, the following year.

The schools founded by Mother Barat multiplied in cities throughout France and across the borders to Belgium, Germany and Italy and, in 1818, to North

America. With humility and a clear understanding of the support her task as superior general now needed, Mother Barat wrote, "I have been only a weak instrument; what would have become of the little grain of mustard seed without the indefatigable zeal of my companions and the enlightened direction of those who have supported and guided me?"[55]

Mother de Sartorius, one of Mother Barat's successors, outlined the core of the society's values in a letter: "We have a unanimous desire to keep the traditions of our first Mothers, and the primitive spirit of the Society which has made it what it is and which must remain sacred for us ... It is a spirit not only of generosity and devotedness but of love, simplicity, humility, interior life ... To keep it let us remain united; let us form but one heart, let us put up with things, forget ourselves, and count as nothing those trifles that harm fraternal charity."[56]

This spirit formed the charism of the Society of the Sacred Heart and was the underlying influence on the students who received their education from the Religious of the Sacred Heart.

Expanding Horizons in the New World

At the age of seventeen Rose Philippine Duchesne (1769–1852) became a member of the Visitation Nuns in Grenoble, France. She lived in this religious community until religious life in France was abruptly ended by the onslaught of the French Revolution. In 1802, after religious freedom had returned to the country, Philippine Duchesne purchased the old Visitation convent with the hope of re-establishing her community. By this time, however, the majority had either died, disappeared, or joined other religious communities.[57]

Philippine Duchesne was to join the Society of the Sacred Heart, inspired by the vision of Mother Barat. With its similarities to the spirit of the Visitation community, the Religious of the Sacred Heart offered a plausible transition from her previous life in community. Both communities were marked by devotion to the Sacred Heart and both recognized their mission as one of education.

Like so many others who answered the plea for missionaries in the New World, Mother Duchesne hoped to partake in a mission to North American Natives. In 1818, after having spent sixteen years with the Religious of the Sacred Heart, Mother Duchesne received permission to join the missionary exodus to the New World. This was a very different calling from the one she heard at the age of seventeen, but at the age of forty-nine she showed the same courage of conviction as when she tried to re-establish the Visitation convent in France.

Accompanied by four other nuns, she endured the long voyage over the Atlantic to New Orleans. These "refined French ladies" eventually established themselves at Saint Charles, Missouri, in a crude cabin in the wilderness just outside of St. Louis. Theirs was the first free school west of the Mississippi, and its students were Creole, French and American children.[58] Thus the traditional spirit of the Sacred Heart took root in the New World.

New religious missionaries from the Society of the Sacred Heart made their way across the ocean to continue the work of Mother Duchesne, opening numerous schools throughout the United States. In Canada, the first school opened in 1842 at Saint Jacques de l'Achigan near Montreal. Seven years later, a foundation was made in Halifax, and subsequently between 1858 and 1935 seven convent schools, including the one in Vancouver, were opened across Canada. New Sacred Heart missions also started in South America, Australia, Asia and Africa. Even before Mother Barat's death in 1865, the Religious of the Sacred Heart had established themselves throughout the world.

To ensure that their widespread community maintained its charism, each mission dedicated itself to education and to their foundress's inspirational legacy. Mother Digby, a superior general in the early twentieth century, wrote:

> It is specifically for the work of education that we have been approved by the Church; . . . In each country we must take into account the programs and requirements of the government and the desires of the parents who now often ask that their children take state examinations.
>
> Yet how regrettable it would be if the character proper to our education should be lost! What has secured its recognized superiority up to now is the primary end which it has proposed to itself from the beginning: to form for the Church and for the home women of solid faith and attractive virtue, whose good judgments and minds cultivated by all the learning fitted for their situation will give them a strong influence for good. If we wish to remain on this level we must hold strongly to the traditions to which we owe it, not be content with simply useful results but, above all, cultivate the faculties of the children, "bring them up" in the best sense of the term. At a time when the sciences have made such progress we must necessarily give them due importance while still placing upon our studies that literary stamp which is its distinguishing mark.[59]

The Religious of the Sacred Heart of Jesus Come to Vancouver

Archbishop MacNeil wanted the Religious of the Sacred Heart to instill the spirit of their community in the hearts of young girls in his Diocese of Vancouver and he asked the society to supply him with teachers. They accepted the mission and chose six religious to go to the Pacific Coast. Three of the sisters, Sister Jeanne Bessette, Sister Catherine Hoban and Sister Lillian Cable, waited in Montreal for the others to arrive. Sister Mary Ellen Powe came from

London, Ontario, and Sister Marie Gallant from Halifax, Nova Scotia. Mother Mary Gorman, although still recovering from influenza, had departed from Missouri and arrived in Montreal on February 4, 1911. The group of six left the following day for their new mission in Vancouver: "...At half past nine the Vancouver community met in Reverend Mother Vicar's room, where her parting words filled our hearts with gratitude for having been chosen to carry the knowledge and love of the Sacred Heart to a new county. Then came the signal for departure and half an hour later with the 'God Speed' and blessings of loved Mothers and Sisters yet ringing in our ears our little party of six boarded the West bound Express..."[60]

Accompanying this farewell were gifts for the sisters' new mission from various houses within the Vicariate. Included among many other items were a silver tea service and four hundred volumes for their library.

After a long journey across the Prairies, they had the good fortune to approach the mountains for the first time at sunrise and were spellbound by the beauty of the snow-capped mountain peaks. They continued on through the Rockies and into the Fraser Valley, where "the Vancouver lights were welcoming us and with hearts full of thankfulness we entered the City of our Desires on Sunday, February 12th at 1:45 a.m. The Archbishop had sent his nephew Mr. MacDonald with carriages to meet us and he conducted us without delay to St. Paul's Hospital, where the kind Sisters of Providence received us with the warmest hospitality..."[61]

The archbishop mistakenly believed only two sisters would begin the new mission and upon seeing six religious, realized the small house he had rented would not suffice. The Sisters of Providence set aside a dormitory for the Religious of the Sacred Heart until a suitable residence was found. Anxious to begin their work, within three weeks of their arrival the sisters received their first two pupils in temporary rooms at Saint Paul's Hospital. The two students, who were sisters, had previously attended a school operated by the Religious of the Sacred Heart in Seattle.

On March 20, 1911, the sisters opened their first convent and school on nearby Burnaby Street. By July 1 the sisters and students relocated from 1075 Burnaby Street to the Coleman Mansion, also on Burnaby Street. In September 1911 thirty day students and five boarders were registered. A year later enrolment had climbed to fifty-six pupils, warranting the construction of a new convent school in the recently-opened district of Point Grey:

> Property had been obtained at Point Grey, which in those days, was considered to be almost at the other end of the world. On one occasion, I accompanied Reverend Mother Gorman on a visit to the new

property. We drove by horse and carriage out to the west end, through sparsely settled Kitsilano to Point Grey and then down a muddy little road known as "Dunbar St." to a spot which is now 29th Avenue. There we had to alight and make the rest of the trip on foot over a trail until we reached the property. This trail wound through woods and underbrush so dense, that it was only when we reached a little clearing, which now marks the West Gate, that we could see the sky.[62]

On the Feast of the Sacred Heart, June 14, 1912, Bishop Casey officiated at the laying of the cornerstone for the new building. The Society of the Sacred Heart's Point Grey School opened in September 1914. For the opening, Reverend Mother Stuart, the superior general, sent a message that read, "…to make the Sacred Heart of Jesus known and loved, so that, for all who come to this Convent, it may truly be to them the very Gate of Heaven."[63]

Point Grey School, Convent of the Sacred Heart. Point Grey School

Although the sisters were semi-cloistered and so dedicated to a life of prayer, they also had a mission: the apostolic work of teaching. In keeping with their semi-cloistered life, they invited the students into their convent home rather than going out to teach. Point Grey operated as a girls' boarding and day school, open to weekly, monthly and annual boarders as well as day students.

The socio-economic status of the majority of students at the Point Grey School was higher than that of the general population. This was reflected in the school itself: "The types of school established in the beginning necessarily

School gathering, 1940. Point Grey School

reflected the social spectrum of that day, and as time passed these types tended to harden—which accounts for many present-day anomalies. The boarding schools...were the primary work. They were for children of 'good families' who could pay tuition..."[64]

Mother Barat always wished that a school for the less affluent should be established near the boarding schools. In Europe they were called "poor schools" and in North America they were often parish schools. Thus the religious in Vancouver began to teach in the nearby parish school in 1925: "...Those who work with the rich should always be eager to work with the poor, and those who work with the poor should never refuse to serve the rich, since all souls are dear to Jesus Christ...We must do all the good that we can. Spend yourself for the rich and poor alike."[65]

The Sacred Heart Community in Vancouver also had the opportunity in 1956 to include the less fortunate in their Point Grey School when they welcomed a number of Hungarian refugee girls, who were non-paying students. Although the majority of students at the school constituted a homogeneous group of white upper-class girls, the school welcomed diversity. They held cultural nights to encourage those of different backgrounds to express their heritage. This included Mexican students who attended, often for a term or two, to learn English. Some of these students enjoyed their education in Vancouver to the extent that they continued on to graduation.

Life with the Religious of the Sacred Heart

In addition to the regular intellectual pursuits typical of the rigorous Sacred Heart curriculum, the Society included sodalities as part of the character formation of girls who wished to further their spiritual growth. The first sodality, formed at the Paris school in 1818, was that of the Children of Mary. The Rule Book of the Children of Mary stated, "...the mission of a Child of Mary: what we cannot do on account of our enclosure, that is your work. We have gathered you together like an advance guard to replace us in the world."[66]

The young women of the sodalities, who spread the spirit of the sisters in the world, often continued their work long after they completed their school days. Many did so as members of Sacred Heart alumnae associations. Whether raising cash to send to the Poor Clares, helping the Sacred Heart School in Uganda, holding a candlelight ball to help a girl with tuition or finding funds to assist a needy child in some far-off country, the international efforts of Sacred Heart alumnae associations continue the charitable tradition to this day. It seems that wherever former students of the Sacred Heart live, an alumnae association follows. Even in Ottawa and Arizona, where a Sacred Heart school never existed, an alumnae association operates today.

First communicants, 1917. Point Grey School

At Point Grey there was an enthusiastic desire to spread the spirit of the Sacred Heart, but not necessarily a desire for converts. Not all who attended the school belonged to the Catholic faith, but the opportunity to experience the omnipresent spirit was available to all. A Presbyterian president of the Point Grey Alumnae Association attests:

> The love of the Sacred Heart was a basic thing that we were taught and that love absolutely went over the whole school. That's how I felt. I walked in that door and the love of the Sacred Heart was there...There was never a time when I didn't feel at home. We felt

and were told and I think some of us believed, certainly I, that we were children of the Sacred Heart and it was a worldwide family... It wasn't just a school. We were never thought of as insular, as just one little school in Vancouver. We very much felt very much part of the whole world. I wasn't a Catholic... In grade twelve I thought that I would like to be a Catholic... I loved the nuns. They never let me down. Not one day.[67]

The educational legacy remains in the hearts of the students who remember a home-like atmosphere: "When Saint Madeleine Sophie Barat founded the Society of the Sacred Heart over a century and a half ago, she intended it to be more of a home than a school. The Religious of the Sacred Heart are the loving mothers and we the privileged children. Yes, we are privileged in being the ones chosen to attend a school founded and modelled after the Heart of Christ Himself."[68]

The spirit that pervaded the Point Grey Convent School originated in the attention the sisters devoted to each student, though it was not always immediately apparent. As a new student entering the imposing edifice for the first time and meeting "a tall, stern-visaged nun," Patricia Prowd recalled, "...behind that sterness was a particular brand of greatness, understanding and wisdom, tempered with justice and love; but on our first day... I [was] paralyzed with fright at that first glimpse of—Mother Jensen."[69]

Point Grey School in the late 1950s. Point Grey School

The sisters approached recreation as an integral part of the formal curriculum. Apart from fencing, tennis, horseback riding, jumping and other organized sports, the girls participated in cultural activities such as dance, plays and musicals. The school also owned a printing press where, in the early days, the students printed their yearbook called *The Gleam*, along with other literature. Religious ceremonies, also integral to student life, included beautifully celebrated events such as the Procession of the Lilies on December 8 and the Procession of the Blessed Sacrament for the Feast of Corpus Christi.

The convent grounds provided a beautiful setting for these grand occasions and also provided both the sisters and the students with a place to enjoy religious and recreation activities. A grotto to "Our Lady" existed on the grounds, and trails through the adjacent woods allowed the nuns to say their beads or prayers in nature's solitude. An orchard encompassed by a stand of conifers provided fruit for the sisters and boarders. At recess the students often played in a gazebo at the end of "Pine Alley." In the school's early years one recreational activity held particular appeal for the children:

> There were wonderful picnics when he (Merrylegs, a shaggy little Shetland pony, blind in one eye) pulled a basket-cart full of food . . . I remember especially the water melons! Accompanied by one or two of our mistresses, we went in a two-by-two crocodile through miles of thick woods to the sea on these excursions; 29th Avenue was not much more than a cart track, and there was not a house all the way. I could see the Fraser Delta from my cubicle window, and could count the houses in-between on my fingers.[70]
>
> We would set out early in the morning with two mistresses, one heading the band and one in the rear, and after a thrilling hike over stony paths and through deep woods, we would reach Spanish Banks and there we lunched on the beach. The university area was completely uninhabited and one could easily get lost by wandering from the path.[71]

While primarily a residence for the cloistered sisters and a boarding school for the children, the stately edifice of the Convent of the Sacred Heart also served other needs of Vancouver's Catholic community. The convent doubled as the first parish church for the Immaculate Conception Parish, which had been initiated in 1924. In that same year the Catholic Women's League was inaugurated at the convent. Meetings of outside groups such as the Saint Thomas Aquinas Club (UBC Newman Club) also met at the convent. The Religious of the Sacred Heart also offered closed retreats for women, beginning in the summer of 1914. These became an annual event until the arrival of the Religious of the Cenacle in 1947, when they opened their own retreat house in Vancouver.

Point Grey School closed its doors the decade after Vatican II. Although the enrolment of the school had continued to increase, the numbers of sisters had diminished and the Society of the Sacred Heart decided to withdraw its services from Vancouver in 1979. Sadly, the sisters left Vancouver for other missions, but like so many other schools, the spirit of the Sacred Heart lives on. In that same year, a community was founded in the Diocese of Whitehorse in the Yukon Territory, at the request of the bishop.

After Point Grey girls' school closed, a new student body and administration reopened the facility as Saint George's boys' school, and the respect for the spirit of the Society of the Sacred Heart remained. Saint George's School administration allowed the Sacred Heart Alumnae to hold their meetings there each year. In 1993 an "Extra-Special Reunion" of the Sacred Heart Alumnae took place within its hallowed halls and three hundred women returned to Vancouver from various parts of the world to celebrate the spirit of the Sacred Heart.

In 1988 two religious of the Sacred Heart returned to British Columbia to work in Kitimat at Christ the King Parish in catechetics and parish work. In 1991, two more sisters came to Prince George to work in catechetics and supervision in the Catholic school system. Later, two others came to work in a renewal centre, where programs of adult faith education were offered, and thereby their work of education was offered in new ways for a new world.

CHAPTER THREE NOTES

1. Andreas Eckerstorfer, "To Do Some Good Among the Indians" (thesis submitted to the Theological Faculty of Mount Angel Seminary, St. Benedict, Oregon, March 1994), 27.
2. Ibid., 27.
3. Ibid., 28.
4. "Benedictines Sisters Celebrate 110 Years of Service" in *Reflections of the Benedictine Sisters* (Queen of Angels Monastery, Mt. Angel, Oregon, Fall 1992), Vol. XXI, No. 2, p.1.
5. Father Brabant, *Vancouver Island and Its Missions* (Hesquiat, W. Coast, Vancouver Island,Canada, 1899), 86
6. Ibid., 3
7. Ibid., 25
8. Ibid., 31
9. Ibid., 7
10. Ibid., 33
11. Letter to Father Maurus from Sister M. Placide, October 29, 1934, (recounting first trip to Kakawis, from Queen of Angels Monastery, Mt. Angel, Oregon).
12. Reverend Maurus Schneider, *Golden Jubilee of Christie Indian Residential School 1900–1950*, (Queen of Angels Monastery, Mt. Angel, Oregon), 3.
13. Ibid., 3.

14. "Sisters Celebrate 110th Anniversary" in *Reflections of the Benedictine Sisters* (Queen of Angels Monastery, Mt. Angel, Oregon, Winter 1992), Vol. XXII, No. 3, p.3.
15. Ibid., 3.
16. Ibid., 6.
17. Letter of May 11, 1912, Sister M. Elizabeth to Father Maurus Schneider, (Queen of Angels Monastery, Mt. Angel, Oregon).
18. Letter of April 16, 1912, Sister M. Clare to Father Maurus Schneider, (Queen of Angels Monastery, Mt. Angel, Oregon).
19. Letter of May 11, 1912, Sister M. Sophie to Father Maurus Schneider, (Queen of Angels Monastery, Mt. Angel, Oregon).
20. Kay Cronin, *The Last of the Vanguard: What these Benedictine Sisters gave you could not by for a million dollars* (September 1960), 7.
21. Andreas Eckerstorfer, "To Do Some Good Among the Indians" (thesis submitted to the Theological Faculty of Mount Angel Seminary, St. Benedict, Oregon, March 1994), 33.
22. Hugh Johnston, "Native People, Settlers and Sojourners, 1871–1916" in *The Pacific Province*, edited by Hugh J.M. Johnston (Vancouver: Douglas & McIntyre, 1996), 175.
23. Jean Barman, Neil Sutherland, & J. Donald Wilson, *Children, Teachers and Schools: In the history of British Columbia* (Calgary: Detselig Enterprises Ltd., 1995), 68.
24. Ibid., 57
25. Ibid., 66
26. Interview with author (and handwritten notes) from Sister Amelia at Queen of Angels Monastery, Mt. Angel, Oregon, August 1995.
27. Jean Barman, Neil Sutherland, & J. Donald Wilson, *Children, Teachers and Schools: In the history of British Columbia* (Calgary: Detselig Enterprises Ltd., 1995), 67
28. Ibid., 58
29. Ibid., 69.
30. Author's correspondence (telephone interview) with Sister Alberta Dieker, Queen of Angels Monastery, Mt. Angel, Oregon, January 11, 1999.
31. Jean Barman, Neil Sutherland, & J. Donald Wilson, *Children, Teachers and Schools: In the history of British Columbia* (Calgary: Detselig Enterprises Ltd., 1995), 190 and 308.
32. Letter to Reverend Mother Edith, from Joseph R. Birch (and vice-provincial) sent from Saskatoon, Saskatchewan, August 14, 1938.
33. Letter to Mother M. Gemma from Sister M. Loretta, May5, 1956.
34. Letter to Reverend M. O'Connell, (in Victoria, BC) on June 13, 1960, from Sister M. Loretta.
35. Letter to Father Kearney, Jan.13, 1958, from Mother M. Gemma.
36. Letter to Father Kearney, Feb. 3, 1958, from Mother M. Gemma.
37. "Sisters Celebrate 110th Anniversary" in *Reflections of the Benedictine Sisters* (Queen of Angels Monastery, Mt. Angel, Oregon, Winter 1992), Vol. XXII, No. 3, p.6.
38. Telephone conversation (interview) with Sister Alberta Dieker, Archivist, January 11, 1999.
39. "Benedictines Sisters Celebrate 110 Years of Service" in *Reflections of the Benedictine Sisters* (Queen of Angels Monastery, Mt. Angel, Oregon, Fall 1992), Vol. XXI, No. 2, p.7.
40. Letter to Sister Marie-Patricie from Father L'houmeau, June 26, 1904 (Daughters of Wisdom, Edmonton, Alberta).
41. *The Daughters of Wisdom Presence in North America*, (Daughters of Wisdom, Edmonton), 8.
42. *The Gospel Way of Clare: The rule and general constitutions of the Order of Saint Clare* (1989), 27.
43. Ibid., 27
44. Ibid., 78
45. Those who profess the primitive rule do not have a dowry or fixed revenue, as opposed to the Urbanists who may own property in common and receive fixed revenues—the latter obtaining their name from Pope Urban IV.

46. "Our Roots," (pamphlet), "The coming of the Poor Clares to America" (originally this appeared as an article in *The Provincial Annals*, Winter, 1975, a semi-publication of the Province of the Most Holy Name of Jesus.) Reprinted exactly as published.

47. The term "nun" refers specifically to a cloistered woman, however, the terms "nun" and "sister" are sometimes used interchangeably.

48. *The Gospel Way of Clare: The rule and general constitutions of the Order of Saint Clare* (1989), IX.

49. Ibid., XIX.

50. Ibid., VII.

51. Author Interview with Sister Clare Lewis, St. Clare's Monastery, Duncan, BC, February 21, 1995.

52. *The Gospel Way of Clare: The rule and general constitutions of the Order of Saint Clare* (1989), X.

53. Ibid., 77.

54. Author Interview with Sister Clare Lewis, St. Clare's Monastery, Duncan, BC, 1995.

55. Pauline Martin, *Saint Madeleine Sophie Barat* (booklet, December 1985), 19.

56. Margaret Williams, *The Society of the Sacred Heart: History of a spirit 1800–1975* (London: Darton, Longman and Todd Ltd., 1978), 110.

57. George C. Stewart Jr., *Marvels of Charity: History of American Sisters and Nuns* (Huntington, Indiana: Our Sunday Visitor Publishing Division, 1994), 66.

58. Ibid., 67.

59. Margaret Williams, *The Society of the Sacred Heart: History of a spirit 1800–1975* (London: Darton, Longman and Todd Ltd., 1978), 176–177.

60. House Journal of Vancouver, 1911 (from the Religious of the Sacred Heart Archives, Montreal), 8.

61. Ibid., 12.

62. *The Gleam* (yearbook), Convent of the Sacred Heart, Vancouver, BC, 1955, (Frances Bartley), 7.

63. *The Gleam* (yearbook, Convent of the Sacred Heart, Vancouver, BC, 1955), 8.

64. Margaret Williams, *The Society of the Sacred Heart: History of a spirit 1800–1975* (London: Darton, Longman and Todd Ltd., 1978), 73.

65. Ibid., 73–74.

66. Ibid., 78.

67. Author interview with Airlie Ogilvie, president of Point Grey Alumnae Association, Vancouver, BC, July 18, 1995.

68. *The Gleam* (yearbook, Convent of the Sacred Heart, Vancouver, BC, 1955, Mary O'Malley), 24.

69. *The Gleam* (yearbook, Convent of the Sacred Heart, Vancouver, BC, 1955, Patricia Prowd), 9.

70. *The Gleam* (yearbook, Convent of the Sacred Heart, Vancouver, BC, 1955, Mrs. S.D.Markham, nee Kathleen Underwood), 8.

71. *The Gleam* (yearbook, Convent of the Sacred Heart, Vancouver, BC, 1955, Frances Bartley), 7.

PART II

Community Building

1913–1945

CHAPTER FOUR

Education and Health

Introduction
Demographic Changes

etween the completion of the transcontinental railroad in 1886 and the First World War, British Columbia underwent a demographic transformation. The federal government's campaign to settle western Canada, combined with the national transportation system, resulted in an increase of the non-Native population from approximately 100,000 to 450,000.[1] During this time the Native population in the province decreased from an estimated 27,000 to 20,000, and dropped from twenty-seven percent to five percent of the total population.

The new demographic profile resulted in a new era and identity for British Columbia. The previously British-dominated colony was now considered "more Canadian." Of the congregations of women religious who arrived in British Columbia between 1858 and 1958, approximately one half were founded in Canada. These communities of women religious had been established during the nineteenth century and originated mostly from eastern Canada, although at least three of the communities were founded in British Columbia.[2]

A decade after British Columbia joined Confederation, Catholics in the province numbered about 14,000, approximately thirty percent of the total population. When the First World War began in 1914 the numbers of Catholics had increased more than four fold, but decreased to fifteen percent of the total population. By this time the Protestant population (Anglican, Presbyterian, United, Lutheran, Conservative Protestant) rose from less than half to almost three quarters of the total population. Those of "other or no religious affiliation" plummeted from twenty-five percent to less than ten percent of the total population. Although the Catholic minority was outnumbered by the many other religious groups, their influence in the fields of education and health care continued to be substantial. They received notoriety on provincial, national and international levels.

Numbers and Roles of Women

In the non-Native adult population, men outnumbered women three to one until the First World War. With subsequent changes, by the early 1950s the population of women was approaching the fifty percent mark. It has been suggested that the enduring male majority may have resulted in women's "lack of power and the reaffirmation of roles limited to wife and mother or sexual commodity."[3] These stereotypes did not apply to women religious who, by adhering to their vows of poverty, chastity and obedience, achieved a degree of power, status and communal wealth from which laywomen of their day were regularly excluded.

Although the sisters found themselves in typical female roles—namely nursing and education—they also found themselves in positions of power to which laywomen rarely had access. The sisters directed hospitals and schools and managed the multi-million-dollar institutions they had created under the most impoverished conditions.

The exemplary lives of the sisters, whether as managers, nurses, teachers or in supporting roles, continually provided young women with an opportunity to view themselves, to some extent, in non-stereotypical ways. Women religious as exemplary female role models were recognized by Germaine Greer, one of the renowned feminists of the twentieth century. Marcia Cohen describes Greer's experience at the Star of the Sea Convent in Australia:

> Somehow the convent sisters managed to impress her with the possibility of another way of life. "Not that it had to be theirs," she would remember, "following their rules." Just that there was another way… Germaine observed a simple sense of community, a particular kind of sisterhood. The nuns were women alone, living in a female society. They were committed to their teaching and had no husbands or children on their minds. Not unlike the farm women Germaine had taken to her heart, the sisters worked together, they were intelligent and respectful of one another…"The nuns were…too big and too special to be some man's menial. Certain women could only be satisfied with God Himself!"… And so it happened that the celibate nuns in the Star of the Sea Convent became Germaine's guide to a more emancipated way of life.[4]

These insights fuelled Greer's continued development as a woman and inspired her to create a different life for herself and for many others who would follow.

Community Aspirations

In the frontier days of the early and mid-nineteenth century, missionary sisters were interested in converting Protestants, evangelizing what they considered to be "heathen Natives" or bringing back to the fold those who had fallen from the "true faith." They approached their missions with a zeal motivated by faith, the intentions of the foundress of their community and the "providence of God." The results of their communal efforts prompted further requests for their continued work across British Columbia.

They could always be counted on to expand their vision in order to respond to current needs, particularly in the frontier days when material needs were often neglected. When the services of sisters were requested by the provincial or civic governments, by priests or by bishops, little financial support was available to assist them in performing their works of charity. The sisters had often depended on their own resourcefulness to establish whatever social service they came to provide and, more often than not, this included varied and innovative forms of begging. As provincial funding became available, particularly in the area of health care, the sisters took advantage of government assistance. For services not similarly supported, such as in the field of education, they relied on whatever means were available to them, including gifts, donations and community support of every kind.

As the province developed, teaching missions focused on providing a Catholic-based education for children who would have otherwise attended the public school system, which excluded religion from the curriculum. Catholic education focused on the mind and soul and welcomed children of other religious affiliations. Similarly, the sisters did not discriminate against other denominations in the health-care facilities they owned and operated. These were set up as charitable institutions, often serving those who were not provided for by mainstream facilities.

Many of the Catholic women religious who arrived in British Columbia between the mid-nineteenth and mid-twentieth centuries were members of communities founded during the nineteenth century. These communities had initiated a trend of establishing foundations that focused on active ministries with specific missions. Although many sisters were involved in health care and other social services, the predominant mission was education. In North America the period between 1850 and 1950 has been termed by Lawrence Cada as the "Age of the Teaching Congregations."[5]

Schools

In late nineteenth-century British Columbia, the non-Native population was predominantly British and Protestant. In the first half of the twentieth century an average of approximately seventy percent of the non-Native population were of a British heritage and were affiliated with Anglican, United, Presbyterian, Lutheran or Conservative Protestant congregations: "...most of the wealth and positions of influence were in the hands of Protestants. Church authorities perceived Catholic Education as the primary need in order to preserve the faith of Catholics in a predominantly Protestant culture."[6]

Catholics, despite a population share of only about fifteen percent in the first half of the century, sought education for their children that included religion in the curriculum. Only non-denominational schools were funded by the government, so parents who wanted their children to receive a Catholic education were required to pay taxes into the public school system as well as pay for their children's Catholic education. This situation would continue through the 1960s until the Federation of Independent School Associations (FISA) was formed, and on into the 1970s. After much lobbying by FISA, the School Support (Independent) Act was enacted in 1977, finally allowing private and other independent schools to receive financial assistance from the provincial government.

The interest in free non-denominational education had begun in the mid-nineteenth century as a result of the "English practice ... [of] ... class and religious divisions between schools."[7] One side of the public funding debate was described by a Non-Conformist English minister in 1865: "... There are individuals of every race, and members of every religious persuasion in the colonies; and it is maintained; as in Canada and the United States—that it would be unjust to Jews, Catholics, Buddhists, and Mohammedans, to adopt exclusively the text-books of any one religion."[8]

The Catholic side disagreed with the nineteenth-century notion of taking religion out of the school curriculum: "Religion is the atmosphere of the soul, and must be inhaled in imperceptible and continuous draughts. It is not a special science to be taught at determined hours in the week or day; it is the universal science which must permeate the entire teaching."[9]

Thus the Catholics operated their own school system, sometimes referred to as private, separate, parochial or parish schools.

By 1865 the free non-denominational education had become law. Within fifteen years the notion of free schools and a non-sectarian (non-denominational) system of education was broadly encompassed.

In the late-nineteenth century and early-twentieth century, private Catholic schools employed sisters who were invited by the bishop and/or parish priests to provide Catholic education for the children who lived in the area. The sisters worked for extremely small sums of money or for no pay at all. That their salaries were often referred to as stipends reflected the charitable view of their service. It is well known among the Catholic community that private Catholic schools could not have survived without the virtually unpaid work of the sisters who taught at these institutions: "A parochial school system in British Columbia would have been impossible at that time without sisters who were willing to work for a pittance, supplementing their earnings by other means such as boarding schools, private commercial classes, and music lessons. Not until the 1960s did the parochial schools hire lay teachers in substantial numbers."[10]

The majority of the first teaching sisters arrived in British Columbia in poverty. The motherhouse could on occasion funnel funds from their more established and financially viable operations, and the sisters sometimes earned extra income through activities such as teaching music lessons. However, the rallying support of parishioners was probably the most encouraging determinant for sisters, who essentially provided a volunteer workforce. The community efforts of the Catholic laity, combined with the sisters' efforts, worked together to provide a Catholic education for children in British Columbia.

The first Catholic school in British Columbia was established in 1849 in Victoria and was run by an Oblate, Father Lempfrit. That same year the Anglican minister Reverend R. Staines and his wife started a school for the Hudson's Bay Company employees. Father Lempfrit's main mission was to minister to the Native population, but he added the education of the wives and children of the French-Canadian servants to his mission. The Anglican minister received "340 pounds plus 100 pounds for the support of the school from the company," whereas Father Lempfrit "relied on the generosity of his parishioners," a situation that would remain virtually unchanged for a century.[11]

Sisters of Saint Joseph of Toronto

The centuries-old tradition of the Sisters of Saint Joseph of Toronto has its roots on Montferrand Street in Le Puy, France, in 1650. Here they opened a hospital that functioned as a refuge for orphans and homeless women. Although Father Jean-Pierre Medaille is considered the founder of the sisters' community, Bishop de Maupas of Le Puy notes that the initiative came from the sisters themselves. In keeping with the vow of obedience, the sisters organized under the blessing of the male hierarchy as described in the bishop's letter dated March 10, 1651: "...having learned that some generous widow and young women wished to consecrate themselves to laudable works of charity...and that to accomplish this...they wish, with our good will and approbation to organize a society and congregation; this plan seems so praise-worthy to us that we have heartily accepted, permitted and authorized it.[12]

As the spirit of their community grew, the virtues of humility, charity and simplicity spread throughout the region. When establishing new missions, they typically took charge of a hospital or orphanage first and then would open an

Mother Saint John Fontbonne. Courtesy of the Sisters of St. Joseph of Toronto Archives

associated school. Their charitable works were interrupted when the French Revolution ignited in 1789 and a number of the Sisters of Saint Joseph were imprisoned and martyred.

One of the imprisoned sisters, Mother Saint John Fontbonne, the Superior of the Monistrol community near Le Puy, escaped the guillotine and regained her freedom in 1794. By 1816, at the request of Cardinal Fesch, archbishop of Lyons, Mother Saint John Fontbonne gathered together some scattered groups of sisters and re-established the congregation. To manage the rapid renewal of this congregation, a new motherhouse was established in Lyons, France.

Twenty years later, in 1836, six sisters financed by a wealthy widow left the Lyons motherhouse to begin a mission in the United States at Carondelet, in the Diocese of Saint Louis, Missouri. The sisters at Carondelet established a Philadelphia foundation in 1850 and the following year sent a mission to Toronto, Ontario. In 1851 these four women were the first Sisters of Saint Joseph in Canada. They adhered to the community's commitment to health and education as depicted on their coat of arms, which consists of a red cross symbolizing their Christian work in healing and a gold cross symbolizing their Christian work in education.

At a request from Bishop de Charbonnel of Toronto, Sister Delphine Fontbonne, foundress of the Sisters of Saint Joseph of Toronto and also niece of Mother Saint John Fontbonne, arrived with three companion sisters of diverse backgrounds—an Irish sister, a German sister and a converted Quaker from Pennsylvania. These first Canadian Sisters of Saint Joseph assumed the responsibilities of an orphanage started by the women of Saint Paul's Parish on what is now Jarvis Street in Toronto.

Canadian Foundations

Sister Alphonsus Margerum was the first of the Sisters of Saint Joseph of Toronto to open a small school in Toronto in 1852. After only a year, the Toronto mission had expanded by setting up a new motherhouse in Hamilton, Ontario. Although the sisters in Toronto remained affiliated with Carondelet, due to the difficulty of communicating over a long distance, they operated independently. They maintained a strong bond of affection for the Carondelet community but by 1860 the Toronto house was officially independent.

Another mission sent from Toronto resulted in an independent community of the Sisters of Saint Joseph in London by 1868. In 1890 Toronto sent a third mission from their motherhouse to Peterborough, Ontario. From Peterborough, two more missions established independent congregations, in Pembroke in 1921 and in North Bay in 1937. The expansion resulted in six independent congregations of the Sisters of Saint Joseph in Canada, originating first from Carondelet. The Federation of the Sisters of Saint Joseph of Canada was formed in 1966 as an association uniting the six autonomous congregations with the establishment of many inter-congregational activities.

The sisters started their first teaching mission in British Columbia in 1916 when they opened a school in Prince Rupert. Their first mission in the province, however, was a hospital they had opened three years earlier in Comox on Vancouver Island. True to the pattern established in the mid-seventeenth century, they first opened a hospital and then a school.

Coastal British Columbia

Shortly after the Sisters of Saint Joseph opened the hospital in Comox, they were asked by Father McLean to reopen the school in Ladysmith that had been run by the Sisters of Saint Ann from 1909 to 1912. Sisters Magella, Ernestine, Francis Xavier and Conisius arrived in Ladysmith to take over in September 1917. Due to a number of circumstances, the sisters stayed only six years in Ladysmith, leaving in June 1923.

Teaching Sisters at Ladysmith. From left: Sisters Canisius, Majella, Francis Xavier, Corsini, Ernestine and Alberta. Courtesy of the Sisters of St. Joseph of Toronto Archives

In the meantime, sisters had been requested in Prince Rupert, a coastal community founded in 1906. By 1916 the increased number of Catholics in Prince Rupert had convinced the Oblate fathers of Mary Immaculate that teaching sisters were needed. The fathers wrote to request the Sisters of Saint Joseph from Toronto, but the response from their motherhouse was not encouraging, and Father Emile Bunoz went to Toronto personally to request their assistance.

During his absence Father Patrick McGrath held public prayers to help the cause, and it seems their combined efforts convinced the sisters in Toronto to come to Prince Rupert to open a school. In August 1916 Sister Lidwina Henry and three companion sisters arrived to a warm welcome in Prince Rupert. The Sisters of Saint Joseph of Toronto opened the first Catholic school in Prince Rupert on August 28. A small cottage became their convent: "... they proceeded to the cottage which was to be their home until something better could be secured. There was further evidence of welcome here, for it had been furnished, the larder well stocked with food, and the whole house was bright with flowers. Here too, they were presented with a beautiful statue of Our Immaculate Mother which, some time before, Lady Laurier had donated, to mark her visit to Prince Rupert on the first train to pass over the newly completed railroad."[13]

In January of the new year the sisters made room for a commercial class. Within two years of their arrival they built a boarding school on a hill with a magnificent view of the Pacific Ocean. They financed the school by soliciting funds from lumber camps in the region as well as through donations and gifts. The sisters' many excursions through northern British Columbia helped the school to become known in outlying areas. The staff quickly grew to nine Sisters of Saint Joseph, which allowed the boarding school to include a kindergarten. When the Spanish flu epidemic broke out in 1918 and all but two students became ill, the sisters mobilized their dual skills of teaching and health care.

During the epidemic, two sisters assisted every evening at the general hospital in Prince Rupert and two sisters ventured out to minister to the sick in their homes. Two more sisters answered a call of desperation from the manager of the lumber camps on the Queen Charlotte Islands. Although many people had died in the camps, with the arrival of the sisters, the death rate plummeted to zero. After the epidemic, the manager of the lumber camp "sent a cheque for a very substantial sum, not, he said, in payment for services beyond human accounting, but merely as a token of gratitude."[14]

Teaching in Vancouver

In Vancouver, the first teaching sisters were Reverend Sister Alberta Martin and her five sister companions, who travelled to Vancouver in 1922 to teach at the newly constructed Saint Patrick's School. With enrolment the first year at fifty

Corpus Christi procession, St. Patrick's School, Vancouver, 1925.
Courtesy of the Sisters of St. Joseph of Toronto Archives

to sixty pupils per class, two lay teachers were hired to take on some students in the oversized classes. By 1924 the Catholic population in the neighbourhood was large enough to warrant a third storey on the school, which allowed the addition of high-school classes.

By this time the increased numbers of sisters also needed more living space. The parish priest, Father Forget, initially had given the sisters his rectory on Twelfth Avenue for their convent. In the summer of 1924, the sisters moved from this donated rectory into two houses opposite the church on Twelfth Avenue. One of these houses had been previously used as a rectory and the other was a dilapidated building. The two residences became jestingly known as "Job" and "Jeremiah." The property they occupied was slated for a convent in the future.

Until the Vancouver sisters became established, they received assistance from their counterparts in Comox. The Comox sisters "sent them frequent supplies of fruit and vegetables from their own fertile gardens, as well as medical and household necessaries."[15] In 1927 construction on the new convent began. When it was completed it served the sisters for almost seventy years, until they left it in the summer of 1995.

In the late 1940s the Sisters of Saint Joseph began to expand their services. In 1947 they taught at Saint Andrew's School in South Vancouver, where they remained until 1965. In 1948 they began teaching at Saint Mary's in Chilliwack, where they stayed until 1993. In the 1950s they were teaching in North Vancouver, Kitimat, New Hazelton and Terrace, and by the 1960s they had moved into Richmond and Victoria. The sisters headed north to the Queen Charlotte Islands and Port McNeill on Vancouver Island in 1980 and to Stewart the following year.

The First Missionary Sisters Continue to Expand Their Services

While the Sisters of Saint Joseph of Toronto were establishing themselves along coastal British Columbia and the lower mainland, four of the five communities of sisters who arrived during the nineteenth century were continuing to expand their educational mission across the province of British Columbia.

The Sisters of the Child Jesus were invited by Bishop Paul Durieu to come to Canada to help with the education of Native children in British Columbia. They arrived at Saint Joseph's Mission near Williams Lake in 1896, with four others joining them two years later. Some sisters went to North Vancouver, where in 1899 the Natives had built Saint Paul's School, which was open to girls. Later the school was enlarged to accommodate boys. In 1903 a group of ten more sisters arrived from France to help. There were many requests for sisters to teach both Native and white children and the following year the foundation of Sechelt was opened. By 1910 the Sisters of the Child Jesus were called to help the white children in Maillardville and two of the sisters living in New Westminster travelled back and forth to teach there. In 1911 a school was built by the Sisters of the Child Jesus for white children at Saint Edmund's Parish in North Vancouver. In the same year the sisters staffed the newly opened school in Our Lady of Lourdes Parish.

Boys Lacrosse with Sister Joan of Arc, St. Paul's School, North Vancouver.
Sisters of the Child Jesus Archives, North Vancouver

Additional recruits of the Sisters of the Child Jesus came from France and also Ireland, allowing more mission schools to be opened in British Columbia. In 1917 the school at Fort St. James was opened and in 1922 this mission moved to Lejac, where the sisters continued to teach Native children. Altogether in the first two decades of the twentieth century the Sisters of the Child Jesus established five new teaching foundations in the province of British Columbia. In the 1930s they staffed Saint Mary's School in Vancouver. Later, in the 1960s and 1970s, the Sisters of the Child Jesus taught at Saint Thomas Aquinas High School in North Vancouver, at Chemainus on Vancouver Island, and at Babine and Burns lakes.

Sisters at Babine Lake, circa 1955. Sisters of the Child Jesus Archives, North Vancouver

The Sisters of Saint Ann were similarly industrious, establishing six new educational institutions within the first two decades of the twentieth century. The combined mission of education and health care culminated at the turn of the century with the foundation of the first Catholic school of nursing in the province of British Columbia—Saint Joseph's School of Nursing. Nine years later the sisters expanded to Ladysmith, where they taught until the school closed in 1912. In that same year Saint Augustine's School opened in Vancouver.

Students at Little Flower Academy. Archives Sisters of St. Ann, Victoria, BC

Little Flower Academy was also opened in Vancouver in 1927. Three years later there was a substantial increased enrolment when high-school classes were transferred from Saint Ann's Academy on 406 Dunsmuir Street to Little Flower Academy. On Vancouver Island the sisters began a boarding school for boys in 1904, with an expansion in 1921. In 1925 they started teaching at St. Louis College in New Westminster.

By 1939 the sisters staffed Saint Catherine's Indian Day School in Duncan and ten years later, Sacred Heart School in Prince George. The 1950s heralded the centennial year of the Sisters of Saint Ann's arrival to British Columbia. During this decade their contribution to education included their involvement in seven new schools located throughout British Columbia in Prince George, Port Alberni, Lower Post, Penticton, Vancouver, New Westminster, Victoria and Vernon.

The Sisters of Saint Joseph of Peace also served in the ministries of health care and education. By the turn of the twentieth century they had established two hospitals and a school in the interior of British Columbia, in the Diocese of Nelson. After founding Saint Joseph's Academy in Nelson, the sisters responded to the request for assistance in Fernie, where they sent sisters in 1922 to staff Holy Family School. The expanding school population in Washington and

Oregon required the return of a number of Sisters of Saint Joseph of Peace to the United States, and by 1956 the four remaining sisters at Holy Family School sadly closed its doors forever.

In 1914 the sisters expanded to the west coast of Vancouver, where they served at Rosary Hall, a residence for young women working in the city. By 1937 the sisters began another convent in the interior when Bishop Martin Johnson asked them to help with religion classes in Trail. Their work expanded and spread to other parishes and towns in the area. In 1953 Saint Michael's School was built in Trail and Sister Lucille of the Sisters of Saint Joseph of Peace became its first principal. The last Sister of Saint Joseph of Peace to serve as principal was Sister Rose Donahoe in 1984. In these later decades individual sisters served in the Nelson Diocese in various capacities relating to religious education.

The Sisters of Providence focused their efforts on health care in the interior, the lower mainland and northern British Columbia, but their involvement in education was limited. They operated two schools of nursing, one in Vancouver and the other in Cranbrook, both associated with their hospital operations. They sent two sisters to the northern part of the province to open Notre Dame School, the first Catholic School in Dawson Creek, which they staffed from 1944 to 1971. The year following the opening of Notre Dame School, Sister Ann Clementine, also a Sister of Providence, opened a business college in Dawson Creek and also taught an adult night school there. Initially the teaching sisters boarded at Saint Joseph's Hospital, which had been operated by the Sisters of Providence since 1932.

Sisters of Charity of Saint Vincent de Paul of Halifax

The Sisters of Charity of Saint Vincent de Paul of Halifax share their history with the Daughters of Charity, who were established by Saint Vincent de Paul in seventeenth-century France. Saint Vincent was dedicated to a life of serving the sick and poor and organized the daughters to help him respond to the desperate need for schools and hospitals.

Saint Elizabeth Ann Seton (1774 –1821) established the Sisters of Charity in America based on Saint Vincent's spirit and rules. Canonized in 1975, Mother Seton is credited with establishing the first parochial school in the United States in Emmitsburg, Maryland. Her work in education began in 1809 when she was thirty-five, only five years after being baptized a Catholic.

In 1814 her community of religious women based their rules on Saint Vincent de Paul's, adapting them to meet the requirements of American children. Although education was the principal work of the congregation, they provided help for others in need by establishing institutions for the elderly, residences for young women and orphans, and hospitals.

Saint Elizabeth Ann Seton, founder of the Sisters of Charity. Archives of the Sisters of Charity, Halifax

In 1817 Mother Seton sent sisters from the Maryland community to New York to care for orphan children. After establishing their own foundation in 1846, these New York sisters answered a request from Bishop William Walsh of Halifax to teach at Halifax's cathedral school, Saint Mary's. Four Sisters of Charity of Saint Vincent de Paul left New York in 1849 to teach in the Diocese of Halifax. They were led by Mother Basilia McCann, who herself had been taught by Saint Elizabeth Ann Seton. By 1856 the sisters in Halifax had established their community as a foundation separate from New York, and in 1873 they opened Mount Saint Vincent, which became their motherhouse.

Exactly half a century later the Halifax Sisters of Charity of Saint Vincent de Paul began their mission in what was eventually called the "Western Province," and would include British Columbia, Alberta, Washington State, the Yukon and the Northwest Territories.

Teaching in British Columbia—Saint Helen's Parish

Nine of the Halifax sisters arrived in British Columbia by train on August 25, 1923, to staff two parochial schools. Five sisters went to Vancouver Island to teach at Saint Mary's Parish in Ladysmith and four stayed to teach at Saint Helen's Parish in Burnaby: "When I was small and growing up in St. Helen's Parish the area was still country-like and quiet. There were woods and inviting grass fields covered with wild blackberries in the summertime. There was, for a long time, no bus service past Boundary, and only the old tram rattled up Hastings Street to carry passengers the formidable distance to Capitol Hill."[16]

This account of North Burnaby's early years illustrates the scene of Saint Helen's newly constructed three-room schoolhouse, which was built in time for the opening of classes in September 1923. The parish priest set up his headquarters in one of the small rooms in the schoolhouse and gave his rectory to the sisters. This left two remaining school rooms for the forty students who registered the first year. In 1929 high-school classes were added and by 1936 a school addition provided more classrooms. Between 1936 and 1948, when the old

St. Helen's Parish School, erected 1923. St. Helen's Parish

St. Helen's Parish School, 1948. St. Helen's Parish

school was razed and a larger new school was constructed, the annual student enrolment remained at approximately 120 pupils.

Although the parishioners welcomed the new school, the old school days, even with their trials were fondly remembered:

At times, the school was often cold and we wore our coats in class, our inkwells froze and the ink bottles sometimes broke in the cupboard. The playground was a mud bog in spring with dirt everywhere in the school. In September, you had to be careful with the newly oiled floors as your leather soles would absorb the oil and you would not only track it home but slip as well.[17]

...but there was something homelike in the old brown schoolhouse. The Sisters made it home; and we all treated it with as much respect...after all we had the care and the devotion of the nuns; we had a wonderful big bell we would fight each other for the privilege of ringing, and there was a genuine hill in the yard, dandy for sleighing in the winter and running up and down the rest of the time...[18]

Class of 1928 at St. Helen's School.

Sisters Maria Bernard (superior), Mary Rose, Mary Sylvanus and Regina Carmel, the four who arrived in Burnaby, transformed the rectory donated by Reverend J.B. MacDonald into a convent housing a library, chapel, living quarters and classroom. The following year the sisters moved into a residence at Esmond Avenue and Triumph Street, where they stayed for six years and took in boarders who attended the school. When there were more boarder requests than space, the sisters began to search for a larger facility.

In 1930 they purchased the Peters' Estate on 401 North Esmond Avenue in Burnaby. Built by the prominent British Columbia architect Samuel MacClure, the stately mansion accommodated ten sisters and twenty-four boarders, the latter providing a stable source of income, particularly during the Depression years. The building commanded a spectacular view and the grounds provided a beautiful setting for the mansion as well as a setting for recreational activities and religious celebrations: "In May there was always a procession around the grounds of Seton Academy. The Rosary was recited and hymns sung as the First Communion class led the way to the Shrine for the Crowning of Our Lady with a floral wreath."[19]

Seton Academy. Archives of the Sisters of Charity, Halifax

The sisters named the institution Seton Academy in honour of their foundress, Elizabeth Ann Seton. Initially a boarding and day school, Seton Academy operated first as a grade school and then as a high school for girls. Some of the sisters who resided at the academy also taught at Saint Helen's School: "[We received] report cards in class from Sister Superior, who came down from Seton for the occasion. They (the sisters) took their lunch alone and the lunch was biked by someone from Seton to the school and it came in a large, black, mysterious looking suitcase and one never knew what it contained!"[20]

After thirty-three years the boarding school was closed, but the private day school continued. In just five years, by 1968, all classes at Seton Academy were discontinued and the mansion returned to its residential role, now for the sisters teaching at Saint Helen's and Holy Cross schools, the latter opening in 1959.

In 1971 Seton Academy was sold. A non-profit society purchased and developed the property as a seniors' residence, renaming it Seton Villa. The four sisters who remained took up residence in a convent that the pastor of Saint Helen's Parish had given to them, repeating the situation of the first days of their arrival. The last sister withdrew her teaching services from Saint Helen's Parish in 1983, although other sisters remained to provide services within the parish and thus continued an association which extended over sixty eventful years.

Ladysmith

While four of the first nine sisters began teaching at Saint Helen's in the lower mainland, the other five sisters travelled on to Vancouver Island to teach in Ladysmith. Sister Maris Stella Murphy, who was experienced in founding earlier missions, led the Ladysmith group of Sister Mary Perpetua, Sister Mary Fabian, Sister Mary Dorotheus and Sister Mary Alphonse.

Their convent had previously housed two communities of sisters. The first were the Sisters of Saint Ann, who began teaching in the twenty-two-room convent in 1909 and stayed until 1912. Three years later the Sisters of Saint Joseph of Toronto took over their teaching duties, until 1922. The Sisters of Charity of Saint Vincent de Paul agreed to replace them and arrived in 1923. They registered seventy-nine students at the school, which was named Our Lady of Perpetual Help. By the end of the first month of school the enrolment had increased to 107.

The convent and school were housed in a "grey fortress-like edifice" built in 1909. The structure provided classrooms for the convent school and served as a parish hall, and required numerous renovations when the sisters arrived in 1923. The parishioners helped complete the repairs and paid a tuition fee of one dollar per month for each child, although not all children could pay. It was said that no one in need was refused an education.

As at Saint Helen's Parish, the Ladysmith sisters took in boarders to supplement their meagre earnings. Later they conducted music classes and concerts to help sustain themselves and the institution. The sisters opened a commercial class in 1924 that further contributed to their livelihood, but luxuries were virtually non existent:"The gardeners of the parish regularly brought fruit and vegetables, and those with farms or acreage were most generous. In the Depression years the enrolment fell as low as thirty-seven. When the Sisters of Charity arrived in 1923 they were given a hen shower! There was a poultry house at the convent earlier. It was repaired and the donations of the chicks were joyfully received by Sister Mary Alphonse."[21]

In 1956 the tuition fee was raised to two dollars per child per month. Three years later, in 1959, additional funding came from the Canadian federal initiative to integrate aboriginal people into mainstream education. The additional revenue helped extend the school's life. Although enrolment peaked in the 1950s at 165 students, it began to decline in the 1960s, as did the number of teaching sister personnel. Finally, in 1971 the school was closed permanently.

The Sisters of Charity in Vancouver

In the next few years, after 1923, the opening of three parochial schools staffed by the Sisters of Charity of Saint Vincent de Paul followed in quick succession. The first of these, Saint Joseph's Convent and School in Vancouver, opened in 1924. The sisters followed the typical pattern of teaching in a parochial school, living in a parish-owned house and participating in typical extracurricular parish activities such as teaching catechism to public-school children, preparing them

Sisters of Charity at St. Joseph's, Vancouver. Archives of the Sisters of Charity, Halifax

for first communion and confirmation, directing children's choirs, ladies' sodalities and assisting in the sacristy. In the late 1960s a decrease in numbers of sisters made it necessary to hire lay teachers and by 1969 only two sisters remained on staff. After forty-eight years of teaching in Saint Joseph's Parish, the last two sisters were withdrawn. Their teaching responsibilities were assumed in 1972 by the Sisters of Saint Joseph of Peterborough.

A few years after Saint Joseph's opened, the sisters were invited to staff two more parochial schools in Vancouver, Our Lady of Sorrows School in 1926 and Our Lady of Perpetual Help the following year. Sister Rose de Lima, Sister Maria Patricia, Sister Angela de Lourdes and Sister Maria Baptista were the first sisters at Our Lady of Sorrows School. In September 1926 they registered ninety-two students, thirteen of whom were non-Catholic.

The first year, the four sisters teaching at Our Lady of Sorrows School resided at Saint Helen's Convent in Burnaby, but soon moved into a house near the school. They moved again in 1928 and 1929 to a convent, where they remained for twenty-four years. In 1953 the seven sisters who taught at Our Lady of Sorrows School relocated to a modern convent on Venables Street. They shared this accommodation with their teaching counterparts at Notre Dame High School, which opened the same year.

School enrolment at Our Lady of Sorrows peaked at 265 students. Enrolment declined somewhat when Saint Jude's School opened in the neighbouring parish in 1958. Over the next ten years, seven teaching sisters staffed Our Lady of Sorrows School; one dedicated herself entirely to music education. By the end of the 1960s, however, the number of teaching sisters had decreased, and at the end of the school year in 1982 the Sisters of Charity of Saint Vincent de Paul of Halifax withdrew entirely, ending fifty-six years of service.

Unlike the east-side schools of Vancouver and Burnaby, where parish funds had to be closely budgeted for their schools to continue operation, Our Lady of Perpetual Help Parish was regarded as somewhat better off, although the Depression of the 1930s affected this area, as it did all sectors. At considerable sacrifice the parish community, with the assistance of a generous donor, Mrs. Lillian Lefevre, opened a four-room grade school in 1927. It was located in the more affluent Point Grey area of the west side of Vancouver: "In the 1930s they (the sisters) were paid a salary of twenty-five dollars a month, and the pastor paid for organ services, took care of medical insurance, and gave an extra cheque at Christmas."[22] "...I am almost embarrassed to think of the terms under which the good Sisters came from Halifax. The Parish provided them with a rented residence. They (the sisters) paid the heat and light bills, the water, etc. and they (the parish) paid the Sisters...the ENORMOUS SALARY OF TWENTY-FIVE DOLLARS A MONTH!"[23]

Sister Francis Clare, Sister Marie Clare, Sister Maria Vincent and Sister Rose Clare from Our Lady of Perpetual Help in Point Grey resided at Saint Helen's Convent in the first years. They commuted fourteen miles through Vancouver by streetcar and returned each night to their convent home in Burnaby. This continued until the following summer (1928) when the parish rented a house on 3894 West Eleventh Avenue. As the sisters had little in the way of household articles, a "shower" where they received various necessities was held for them in September of that year.

The grade school opened in 1927 with four sisters and seventy-five students. In the following years this developed into an elementary and high school with over four hundred students. In 1947 an addition was made to accommodate the high school initially located in the convent and rectory. The school was enlarged again in 1956 to adjust to increased enrolment. The staff had increased from the original four sisters to fourteen sisters and one lay teacher.

In the late 1950s renovations were made to the sisters' residence. However, by 1960, because of some inadequate heating and limited space, the old convent was finally demolished and in 1964 a spacious new convent was built. By the end of the decade circumstances resulted in closure of the high school and the years following saw a marked decrease in teaching sisters at the grade school. It was with regret that, by 1986, after almost sixty years of service to the parish community, the sisters had to withdraw, leaving the school to be administered by dedicated lay people.

The Diocese of Nelson

The Sisters of Charity of Saint Vincent de Paul were asked to staff five schools in the province in the 1920s. In the 1930s they were established in three new locations in southeastern British Columbia in the Diocese of Nelson. The first of these was a mission in which they were to assist with the teaching and the care of First Nations children.

In 1936 six sisters left Halifax to staff the Kootenay Residential School, located a few miles outside of Cranbrook . The Sisters of Providence had worked from 1890, when it was known as Saint Eugene Mission, until 1929. After the Sisters of Providence left, lay people took over their duties until the Sisters of Charity of Saint Vincent de Paul of Halifax arrived.

The Oblates asked the sisters to staff the girls' division and specifically requested "teachers, a nurse, a housekeeper, a wardrobe-mistress and a girls' supervisor." Sister Mary Rose noted that although they provided the students with opportunities for many extra-curricular activities, "such did not ease the urge to be 'home', hence the need to run away was sometimes the order of the day. Life was not easy apart from their native environment."[24]

147

During their years at the Kootenay Residential School, the sisters also travelled throughout the Cranbrook area to assist other parish communities in catechetical work.

In September 1965 Saint Mary's Parish opened a grade school in Cranbrook. For the next five years, the teaching sisters and children from the Kootenay Residential School travelled to Cranbrook for classes, which were also attended by Cranbrook area children. By 1970, policy changes within the Department of Indian Affairs resulted in closure of the residential school and the teaching sisters found accommodations in Cranbrook. During the previous thirty-four years, over forty sisters had served at the Saint Eugene Mission.

In 1938 the sisters were invited to staff parish centres in Kelowna and Kimberley. At Immaculate Conception Parish in Kelowna and Sacred Heart Parish in Kimberley, sisters taught religious instruction and made home visits, but to sustain themselves they opened a kindergarten and taught music classes. Although both these latter missions began as a break from their traditional teaching ministry, the mission in Kelowna grew to include teaching services in a parochial grade school and later a high school. The sisters eventually withdrew from Kimberley but continued involvement in education and parish ministry in Kelowna. Later, service in the area included assistance in a retreat centre and in the diocesan offices.

Toward the end of the twentieth century over nine hundred Sisters of Charity of Saint Vincent de Paul were working throughout Canada, the United States, the Dominican Republic and Peru. Forty were located in the Western Province, which included British Columbia, and all still followed the original spirit of the community as expressed in their constitution: "The Principal end for which God has called and assembled the Sisters of Charity, is to honour Jesus Christ our Lord as the source and model of all charity, by rendering to him every temporal and spiritual service in their power, in the persons of the poor, either sick, children, prisoners, or others who through shame would conceal their necessities."

Sisters of Charity of the Immaculate Conception

The Sisters of Charity of the Immaculate Conception arrived in British Columbia in 1929. Their first two decades in British Columbia focused on the ministries of education and health care. Similar to the Sisters of Charity of Halifax, the Sisters of Charity of the Immaculate Conception established a separate congregation that originated from Mother Seton's New York foundation.

In 1852 Honoria Conway, on the invitation of Bishop Connolly of Saint John, New Brunswick, entered the novitiate of the Sisters of Charity of New York. After previous appeals, the bishop again went to the New York Sisters for help in 1854 to care for the Irish immigrant children orphaned by the cholera epidemic.

Honoria Conway 1815–1892.
Sisters of Charity of the Immaculate Conception

No sisters were available at that time but the bishop invited volunteers from among the novices. Honoria Conway and three other novices took up the challenge and arrived in Saint John, New Brunswick, in August. In October 1854 these novices took the vows of chastity, poverty and obedience, forming the nucleus of the new community.

Honoria Conway (Mother Mary Vincent, 1815–1892) founded the community in Saint John at the age of thirty-nine, giving spiritual guidance and inspiration to her three colleagues, Sister Mary Francis, Sister Mary Joseph and Sister Mary Stanislaus. They opened an orphanage and established their religious community, known as the Sisters of Charity of Saint John. Born in Ireland, Mother Mary Vincent zealously carried out the exhausting task of running the orphanage, teaching, cooking, sewing and nursing the children with the help of her companions. The children of the orphanage were from the seventeen thousand Irish families who, upon arriving in Saint John, were decimated by a cholera epidemic ravaging the city. Though children survived, many lost their parents to the disease and found refuge in the orphanage.

In 1914 the sisters changed their name to the Sisters of Charity of the Immaculate Conception to honour the Declaration of the Dogma of the Immaculate Conception. After half a century in New Brunswick, and at the request of the Oblates of Mary Immaculate, the sisters headed west to establish an orphanage in Prince Albert, Saskatchewan. Their charitable services continued to develop across the Prairies in the form of hospitals, schools and orphanages until the sisters reached the Rockies. They crossed into British Columbia in 1929 and within a year had established three different missions involving health care and education.

Teaching on the Mainland

Archbishop Duke had asked the Sisters of Charity of the Immaculate Conception to initiate health care ministries in Vancouver and teach in parochial schools. In 1929 Sister M. Ethelreda (Gorman), Sister M. Roberta (Shea) and Sister M. Gertrude (Keohan) opened Sacred Heart School. They set up residence on 940 East Pender Street in Sacred Heart Parish, the oldest Catholic parish in Vancouver. Although the parishioners attempted to make the former rooming house presentable as a residence, they could not disguise the surroundings of the little slum dwelling.

In the beginning the sisters themselves received charity from this poor parish community. Grocery collections were taken up on Sundays at the church doors and they received generous donations of every kind from the parishioners. The sisters received a paltry salary of fifteen dollars a month from parish funds.

After just over a decade, student enrolment at Sacred Heart School increased to the point where the construction of another school was warranted. The sisters opened Guardian Angels School in 1942 and more teaching sisters arrived to help with the students. Fortunately, the sisters were able to move from their humble convent on Pender Street to Keefer Street when the priests gave up their new rectory to accommodate the sisters growing numbers. By 1947 a new residence, Immaculate Heart Convent, was opened in the west end of Vancouver for sisters teaching at Guardian Angel School.

By this time, Archbishop Duke had asked them to expand their teaching services to encompass the community at Powell River. Four sisters arrived there in

Guardian Angels School, Vancouver. Sisters of Charity of the Immaculate Conception

1938 to visit the sick, conduct classes in Christian doctrine and open a kindergarten class. The sisters remained in Powell River until 1960.

In 1940 the sisters started teaching at Saint Anthony's School in the Marpole community in south Vancouver. They lived at Our Lady of Mercy Home in the South Shaughnessy area of Vancouver and helped out with household tasks there during non-school hours. By 1946 the sisters had opened Saint Clare's Convent on the east side of Vancouver and were teaching at Saint Francis School, where they stayed until 1983. The Sisters of Charity of the Immaculate Conception staffed three more schools in the lower mainland in the 1970s.

The Boys' Orphanage—Saint John's School

Sisters of Charity of the Immaculate Conception arrived at the Burnaby Boys' Home (Saint John's Boys' Home) in 1930 to operate the orphanage on a seven-year trial basis. Archbishop Duke requested they care for fifty boys ranging in age from six to eighteen who came from orphanages and broken homes. When Sister Rose Anna Goan arrived in 1930 the home was under the direction of the Catholic Children's Aid Society and was run by Mr. and Mrs. Goullett.

The Goulletts remained to care for the boys until December 1931. Two sisters were loaned from Our Lady of Mercy Home to aid Sister Rose in "training

Sisters in front of St. John's Boys' Home. From left: Sisters Antonia, Martha, Kathleen and Roberta. Sisters of Charity of the Immaculate Conception

the boys in their religious duties and in being respectable citizens; not to mention the amount of mending that was piled so high and deep that Sister Martha had room only for her sewing machine and herself."[25] By August 1931 Sister Ruth (Helen Ross), Sister Henrietta Maria (Mary Ell) and Sister Antonia (Barbara Schatz) had joined the staff of the orphanage.

In September Sister Henrietta and Sister Antonia began teaching the boys from grade one to seven. They taught together in the same classroom until Sister Antonia was provided with a separate room to teach grades one to four. The grade-eight boys were sent to Sacred Heart School, where the sisters had begun teaching the previous year. The high-school boys were sent to either Vancouver College or Saint Patrick's High School.

The following year Sister Henrietta was transferred to Edmonton. Sister Kathleen (Mary Dunn) replaced her and began teaching grades one to seven in a single classroom again. Sister Antonia taught the boys music and helped with their general care. Many sisters were transferred elsewhere as they were needed in other missions, but replacements allowed the orphanage to continue to operate.

By 1939 the sisters had stayed two years past their seven-year trial period and they withdrew their services. It was decided that the home should be run by men rather than women, so it returned to the care of the Children's Aid Society, which disbanded it after a few years. Sister Ruth, who had been superior of the sisters at the boys' home since 1935, was directed to undertake the administration and opening of Saint Vincent's Hospital, thus officially beginning the sisters' health care mission in Vancouver.

Sisters of the Immaculate Heart of Mary

Reverend Masmitja y Puig, founder.
Immaculate Heart Community
Archives, Los Angeles, California

The history of this foundation began in 1848 in the Catalonian region of Spain with Reverend Masmitja y Puig as the founder. A community of their sisters was established in the United States in 1871 in response to a request from the bishop of Monterey, California, who wanted the sisters to teach in his missionary diocese. The nine Spanish sisters began their first foundation in Gilroy, California, with Mother Raimunda as the Prioress.

In 1924 the American foundation became a separate institution and changed its name to the California Institute of the Sisters of the Most Holy and Immaculate Heart of Mary. Health care and the education of Christian youth were their prime missions.

Vancouver Island

In 1943, at the request of Bishop John Cody, four sisters left their motherhouse in California to teach in Victoria. Sister Mary Rita and Sister Mary Jane Frances began by teaching eighth-grade students at Sacred Heart School, which was staffed by the Sisters of the Immaculate Heart of Mary until June 1970. Sister Elizabeth Ann and Sister Maureen, who was appointed principal, taught at the Tsartlip Indian Day School on the Saanich Peninsula on the outskirts of Victoria.

The Tsartlip school was located on the west side of the Saanich Peninsula and consisted of two one-room schools. Classes for the junior room, which included grades one to four, were held in the old rectory of the Assumption Church. Classes for the senior room, which included grades five to eight, were held one mile south on West Saanich Road. The East Saanich Day School, which included grades one to eight, was four miles away on the east side of the peninsula.

In 1951 Sister Socorro, Sister Catherine Sienna and Sister David went to teach at the new school that was built for Native children. It was a consolidation of the Tsartlip and East Saanich schools and was built near the location of the senior room on the Tsartlip Reserve. Although the school was originally called the

Founding Sisters from California, 1943. Immaculate Heart Community Archives, Los Angeles, California

Saanich Indian Day School, it was renamed the Tsartlip Indian Day School.

The school served four reserves on the peninsula—Tsartlip, Pauquachin, Tseycum, and Tsawout—and it garnered support from a women's organization formed to benefit Native students:

> The school (Tsartlip Indian School) mothers and women of the four reserves on the Saanich Peninsula have formed the Saanich Homemakers' Club of the Cowichan Agency, under the leadership of Alfreda Cooper, president; Mrs. Stella Paul, vice-president; and Mrs.

Audrey Sampson, secretary-treasurer. The aim of the organization is to improve living conditions on the reserves by cooperating in all projects which will help to attain this objective ... During the week prior to the feast of St. Valentines, every spare moment in the school day was given to making Valentine greeting cards for our sick friends at the Nanaimo Indian Hospital.[26]

In the late 1980s a new school was built next to the Tsartlip Indian Day School, which then became administrative offices.

Replacements for Christie School

Father Bradley, Victoria diocesan superintendent of Indian mssions, needed new missionary sisters for Kakawis when the Benedictine sisters announced their withdrawal from Christie School. He knew of the Sisters of the Immaculate Heart of Mary through their work in Victoria and Saanich and wrote the superior general of their community to ask for help. Mother Regina from the California motherhouse recalled part of Father Bradley's letter: "One hundred years of Christianity will slide into the sea, if you don't come."[27] Mother Regina agreed to send three sisters the first year and three sisters the following year.

Sister Ruth Anne teaches grades one and two. Immaculate Heart Community Archives, Los Angeles, Califronia

These first three sisters left their motherhouse in Hollywood, California, to arrive in Kakawis on August 12, 1959. Sisters Peter Damian, Ruth Anne and Juan Diego worked with the Benedictine sisters for the first year to ease the transfer of administration. Sister Juan Diego had originally come from Saanich and was the first Native to become a professed sister of their community. The Benedictine sisters left Kakawis at the end of the school year in 1960.

When the Sisters of the Immaculate Heart of Mary replaced the Benedictine sisters, there were seventy-five boys and seventy-five girls at Christie School. These Native children came from the north island territories and remained at the school for nine months of the year, going home only for Christmas, Easter and summer holidays. Travel off the island, still cumbersome, required a tractor trailer to transfer to a flat-bottom canoe, and a connection to a motor boat. By this time the Oblates had purchased an airplane to make their missionary visits in the area easier and faster.

As well as teaching at Christie School, the Immaculate Heart Sisters assumed teaching duties on the nearby Opitsat reserve, which was "regarded by the Oblate fathers as one of the most challenging missions on their four-hundred-mile coastline beat."[28] Opitsat was the first Native day school on the West Coast to be staffed by sisters. Sister Mary Laura arrived to teach at the Indian Day School in November 1959, and the following year was assigned to Christie Residential School:

> This extra-curricula missionary endeavour entails two sisters [Sister Mary Laura and Sister Juan Diego] having to forgo daily mass from Monday to Friday each week, during which time they live alone on the Opitsat reserve. It also entails the weekly round trip from Kakawis to Opitsat—either by dug-out canoe and missionary boat, or over a mile-long bulldozer trail which has been cut through the coastal wilderness between the two points and is so rough that any form of transport, even a jeep, is out of the question, and "walking" often means scrambling on hands and knees. Torrential rains, a frequent occurrence on the west coast, render this road impassable, at which times there is no alternative but to head for the dug-out canoe, the missionary boat, and the open sea in order to circumvent the rugged peninsula separating Opitsat from Kakawis.[29]

The sisters recorded many happy moments with the children, recalling Easter egg hunts, swimming in the nearby lake, parties "smashing the pinata," hiking, playing ball on the beach, school picnics and many other memorable activities. Toward the end of the 1960s, however, the building was beginning to show its years. The Immaculate Heart Sisters and the Oblate fathers and brothers did their best to renovate, retiling the kitchen floor, replacing curtains and table tops and repainting with the help of the older boys.

In June 1971, Christie Residential School was officially closed. At the request of the Native people a new Christie Residence, and a new school separate from the residence, were built in Tofino. The Native students were later integrated into Wickaninnish Elementary School, a public school. Sister Laura Distaso and Sister Anita Lucia Tavera were asked to join the staff of the new school to facilitate the move for the Native children. Sister Margaret Baumann took a position at the new Christie Residence.

The new Christie Residence closed in 1982 when the Native students from the north island communities were accommodated in schools closer to their homes. Three members of the Immaculate Heart Community, Laura Distaso, I.H.M., Anita L. Tavera, I.H.M. and Margaret Baumann, I.H.M., continue their work today with the Native people, the parish and the school in Tofino.

The School Sisters of Notre Dame

Blessed Mary Theresa of Jesus Gerhardinger 1797–1879. Archive, School Sisters of Notre Dame, Waterdown, Ontario

In 1833 Caroline Gerhardinger (1797–1879), later known as Mother Mary Teresa of Jesus, re-established the Order of Notre Dame originally founded by Peter Fourier in sixteenth-century France. She re-established her community in the last of their houses to be confiscated during the French Revolution, at Stadtamhof, Germany. The revived community followed the same rule as "the original Order of Notre Dame, modified so as to allow the sisters to teach in small rural parishes and among the poor, and was called the School Sisters of Notre Dame."[30]

The sisters expanded their mission to North America in 1847, establishing their first permanent foundation in Baltimore, Maryland, and eventually a total of seven provincial houses in the United States. The School Sisters of Notre Dame had been ministering in Canada since 1871 when Mother Caroline Friess had assumed responsibility for the orphanage in Saint Agatha, Ontario. The missions of Canada were under the jurisdiction of the Milwaukee Province until the foundation of the Canadian Province in 1927. At this time Mother Mary Baptist of the School Sisters of Notre Dame was given the task of building their first motherhouse in Canada. From there they expanded across Ontario and, in 1944, to British Columbia.

Teaching in British Columbia—Our Lady of Consolation School

The Augustinian fathers who lived at the monastery in Ladner invited the School Sisters of Notre Dame there to teach. Mother Mary Pius, the provincial superior from the motherhouse in Ontario, accompanied three sisters who would remain in Ladner to teach at Our Lady of Consolation School and help with the retreat apostolate of the fathers. The sisters arrived in Vancouver at the Canadian Pacific Railroad station on August 25, 1944. From there the fathers drove them sixteen miles to Ladner, where they stayed at Our Lady of Consolation Convent, located in a little building near the monastery: "...Sister M. Eileen had been appointed Superior and teacher of the Upper Grades; Sister Mary William was destined for the Lower Grades while the domestic duties were assigned to Sister M. Martha...During the following day a tour of inspection which included school quarters, retreatant's quarters and kitchen, was made. It became clear to Mother that the work required could not be done without the assistance of a fourth Sister."[31]

Original convent, Ladner, circa 1944. Archive, School Sisters of Notre Dame, Waterdown, Ontario

In early October Sister Bernice Volk arrived to become the fourth founding sister of the new mission, easing the workload for Sister Martha in the monastery kitchen. Although teaching was their first apostolate, assisting the fathers with retreats also consumed a great deal of their time. They prepared and served meals, cleaned the retreatants' rooms and did the laundry. They also washed, ironed and mended for the Augustinian fathers. The increasing numbers of students in conjunction with the increasing numbers of brothers resulted in the brothers relieving the sisters of retreat work in 1957, allowing the sisters to concentrate on their teaching apostolate.

The workload during those first years was heavy, as Father Othmar Mussmacher recalled: "Looking back on the years before my arrival I marvel at the great work the four Pioneer Sisters accomplished without the help of modern equipment. No refrigerator, an old stove in the kitchen, that took hours to replace the heat, once the heat was used up, no washing machine or dryer, an old sawdust burner in the Convent. Slowly, we were able to improve the condition to make work and life a little easier."[32]

Registration for the students took place on September 3, the Feast of Our Mother of Consolation. School opened on September 5, 1944. Twenty-seven pupils enrolled, and a short while later the number increased to thirty-four, with five of the new students coming from the nearby Tsawwaasen Indian Reserve. The first classes ranged from grade one to seven. Six years later classes went up to grade ten.

The first lessons in this Catholic school were held at the monastery, formerly a junior seminary at Ladner, in two old unused bedrooms. The entire building had been renovated to accommodate a school and retreat facility. Upgraded bathrooms had new tile and wainscoting, which helped to evoke "a warmer and more home-like appearance."[33] New heating and electric systems were installed and insulation was added. On the weekends the building doubled as a retreat facility, and usually on Friday nights, "classrooms were changed into retreat bedrooms and back to classrooms again on Sunday evenings."[34]

Although alterations and additions to the monastery were ongoing, a new school was built in 1959. The name changed from Our Lady of Consolation School to Sacred Heart School. As the government did not assist with funding except in the form of a grant for textbooks, the sisters participated in numerous fundraising events.

Students of all religious affiliations were accepted. Sometimes even when only half the student population was Catholic, it was understood that religion would be taught on a daily basis. The sisters demonstrated their religion through example, not limiting themselves to teaching and retreat work, as the Rumpel family remembers: "The Sisters that we knew, Sisters Rose Marie and Rosanne, were like mothers to our family during a period of unemployment. The door bell rang many times and there they would be, with extra food to help us get by…The Convent is now dark and empty, but like the Easter tomb of Our Lord, it has sent forth into our parish community His real presence that lives among us— the fruit of all the Sisters' years of service and dedication."[35]

The sisters passed on their communal spirit to the students and parishioners: "The whole school was like a family…I could go on about all the concerts and bazaars and how much fun the Sisters made them ... Many a time those Sisters made lunch (with a smile on their faces) for children who did not have lunch ... The Sisters were a role model for me and have always been with me, to this day. They always made me feel special."[36]

In 1951 one of the young women who had made a retreat there decided to join the sisters, becoming the first vocation of a Sister of Notre Dame in British Columbia. Later a number of young women who had been taught by the sisters joined their community.

Twenty years after the opening of Our Lady of Consolation School, Sister Louise Vanderploeg arrived to serve as principal and teacher. In her memories of Our Lady of Consolation School, she recalled her leadership as being based in a "faith vision" rather than a "world vision": "My inspiration was and still is—the mountain range that encircled us, and the beauty of Mount Baker, so real, ahead of me as I walked down the lane behind the Monastery. Those mountains became a symbol of God for me. Some days they were so visible, I could experience them with all their majesty and glory. Other days it was as if they were not there because the weather conditions blocked them. So too with God. Some times God is so real, so visible, so close. At other times, He seems so far away, yet He too is there, just like those mountains are also there."[37]

Cloverdale

The newly established Catholic parish in Cloverdale had incurred a large debt when they built Cloverdale Catholic School. The parish could provide little financial security, but the School Sisters of Notre Dame still chose to accept this teaching mission, and replaced the lay teachers who had been there.

In 1958 Sister Adelaide Folick, Sister Hyacinth Reiter and Sister Marie Schneider opened the Cloverdale Convent: "After Holy Mass Father blessed our new home which was formerly a poor old private home in which lived a family of nine children. Only those who saw the house before can appreciate the tremendous change ... Lovely gas stove, refrigerator, deep freeze, automatic washer and drier, desks, comfortably long beds, beautiful furniture are just a few of the things with which this parish has provided us. One kind farmer asked if he could provide the milk we need; another is bringing us two dozen eggs each week. Many others are providing chickens, berries, even Watkins salves ..."[38]

Open house for the parish-owned Cloverdale Convent was held on August 17 and in conjunction with this was a shower, typical in those days when there was a new convent. On the advice of the parish priest the sisters requested money rather than articles, however, they were provided with useful gifts such as floor lamps, blankets, mixing bowls and food supplies.

Sister Adelaide Folick took over as principal of Cloverdale Catholic School and taught grades nine and ten. Sister Marie Schneider taught intermediate grades and Sister Hyacinth Reiter was the housekeeper. The school initially ranged from grade one to ten, but grades seven, eight, nine and ten were soon discontinued. Teaching only the lower grades mitigated crowded conditions and allowed more space for more progressive and practical approaches to education.

Increased school attendance necessitated the addition of prefabricated classrooms, a library and other resource rooms. Because of the underfunding of Catholic schools in British Columbia, monetary concerns were a continuous problem. From 1958 to 1967 each teaching sister received a salary of fifty-five dollars a month. In 1969 the amount was increased to one hundred dollars a month. In 1969 the Congregation of the Sisters of Notre Dame subsidized the parish by limiting their total income to five hundred dollars per month, contributing to the cause of Catholic education in British Columbia. Income from bingos helped to support the operation of the school. Tuition for each child was ten dollars per month, and for a family, fifteen dollars per month regardless of how many children.

Thirty sisters lived and worked in the Cloverdale Parish until they closed their convent in 1991. The 1990s, however, did not end the service of the School Sisters of Notre Dame in British Columbia. Sisters still serve today in the Diocese of Prince George at Dawson Creek and Kelly Lake.

Hospitals
By the turn of the twentieth century in British Columbia, a province populated predominantly by Protestants, Catholic nursing sisters operated twenty-five percent of the hospitals. The Royal Jubilee, the first hospital in British Columbia, opened in 1858, the year the Sisters of Saint Ann arrived in Victoria. It was followed by two more non-denominational hospitals, one in 1862, and the other in 1870.[39]

British Columbia's first Catholic hospital, Saint Joseph's Hospital in Victoria, was opened in 1876 by the Sisters of Saint Ann, whose legacy of Catholic health care played an important role in British Columbia. Ten years later the Sisters of Providence arrived to build the first Catholic hospital on the mainland in British Columbia, Saint Mary's in New Westminster.

Of the twenty-four hospitals in British Columbia in 1901, six were operated by Catholic nursing sisters. These early health care facilities were both owned and operated by the Sisters of Saint Ann, the Sisters of Providence and the Sisters of Saint Joseph of Peace. They were located in urban centres near the coast in Victoria, Vancouver and New Westminster, and clustered in rural areas of the southern interior in Rossland, Greenwood and Cranbrook.

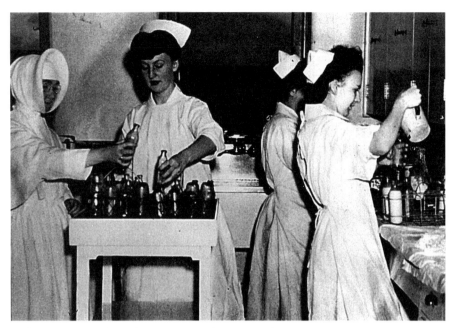

In the baby formula lab with Sister Anne and nursing students. St. Paul's Hospital Archives

Nursing sisters in these early years treated patients both in and out of hospitals, frequently tending to the sick in their homes. The sisters did not operate their hospitals for profit and provided health care irrespective of the ability of a patient to pay. In addition to patient care, the sisters also provided for the many indigents who came to their hospitals on a daily basis for meals and a handout.

In 1888 the provincial government in British Columbia exempted hospitals from taxation by implementing the Assessment Act. Provision for municipal assistance began in 1896 with the Municipal Clauses Act.[40] Although the latter bill also exempted hospitals from taxation, the *Monthly Bulletin* in 1917 recorded that Saint Paul's Hospital "received no help from the city although the sisters are paying heavy taxes each year to Vancouver."[41]

The small stipends the sisters had received for indigent patients in the mid-nineteenth century developed into larger government grants by the turn of the century. Decades later, in 1949, the British Columbian government took responsibility for health care insurance when it implemented the British Columbia Hospital Insurance Service. This helped to reduce expensive medical bills for individuals and provided "payment to be made to the hospitals on an actual operating cost basis."[42] This meant that the sisters who routinely accepted non-paying patients were to some extent now being reimbursed for services to these patients.

On April 12, 1940, the Sisters of Providence in Vancouver hosted the inaugural meeting of the British Columbia Conference of the Catholic Hospital Association for the United States and Canada (later called the Catholic Health Association of BC). Participants included representatives from women religious operating fourteen Catholic hospitals in British Columbia. The association recognized a need for the Catholic hospitals to unite and develop a professional relationship with each other as well as with Catholic hospitals across Canada, which by 1964 numbered approximately three hundred. The conference functioned as a platform to discuss major issues relating to the operation and management of their hospitals. These meetings continued for thirty years, with the executive comprised entirely of women religious until their dwindling numbers necessitated the inclusion of lay administrators.

Inauguration of the British Columbia Conference of the Catholic Health Association of the United States and Canada, Vancouver, April 12, 1940. Catholic Health Association of BC

While the appointment of lay administrators in Catholic hospitals increased during the 1950s and 1960s, the number of women religious administrators accordingly dwindled. This was a result of the decreasing numbers of sisters as well as the decision in the 1960s by Vatican II, which directed the sisters to begin divesting themselves of hospital ownership and administrative involvement, thus enabling transfer of control to the laity. Lay administrators acquired power in finance, expansion and personnel relations while the sisters dealt with the ethical and spiritual matters referred to today as "mission effectiveness."[43] In the mid-1990s, under the direction of the provincial government to form regional hospital boards, some Catholic hospitals in the lower mainland organized to retain their religious identity and affiliations by amalgamating into one board called CHARA (an old German word meaning "caring presence").

Sisters of Saint Joseph of Toronto

The teaching Sisters of Saint Joseph of Toronto who arrived in Comox in 1913 derived their North American legacy from the first six sisters who arrived in the United States from Lyons, France in 1836. In Carondelet, outside of the French frontier settlement of Saint Louis, they taught catechism to children and cared for the deaf. By 1851 their dual mission of education and health had spread to Canada.

Their first mission north of the forty-ninth parallel began in 1851 with the orphanage administered by Sister Delphine Fontbonne in Toronto, Ontario. Along with the orphanage work, caring for the elderly, the destitute and those in need resulted in an increased need for health care. In 1857 the sisters established the House of Providence in Toronto for the poor and destitute of every faith. The orphans were moved to a wing of the House of Providence in 1859. From 1881 to 1921 the orphans were in residence at the Sacred Heart Orphanage, later to become Saint Joseph's Health Centre. On Bond Street in Toronto, in an abandoned church, the sisters opened (in 1885) a hostel for working women, Notre Dame des Anges, which later became the site of Saint Michael's Hospital in 1892. Two decades later the community expanded its horizons to the West Coast.

Sisters of Saint Joseph in Comox

The plea for nursing sisters to care for injured lumbermen in the Comox Valley on Vancouver Island came from J.D. McCormack, president of the Comox Logging Company. Bishop MacDonald of Victoria had suggested the Sisters of Saint Joseph of Toronto. In response to this request Sister Majella, Sister Claudia, Sister Praxedes and Sister Saint Edmund of the Sisters of Saint Joseph of Toronto arrived at the lumber-camp site in early July of 1913. Accommodations promised to the sisters did not materialize. Thus the seventy-six-year legacy of Saint Joseph's Hospital began in an old farmhouse that accommodated four sisters and two patients. By October they had moved to a second larger farmhouse. By February of the following year the hospital capacity increased to ten patients and by August, to twenty-five patients.

The five-acre Comox property allowed for the growing of a productive garden. Typical of their communal spirit, the Sisters from the Comox hospital often sent medical supplies from the hospital and fruit and vegetables from the garden to their companions at Saint Patrick's School in Vancouver.

First farmhouse hospital, 1913. Courtesy of the Sisters of St. Joseph of Toronto Archives

Second farmhouse hospital with Sisters Majella, Praxedes, Claudia and Saint Edmund at front porch, 1914.
Courtesy of the Sisters of St. Joseph of Toronto Archives

The sisters found ways to adapt to changes in the community's needs. When a training camp was set up in the area in November 1915 during the First World War, many of the soldiers of the 102 Battalion were treated in their farmhouse hospital for measles. At the end of the war in 1918, the Spanish flu broke out and the hospital temporarily took over a school to care for the large number of patients.

A permanent expansion of the farmhouse hospital was completed in 1923, increasing the capacity to accommodate thirty-five patients. Fourteen years later another addition brought the patient capacity to sixty-eight adults and eleven infants. World War II brought an unexpected number of patients from the nearby air force base.

The hospital accommodated the health care needs of the region until 1967 when a new Saint Joseph's General Hospital was built to serve the region of the Comox Valley. The new seventy-four-bed hospital, with provision for fifty-two additional beds, was erected and included a thirty-five-bed continuing-care unit. By 1989, when the Sisters withdrew from the administration, the hospital had expanded to 220 beds.

Missionary Sisters of the Immaculate Conception

As a child growing up in rural Quebec, Délia Tétreault (1865–1941) had a missionary dream that influenced her profoundly: "In this dream I was kneeling beside my bed, and all of a sudden I saw a ripe wheat field as far as the eye can see. At a given moment all the ears of wheat changed into the heads of children, and I understood that they represented the souls of pagan children."[44]

In 1902 the dream came true when she and two women companions opened a school for missionary vocations in a small house in Montreal. They formed an association, and within two years Pope Pius X approved it as a religious foundation called the Society of the Missionary Sisters of the Immaculate Conception. The message from Rome read "The Church, through the voice of the Holy Father, deigns to transform your

Délia Tétreault, Mother Marie-du-Saint Esprit 1865–1941. Missionary Sisters of the Immaculate Conception Archives, Laval, Que.

little association into a religious institute devoted to foreign missions."[45]

Délia Tétreault became Mother Marie-du-Saint-Esprit and, as foundress of the community, derived her inspiration from "the Blessed Virgin" Mary. During the retreat Mother Marie-du-Saint-Esprit made in 1904, she wrote a letter to her community: "It seems to me the apostolate among infidels was given to us by the Blessed Virgin as an exterior means of manifesting our gratitude. God has given us everything, even His own Son, what better way of making returns—in so far as a weak creature can do so in this world—than to give Him children, chosen ones, who will also sing His goodness for centuries to come."[46]

On September 8, 1909, at the request of Bishop Merel of Canton, China, the Missionary Sisters of the Immaculate Conception embarked on their first foreign mission. Six sisters left their motherhouse in Quebec and journeyed across

Canada to Vancouver, where they said their last goodbyes before crossing the Pacific.[47] Another missionary group left for China's Sheklung Leprosarium four years later, after being trained by the Sisters of Providence at the Hospital for Incurables. While the missions were being established in China, Mother Marie-du-Saint-Esprit was initiating missionary projects for the Chinese living in Montreal, Three Rivers and Quebec City.

A Chinese Mission on the West Coast

In Vancouver, Archbishop Casey had become concerned over the distressing number of deaths among Chinese residents: "...some local citizens feared that the Chinese were dying of some sort of communicable disease. Lack of proper health care for the immigrants served to compound the problem."[48] Archbishop Casey invited the Missionary Sisters of the Immaculate Conception to work in Vancouver: "It seems to be that you could come among us as into a big city in China, make an humble foundation that will grow under Providence, and be a half-way house on your way to China... Two or three Sisters should be enough to start and I am sure, with the Good Lord's blessing the mission can grow indefinitely."[49]

Apart from assisting the needy Chinese on the West Coast, the mission in Vancouver would also become a *pied-à-terre* for missionaries travelling between the Pacific Coast and the Orient. The Vancouver mission would become a second home to these travellers.

Depart Vancouver, September, 1932. Harry Bullen Studio, Vancouver

Mother Marie-du-Saint-Esprit accepted the offer from the archbishop. On May 2, 1921, four sisters left by train for the "foreign" mission of British Columbia to serve the Chinese community in Vancouver. Sister Marie-du-Sacré-Coeur,[50] the appointed superior, was accompanied by her assistant, Sister Marie-du-Saint-Rédempteur, her blood sister, Sister Aimée-de-Jésus, and Sister Marie-de-St.-Georges. Two of the four French-Canadian sisters spoke English.

In Vancouver the missionary sisters stayed with the Sisters of Providence at Saint Paul's Hospital. After six weeks they rented a small house for themselves on Keefer Street in east Vancouver in the Chinese district:

> On the feast of St. Anthony of Padua, patron of seekers, we finally found a house that is neither too big nor too small: eight rooms are distributed on three floors and there is a large cellar. On the ground-floor are found the parlor which serves as a classroom when needed; the refectory which also serve as our community room; the kitchen and a small pantry. On the second floor, we find a chapel, all white and cool, about the size of the linen room of the Mother House (as you see we are rather close to the Lord); a classroom which serves as a sacristy, and Sister Superior's room just large enough to accommodate a bed, a writing desk, and a chair. On the third floor are two low-ceilinged rooms, one for Sr. Marie-du-St. Redempteur, and the other for both Sr. Marie-de-St. Georges and Sr. Aimee-de-Jesus…We have to struggle against anti-Catholic elements…[51]

Here they opened a school for the Chinese children, but found it difficult to recruit a Chinese teacher and pupils, as Chinese parents preferred to send their children to public schools.

As is sometimes the case during the establishment of a new mission, the sisters encountered all kinds of internal and external difficulties and even opposition. Their work with the sick and disadvantaged immigrants, particularly the Chinese, was not accepted and understood by everyone. After almost two years in Vancouver, the first four missionary sisters were replaced by four new recruits from the motherhouse in Quebec.

Soon after the arrival of the new sisters they began visiting the poor and sick Chinese. Realizing the serious need of a shelter for the sick, they received permission to set up a four-bed hospital in the upstairs of their house. In 1924 they also opened a small free clinic.

Discrimination against the Chinese had been overt in British Columbia. By 1886 a head tax of fifty dollars was levied to discourage their entry into the province and by 1903 the tax had increased to five hundred dollars. The majority of the Chinese in British Columbia had worked on the Cariboo Road in the 1860s and on the Pacific Coast portion of the railroad in the 1880s. They were not permitted to work east of the Rockies. Although "most politicians in British Columbia reluctantly accepted the need to use Chinese labour," when the railroad was nearing its completion, they accelerated their "anti-Chinese campaign."[52]

The Chinese were also banned from union membership in the Kootenay mining districts, although they were allowed to work at the mines along the coast and on Vancouver Island. Here the industry relied on a "transient workforce…most controversially, Chinese pit-men."[53] Policies at the Nanaimo colliery excluded Chinese pit-men from benefits offered to other workers of "mainly British stock."

Campbell Ave. dispensary and hospital, 1925.
Missionary Sisters of the Immaculate Conception Archives, Laval, Que.

In 1924 the sisters purchased a small house on Campbell Avenue to operate as a convent and dispensary for pharmaceuticals. Two Chinese men who begged the sisters for shelter were admitted to the convent dispensary, along with two other elderly men. They ranged in age from seventy years old to ninety. In reference to these men, Mother Marie-du-Saint-Esprit wrote from Montreal to the Vancouver community: "…how happy I am that you are admitting a few poor people into your small house…Surround them with respect and tenderness, make them spend their last days happily on this poor earth, and may your kindness allow them to catch a glimpse of God's bounty…"[54]

The Sisters of Providence assisted the missionary sisters. For ten years the hospital kitchen of Saint Paul's provided the "Oriental Home" with "cooked meat, vegetables, pastries, etc.". In addition to these supplies, the sisters went throughout Chinatown to beg for the needs of their increasing number of boarders.

Saint Joseph's Oriental Hospital

In 1925 the sisters purchased the old Woodward House, also on Campbell Avenue, and by November were providing accommodation to eighteen elderly Chinese. Three years later the sisters opened a new thirty-two-bed hospital adjacent to the existing house, calling it Saint Joseph's Oriental Hospital.

On December 19, 1933, fifteen Chinese patients with tuberculosis were admitted to the hospital. The patients were referred to the sisters by the Board of Health, which had recently closed the Oriental Hospital operated by the United Church of Canada. At that time Saint Joseph's Oriental Hospital beds now numbered seventy, "twenty-five of which were reserved for the incurable and the poor."[55]

When the sisters built a new hospital on Prince Edward Street, they renamed the Oriental Hospital the Oriental Home. They operated the Oriental Home until 1972, when the Villa Cathay Care Home Society assumed responsibility for it.

Sister Teresa Fung Arrives in Canada

The sisters' other facilities included a dispensary opened in 1936 in the centre of Chinatown at 795 Pender Street to serve "Chinese, Negroes, Hindus and Indians." In this same year Sister Teresa Fung, Vancouver's first Chinese sister, arrived from Canton, China, to assist the sisters in their health-care mission through visitations and by teaching patients catechism. In 1997, on the occasion of the fiftieth anniversary of Mount Saint Joseph Hospital, Sister Teresa Fung wrote, "The goodness of the Sisters inspired my vocation to become one of them. I remember (the Sisters) who treated patients at the clinic: [they] were so kind and loved by everyone..."[56]

Sisters Teresa Fung and Berthe Surprenant with the Chinese and Japanese tuberculosis children at Campbell Ave. Missionary Sisters of the Immaculate Conception Archives, Laval, Que.

Sister Teresa Fung was born in China and taught by the Missionary Sisters of the Immaculate Conception at Holy Spirit School in Canton. Before she was a student at Holy Spirit School, Teresa received a Christian and biblical formation from Protestant missionaries. When she came to Vancouver in 1936 she had been a Catholic for only one year, and as a "virgin catechist" in Canton, she had made a private vow of chastity. The missionary sisters did not yet admit Chinese members to their congregation, but Sister Teresa "never gave up hope" of becoming a fully professed member of the Missionary Sisters of the Immaculate Conception. After hearing of Sister Lucia Ho's admission to the community in 1942, Sisters Teresa Fung wrote the superior general of the community for permission to enter the novitiate. In February 1949 she entered the novitiate at Pont Viau, Quebec, to become a member of the congregation. She returned to Vancouver in 1951.

During her years in Vancouver, Sister Teresa Fung visited thousands of Chinese families and was considered almost an institution in the Chinese community. She was responsible for gathering support for the building of a new hospital and became the hospital's main fund raiser during that time: "We sisters did everything. We washed the floors, fed the patients, did the cooking. A lot of times we went to the Chinese farms and asked for vegetables. We picked our own, especially the badly grown vegetables that the farmers didn't want. We brought them back and did our own canning. To raise funds I went to all the Chinese stores to ask for donations every year. I even went into the gambling halls, and the men there donated."[57]

Of her fifty-two years of service in Vancouver, Sister Teresa Fung said, "The generosity and the gentleness of my many Vancouver friends leave me with a heart full of thanksgiving for having lived my missionary career there."[58]

Mount Saint Joseph Hospital

Although the Oriental Hospital had increased its number of beds, an average of almost five hundred home visits a year were being carried out between 1940 and 1945. The growing needs of the community demanded a larger facility. The sisters responded with the purchase of a former sheep ranch and orchard at the corner of Kingsway and Prince Edward Road in 1941. The hospital, located at 3080 Prince Edward Street, was only a few blocks from Saint Patrick's church, convent and school. It was opened in 1946 and was called Mount Saint Joseph Hospital.

The hospital was built with funding from the motherhouse and the financial assistance of the Canadian Chinese community, and a grant from the British Columbia government. The private eighty-seven-bed facility served the Canadian Chinese. Its staff of eighteen sisters, six doctors and several service workers provided medicine and surgical, paediatric and obstetric care.

The patients were cared for by Chinese staff. Chinese cooks prepared the food and the majority of staff spoke Chinese. The patients felt at home in the environment and referred to it as the "Chinese Hospital." Dr. Chu, the first Chinese intern in Canada and one of the original six doctors at Mount Saint Joseph Hospital, remembers delivering the first baby in December 1946: "... a little girl, Frances Chew. She was premature and since there were no incubators, we kept her alive with hot water bottles. She weighed only three pounds. We kept her here for six months. And now she is married and has children of her own."[59]

In 1948 Mount Saint Joseph Hospital became a general public hospital serving not only the Chinese, but the entire community. In 1956 the hospital expanded to provide 154 beds with the addition of a fifty-bed wing. In keeping with the missionary charism of the community, the sisters "encourage[d] the Hospital to be progressive and sensitive to the needs of the growing community and develop culturally sensitive health care programs and initiatives which would improve the Hospital's effectiveness in nursing patients from different cultures and various ethnic backgrounds."[60]

Sister Emma Barrette (Sister Anne of Jesus) provided valuable support by founding Mount Saint Joseph's first ladies auxiliary, which was comprised of twenty-five volunteers who helped to raise funds for the hospital. In 1969 the maternity ward was converted into an intensive care unit and day surgery was initiated. A major expansion and renovation program in 1977 increased the number of acute care beds to 150, with new facilities for emergency operating rooms and daycare services with expanded diagnostic and support facilities. A new wing provided quarters for extended care residents. In 1979 the Short Stay Assessment and Treatment Centre was opened. It was the first specialized geriatric service of its kind in British Columbia.

When the hospital celebrated its twenty-fifth anniversary in 1971, twenty-three Missionary Sisters of the Immaculate Conception were working in Vancouver. A short while later a new convent for the sisters was built next to the hospital and it served as a refuge for the many foreign missionaries who travelled through Vancouver on their way to or from missions across the Pacific. By the late 1980s, hospital staff of Mount Saint Joseph could communicate with patients in forty-two different languages. The Chinese still constitute the majority of patients.

By October 1994 Mount Saint Joseph Hospital joined the CHARA Health Care Society, which included Saint Vincent's Hospitals and Youville Residence. By the end of the 1990s Mount Saint Joseph Hospital still maintained an international reputation for serving the needs of multi-faith and multi-ethnic communities, showing continued leadership in culturally sensitive health care. This leadership is rooted in the love and care shown by the many sisters who first dedicated themselves to the Chinese community in Vancouver and who continue to serve the Chinese community, as well as serve other lower mainland communities through parish and school ministries, prison ministry and pastoral counselling.

Expansion by The Sisters of Saint Ann and the Sisters of Providence

Both the Sisters of Saint Ann and the Sisters of Providence, the first two communities to arrive in British Columbia, excelled in the field of health care.

Between the two world wars the Sisters of Saint Ann expanded to include the operation and staffing of hospitals on Vancouver Island and the interior of British Columbia, while the Sisters of Providence opened three hospitals in northern British Columbia.

The Sisters of Saint Ann on the Island and in the Interior

Half a century after the Sisters of Saint Ann opened Saint Joseph's Hospital in Victoria, they travelled north on Vancouver Island to Campbell River, where they reopened the community-owned hospital that had closed two years before. Arriving on the feast of Our Lady of Lourdes, they renamed it Lourdes Hospital. The small community of a few dozen houses started with a hospital of twenty beds, which mainly served the lumber camps and the Native reservations in the area. Only a few years later the sisters built a new wing to more than double the patient capacity of the hospital. The sisters operated Lourdes Hospital until 1957, when a new sixty-bed facility built with provincial government funds was opened.

In 1934 the hospital board of Smithers appealed to the Sisters of Saint Ann through Bishop Bunoz to take over the management and construction of the new Bulkley Valley District Hospital. Calling it Sacred Heart Hospital, Sister Mary Francis of Jesus, Sister Mary Osithe and Sister Mary Geraldine supervised the construction of the forty-bed, sixty-thousand-dollar facility. By the late 1940s a residence for nurses was added. In 1955 the capacity of the hospital was increased to eighty-five beds, following construction of building plans drawn up by Sister Mary Osithe for a new addition. By 1969 the sisters had withdrawn from the hospital after thirty-five years of dedicated and much-appreciated community service.

Mount Saint Mary in Victoria was built in 1941 as a facility for convalescent patients. The opening of this facility enabled nearby Saint Joseph's Hospital to make more beds accessible to new patients. Before Mount Saint Mary was completed, the Provincial Infirmary Authority asked the Sisters of Saint Ann to accept the overflow from their hospital in Vancouver. One hundred beds of the 150-bed hospital were set aside for this purpose. Still owned and operated by the Sisters of Saint Ann, the hospital continues to provide extended health-care services.

Saint Martin's Hospital, located in Oliver, was built in 1942. The government funded one third of the cost of construction while the Sisters of Saint Ann bore the remainder of the cost. The sisters managed the forty-bed hospital, serving the sick from Okanagan Falls to Grand Forks. After thirty years they withdrew their services and closed the hospital, making way for a new government-owned district hospital to be opened in 1973.

The sisters opened Mount Saint Francis Hospital in Nelson in 1949. Their apostolate to care for the elderly in the area had begun two years earlier when, at the request of Bishop Martin Johnson, three sisters took in five elderly residents. One of the first extended-care hospitals in the province, the ninety-eight-bed home for the chronically ill opened in 1950 and served the pioneers of the Kootenays. Three Sisters of Saint Ann withdrew in 1996 and entrusted the ongoing mission of Mount Saint Francis to others.

The Sisters of Providence in Northern British Columbia

The three hospitals operated by the Sisters of Providence during the 1930s in northern British Columbia were known as the "Hospitals of the Great Depression."[61] They met the needs of several isolated northern communities whose financial difficulties, lack of health care facilities, shortages of doctors, nurses, equipment and sometimes basic necessities, were similar. The ability of the sisters to administer, finance and staff these hospitals efficiently and effectively, along with their devotion and courage against seemingly insurmountable difficulties, set an exemplary standard for the community to follow. In their annals the sisters noted every act of kindness by the community with the same gratitude, regardless of how large or small. This was the spirit by which the Depression Hospitals survived.

Requests by the priest and bishop for help from the Sisters of Providence to operate a hospital in Fort St. John were denied by the provincial superior and the superior general in Montreal. Perseverance by those in need finally resulted in the superior general agreeing to send Mother Rustica, the provincial superior, to investigate. The sisters empathized with the citizens who pleaded for their help as the nearest hospital was 150 miles away. In 1931 three sisters opened the ten-bed Providence Hospital in Fort St. John. By 1942 an expansion was required to respond to an influx of one thousand American soldiers who had arrived to construct a highway. Upon leaving in 1945, the soldiers gave the hospital medicine, linen, furniture and vacated army barracks, one of which was purchased by the sisters for use as a coal shed. After more than forty years of service the sisters withdrew in 1973. The Anglican minister, Reverend William Blackstock, who was also a member of Providence Hospital Board of Management, paid tribute to the sisters and remarked, "... the great advantage of having a religious order was that they did not come to the district to make money, but to make sacrifices, only asking payment from the Great Physician."[62]

A year after Fort St. John's Providence Hospital was opened, the Sisters of Providence began a similar mission in Dawson Creek. Three sisters moved into the unfinished Saint Joseph Hospital on September 1, 1932. This was the beginning of the Depression years and the sisters had to borrow a stove to provide themselves with heat. Beds, table, dishes, utensils and a bit of food were brought in. By October two more sisters arrived, one a registered nurse and the other a cook. The following year, the superior general came with the provincial superior to meet the executive of the hospital board, and the sisters agreed to lend the association the money necessary to pay all the debts contracted for the building of the hospital. The board paid six percent interest and agreed to reimburse the sisters in phases. Again, after more than forty years of service and many thanks from the community, the sisters withdrew in 1973.

In 1940 Bishop Coudert of Prince Rupert and the Yukon Territory invited the Sisters of Providence to build a thirty-bed hospital in Vanderhoof, a mostly non-Catholic community of about four hundred with a surrounding community of Catholic English-speaking Carrier Natives numbering eighteen hundred. Sister Joseph Anselm supervised the building of the hospital, located on a twenty-acre plateau overlooking the Nechako River. On Oct. 4, 1941, the sisters admitted the first patient to Saint John's Hospital, formally opening it on October 9. Typically, five to seven sisters staffed the hospital throughout its twenty years, administering, cooking, nursing, and carrying out spiritual and corporal works of mercy.

The community was active in raising funds for the hospital, and in August 1942 the Ladies of Charity in Vanderhoof joined with those of Fort St. James to form the women's auxiliary. They raised money for a portable X-ray machine, laundry press and extractor, vacuum cleaner, stainless steel table, resuscitator, furniture and many other useful items. In this same year a modern well-lit and well-heated chicken coop was built for 193 chickens that were to be a source of revenue for the hospital. Sixteen fruit trees were also planted to help supply the hospital's needs. Not until 1961 did the hospital get an icemaker to end the daily chopping of ice.

The Provincial House finished paying for the hospital debt and remainder of hospital expenses with a cheque of ten thousand dollars in 1954. At the same time, they agreed to build a nurses' residence at a cost of fifty thousand dollars. Ten years later the sisters withdrew their services with the satisfaction of knowing their contribution to health care in the isolated community of Vanderhoof made a difference.

Sisters of Charity of the Immaculate Conception
Vancouver—Our Lady of Mercy Home
Six Sisters of Charity of the Immaculate Conception arrived in Vancouver in 1929 at the request of Archbishop Duke. Three of the sisters responded to the call of education, teaching at Sacred Heart Parish. The other three responded to the call of health care, opening Our Lady of Mercy Home. For the first three

Our Lady of Mercy Home, Vancouver.
Sisters of Charity of the Immaculate Conception Archives, St. John, New Brunswick

weeks Sister Carmel (Power), Sister Mary Margaret (Jeffries) and Sister Aloysius (Nordon) stayed at Sacred Heart Convent on Pender Street before moving to their own convent.

Their convent, called Our Lady of Mercy Home, was also where the sisters cared for unwed mothers and their babies, who were offered for adoption. The magnificent house and beautiful garden located on West Fifty-fourth Avenue and Oak Street had been a wealthy man's home:

> The property is beautifully landscaped and planted with shrubs and towering cedars; it is an ideal spot—the most beautiful the Community possesses—the extreme opposite of 940 Pender Street. There is, however, a Chapel with our dear Lord in the Blessed Sacrament in every house, and the grounds are really very incidental to the religious life; indeed, whatever beauty or drabness they may hold, a busy Sister has little time to look at either. It does make a delightful home for the children and an inviting place for the Sisters of the city to go for a few days rest when vacation days come 'round. The playgrounds are very attractive and spacious...[63]

The sisters fulfilled this mission from 1933 to 1966, operating it in conjunction with the Catholic Womens League, the Catholic Social Services and doctors

Christmas Day, Our Lady of Mercy Home.
Sisters of Charity of the Immaculate Conception Archives, St. John, New Brunswick

from Saint Paul's Hospital in Vancouver. The home was closed when a change in social-service policy placed children under government care and in foster homes.

Vancouver—Saint Vincent's Hospital

During the 1930s, health-care facilities in the city of Vancouver were inadequate. Archbishop Duke appealed to the mother house of the Sisters of Charity of the Immaculate Conception in Saint John, New Brunswick, asking them to open a Catholic hospital in Vancouver. The sisters complied by opening Saint Vincent's Hospital in 1939.

Sister Ruth (Helen Ross), who was appointed administrator of the hospital, had arrived in British Columbia ten years earlier as superintendent of Saint John's School for Boys. She had completed nurse's training and gained valuable experience in administration and in dealing with the aged and youth in Saint John, New Brunswick. To prepare for her new position Sister Ruth went to Seattle, Washington, where she earned a Certificate in Hospital Administration and took a course in personnel management from Providence Hospital and Seattle College.

Sister Ruth oversaw the planning of the hospital, beginning with the site selection on the slope of Little Mountain (Queen Elizabeth Park) across from the Royal Canadian Mounted Police barracks and horse barns on Thirty-third Avenue. Although the likely choice for the sisters to build a hospital would have been on the property at Fifty-fourth Avenue and Oak Street, where Our Lady of Mercy Home was located, rezoning for a hospital had been turned down twice and the Canadian Pacific Railroad, which owned land in that neighbourhood, opposed it. To avoid controversy, the sisters purchased property adjacent to Little Mountain at Heather Street and Thirty-third Avenue for $11,500. It was a beautiful site on a wooded property somewhat removed from the bustle of the city, which had a population at the time of not quite 275,000. The sisters purchased enough land for the hospital's future expansion.

The first phase of the projected two-hundred-bed facility included a five-storey, hundred-bed hospital fronting on Heather Street. The north end of the building's fourth floor

Sister Ruth (Ross), administrator of St. Vincent's 1939–57. St. Vincent's Hospital

served as a convent for the fifteen sisters who staffed the hospital. The other floors accommodated private, semi-private and four-bed wards for patients, a chapel, operating rooms, a maternity department, paediatric department, X-Ray department, pharmacy, administration offices, medical records and of course, a kitchen: "The ground floor contained the main kitchen which was a marvel of up-to-date equipment, elevators for food, and centralized services . . . A special feature of the entire building was the wide entrance doors to every room and ward with double hinges allowing easy moving of the beds and stretchers…solariums on each floor…had special windows that could be let down so that the patients requiring sun treatment could receive the full extent of the sun's rays combined with fresh air."[64]

In the war years there was a shortage of nursing staff as well as linen and other essential supplies. The sisters rationed sugar and always ensured the patients were fed before themselves: "In March, [1941] twenty-five beds provided by the Shaughnessy Military Hospital, for casualties in case of air raids, were set up. Blackout, emergency, and fire protection arrangements were also made by the hospital. [By November it was] more difficult to obtain food and hospital supplies every day."[65]

St. Vincent's Hospital, 1939.

In 1941 a flu epidemic broke out in the neighbouring army barracks. The military hospital could not accommodate everyone, so the sisters patriotically stepped in to care for the ailing soldiers.

Half a century later the Canadian Medical Forces Services Branch recognized the contribution of "Sisters, Nurses and Doctors who have worked on military and humanitarian missions throughout the world" in a ceremony held at Saint Vincent's Hospital. On behalf of all sisters who served during and after the First World War, Sister Rita Lynch of the Sisters of Charity of the Immaculate Conception was given an honorary membership in the Medical Company Unit Association. Sister Rita had served in health care for fifty-five years.

The year following the flu epidemic, the first floor was filled to capacity and the sisters recorded treating an average of almost fifty patients daily. In 1942 they also recorded, "Our little garden by the laundry is springing up—corn, squash, peas, lettuce, tomato plants and scarlet runners...Fruit trees—apple, pear, peach and cherry were planted on the hospital grounds."[66]

By 1948 the sisters opened a little cottage in the woods just west of the hospital, calling it "Fatima." It accommodated up to seven sisters, who used it as a place of respite during their days off and holidays. They also made it available for hospital staff gatherings.

Although the wooded location of the hospital presented a serene ambiance with "freedom from traffic noises, fog and smoke," access for employees was somewhat difficult: "There were no paved roads and no sidewalks...Public transportation was provided by the street car line on Oak Street, the nearest stop being Thirty-Third Avenue, but because of the wooded areas between the stop and the hospital, many employees preferred to use the King Edward Avenue run, get off at Heather Street, and walk the remaining distance. A few years later a shuttle-bus service was provided by the BC Electric Railway which brought the employees to the terminal located at the hospital."[67]

In 1952 the shuttle service for employees was discontinued as the street cars operating on Cambie Street brought trolleys to within a few blocks of the hospital.

Two years later the sisters implemented the second phase of the hospital, opening a hundred-bed, six-floor wing with a new entrance that fronted Thirty-third Avenue. Although the sisters borrowed money for the construction, the provincial and federal governments agreed to contribute to the projected $800,000 cost, while the city of Vancouver provided a tax exemption for the new hospital wing. The new wing featured piped oxygen and suction systems installed in five new operating rooms, renovations to the kitchen, an expanded maternity ward and nursery, extra facilities for the laboratory and X-ray department and a brightly decorated children's ward.

Saint Vincent's Hospital Guild, which began with fifteen women in 1959, had grown to one hundred members thirty years later. On the hospital's twenty-fifth anniversary the guild volunteers raised $8,000 to completely furnish an operating room. By the hospital's fiftieth anniversary, the total amount members had raised for the hospital approximated $285,000. In one year alone (1987–1988) they donated over three thousand hours of volunteer time.

The work of the guild was augmented in 1965 by another group of volunteers called the Pinafores. These young women belonged to the Future Nurses Club and assisted patients under the direction of Sister Vincentia (Loretta Ehman), who was also the operating room supervisor. Approximately seventy high-school students participated at this time. Within four years some boys had joined and the student volunteers were renamed the Vincenteens. Sister Florina

(Philomena Gallant) completed a course in volunteer direction and became their official director.

The sisters also volunteered for a variety of charitable activities outside of their work, giving and receiving help from their colleagues in other ministries. In their annals they recorded assistance from their colleagues at Our Lady of Mercy Home and from the teaching sisters at Sacred Heart, who took part in a sewing party for the hospital. Two of the sisters stayed for a number of days after to assist with the pile of hospital mending to be done. Volunteerism touched the life of every sister as most helped each other outside of their assigned duties, whenever and wherever they could.

Although the teaching sisters received a small wage for their work, in the beginning, the sister nurses at Saint Vincent's Hospital received no compensation. When government assistance came into place in the 1940s, the sister nurses began receiving wages. This enabled hospital sisters to take responsibility for their own living expenses and to contribute any excess funds to their motherhouse in New Brunswick to support new or impoverished ministries.

In the late 1960s the sisters purchased land from nearby Shaughnessy Hospital, and by 1974 Saint Vincent's Hospital added a new wing to its existing facility, which now included a seventy-five-bed extended-care unit, and twenty inpatient and ten daycare bed units for psychiatric patients. The area's changing demographics resulted in the closure of the obstetrics department the same year. At its peak, the department had enabled the delivery of almost two thousand babies in one year. Changes at the hospital continued, with advancements in technology enabling the sisters to acquire ultrasound equipment. As the only hospital in BC using this technique, they received referrals from all over the province.

By the mid 1990s the sisters were again responding to changing political and economic tides. In keeping with the dedication of the founding sisters to provide care, Saint Vincent's Hospital adapted. The sisters and boards of directors of Saint Vincent's Health Care Society, Mount Saint Joseph's Hospital and Youville Residence decided that future patient and resident care at their facilities would be best served by amalgamating into one society with a single governing board. With a new board of directors selected from individuals serving on the three existing boards, they formed CHARA Health Care Society in 1994. The unique identity of each institution was retained, while at the same time the new society brought together the facilities to strengthen the standard of patient and resident care provided at each institution.

Perhaps Dr. Ivan Martianoff best summarizes the quality all three hospitals continue to share even though his remarks were made fifty years ago. His words were recorded in commemoration of the one hundredth anniversary of the Sisters of Charity of the Immaculate Conception in 1954: "... Our English is not as good as we wish it would be…we remember the time…[the] hospital was losing [a] tremendous amount [of] money, and at that time I would call from my office and tell Sister Superior that there is a patient who needs hospitalization, but will not be able to pay for the Hospital. All you would say in your cheerful voice-'bring him in, send him in right away.' Is it not a splendid spirit of charity! you—being poor yourself, you will not refuse to help the other one. This is real Christianity!…"[68]

Sisters of the Love of Jesus

Ethel Cecilia Mary Dodd (1890–1989), known as Mother Cecilia Mary, established the first community of Catholic women religious founded in British Columbia. Her community was called the Sisters of the Love of Jesus and was formed in 1938. Born in England, Ethel Cecilia entered the Anglican order of the Precious Blood in 1910 and in 1912 transferred to the Society of the Incarnation of the Eternal Son.

When her parents moved from England to Vancouver, British Columbia, Sister Cecilia visited them. After returning home from this visit she requested the permission from her superior to establish an order in Vancouver. Her superior refused, so Sister Cecilia left her order and moved to Vancouver and began soliciting applicants to form a new community of women religious there in 1922. In 1929, in compliance with the British Columbia Societies Act, the Anglican Society of the Love of Jesus legally formed their new religious community with four sisters. Shortly after this, Sister Cecilia built a large school for Anglican girls on Oak Street in Vancouver.

By July 1939 Mother Cecilia and the nine members of her community had converted from the Anglican faith to Catholicism and their society was canonically erected in March 1938. The group retained its original name but now followed the Benedictine Rule. Sister Mary Mildred, one of the Sisters of Saint Ann from Victoria, came to help as a mistress of novices and remained one year. Sister Mary Eugenia, a Benedictine sister from Mount Angel, Oregon, replaced her.

Most of the Anglicans had withdrawn their children from the school in 1939, and given its impending closure and the needs of the Vancouver community in 1939, Archbishop Duke suggested the sisters open a facility for elderly care. In the summer of that year the sisters transformed the school on Oak and Twenty-seventh streets into a health-care facility for elderly women called Saint Anthony's Home. The sisters operated the home until 1942, when they sold it to the government for the war effort.

With the permission of the bishop of Victoria, but still under the jurisdiction of the archbishop of Vancouver, the sisters relocated to Victoria on October 1, 1942. Here they purchased the James Bay Hotel at 270 Government Street and opened a facility to care for elderly men and women. When they sold it in 1946, they moved some of the patients to the Glenshiel Hotel on Douglas Street, a property they bought the same year.

During this time the sisters established a convent and novitiate on Simcoe Street and also housed elderly retired women in a house adjoining the convent. In 1944 they bought two properties in Esquimalt, a house on 442 Barnard Avenue and the former Dunsmuir Estate, also on Barnard Avenue. Mother Cecilia had planned for an abbey to be built on these properties but was denied due to zoning bylaws.

In December 1947 Sister Cecilia purchased Clovelly, the former home of a Lieutenant Governor. She turned it into a care facility the following year, calling it St. Gregory by the Sea. When she tried to expand the facility two years later she realized permission from the city would not be granted, which initiated the sale of this property as well as the other two properties on Barnard Avenue and the remaining properties in Vancouver.

After selling these properties in 1951 the sisters purchased eleven acres of land in Langford, including the clubhouse of the Royal Colwood Golf Course. Here they established Saint Mary's Priory, converting the clubhouse into a convent and care facility that could accommodate forty-eight elderly ladies. The property also included the Chez Marcel Restaurant, which had a lease that expired the next year. The sisters remodelled the restaurant into a twenty-four-bed hospital.

In 1954 Mother Cecilia drew up plans for the House of Peace with help from Sister Etheldreda, who had worked as a draftsperson. The following year, they hired local carpenters to build it. Although the hospital was designed to house ninety patients, sometimes their numbers reached 104. At the peak of the facility's operation, a laundry was established in the tool shed and the caretaker's house was converted into a medical and dental centre with an X-ray department. The facilities were in operation until 1962, when the doctors moved into a newly built centre in Colwood.

Mother Cecilia purchased the Royal Auto Court, located on five acres of land across the street from Goldstream Avenue. Sixteen individual units were joined together by a two-hundred-foot hallway, creating Saint Anthony's Home for the elderly. The sisters now operated "a full range of care from rest home to extended care" and could care for two hundred patients.[69]

As an Anglican sister, Mother Cecilia had owned a dog, and as a converted Catholic she continued to do so, although the practice was considered unusual. When Mother Cecilia's dog died in 1957, she bought male and female pups. Their proliferation resulted in the House of Peace convent being overrun by new pups that eventually grew up and required more space and care. The municipal health authorities ordered the dogs off the premises and Mother Cecilia, with five of the professed sisters, moved into 4151 Borden Street, calling it the Good Shepherd Shelter. They lived there in a house that also had kennels to accommodate fifty dogs. They then requested money from the community to operate it.

Due to zoning, Mother Cecilia sold the property on Borden Street and purchased a twenty-three-acre property on Duke Road in Metchosin, eighteen miles southwest of Victoria. Now the Metchosin neighbours rallied against the uproar of some 250 dogs.

Although Mother Cecilia had been the superior of the community since 1937, Sister Ursula was elected new superior in 1961 as the bishop had suggested Mother Cecilia step down. Mother Cecilia continued the kennel enterprise and requested large sums of money to operate it. She wrote of her plight to the Pope and in turn, the residents of the neighbourhood in Metchosin also wrote to the Pope. They did not appreciate the expansion of the kennel operation.

The situation became an international incident as the media took the opportunity to write headlines about a sister in conflict with the Pope. Designated church authorities advised Mother Cecilia they could not approve her "new ministry." A great deal of discussion ensued, including legal battles and offers of dispensations to those sisters who would not leave the kennels and return to the priory.

Reverend Andrew Keber, a Benedictine from Mission, BC, was appointed by the Holy See in Rome to report on the situation. On April 27, 1964, Reverend Keber submitted his report, which resulted in ordering Mother Cecilia and her sisters to return to community life. They all refused and Mother Cecilia joined a protestant religion the following year. Mother Cecilia purchased two houses on fifty-eight acres at Mill Bay and continued with her animal enterprise.

In 1965 Sister Leonette Hoesing, a Benedictine sister from Yankton, South Dakota, was brought to the priory to take over as the new superior, duly elected. In 1966 nine of the sisters from the priory transferred to a Benedictine convent in South Dakota, while the remaining sisters continued to operate the House of Peace, the twenty-four-bed hospital, and Saint Anthony's Home. At that time a number of Benedictine convents were given the opportunity to take over the operations, but they all declined.

Sister Leonette established an advisory board to assess the finances and future of Saint Mary's Priory. Ultimately the twenty-four-bed hospital was taken over by the government in 1967. That same year the House of Peace, which once accommodated ninety patients and sometimes more, was designated an extended-care unit with accommodation for seventy-one patients. Sister Elizabeth of the Sisters of the Love of Jesus directed this facility as it underwent other improvements: "The Canadian Council of Accreditation used the Priory in helping to establish standards for longterm care facilities and on November 24, 1971, the Priory received full accreditation, lauding the work being done. The Priory became a leader in the field of health care for the elderly and became known nationally and internationally for its innovative concepts."[70]

In 1975 the Sisters of the Love of Jesus sold their property to the government, and the Juan de Fuca Hospital Society began to operate the facility. A number of doctors purchased Saint Anthony's Home, establishing it as a medical centre by the same name.

The Society of the Love of Jesus was officially dissolved on March 9, 1977. At the end of the 1970s Mother Cecilia, having since left the Catholic Church, returned to her faith and was admitted to the priory in 1981. In 1989 Mother Cecilia died at the age of ninety-eight, in the hospital that she founded.

CHAPTER 4 NOTES

1. Jean Barman, *The West Beyond the West: A history of British Columbia* (Toronto: University of Toronto Press Inc., 1996), 129.
2. Three of the communities originally founded in British Columbia that no longer exist today were the Sisters of the Love of Jesus, the Sisters of Charity of the Holy Rosary and the Sisters of Mary Immaculate.
3. Veronica Strong-Boag, "Society in the Twentieth Century," in *The Pacific Province*, edited by Hugh J.M. Johnston (Vancouver: Douglas & McIntyre, 1996), 273.
4. Marcia Cohen, *The Sisterhood: The true story of women who changed the world* (New York: Simon and Schuster, 1988), 35.
5. Lawrence Cada, et al., *Shaping the Coming Age of Religious Life* (New York: Seabury Press, 1979), 43.
6. Sister Marilla Silver, "Ministry in the Western Province 1923–1978" (paper prepared for Congregational Ministry Weekend, Long Island, New York, from Sisters of Charity of St. Vincent de Paul of Halifax Archives, Halifax, Nova Scotia, October 1978), 1.
7. Jean Barman, Neil Sutherland, & J. Donald Wilson, *Children, Teachers and Schools: In the history of British Columbia* (Calgary: Detselig Enterprises Ltd., 1995), 15.
8. Ibid., 21.
9. *Monthly Bulletin,* "Catholic Schools" (article from Catholic Information Centre Archives, Vancouver, BC, April 1917), 33.
10. Sister Marilla Silver, "Ministry in the Western Province 1923–1978" (paper prepared for Congregational Ministry Weekend, Long Island, New York, from Sisters of Charity of St. Vincent de Paul of Halifax Archives, Halifax, Nova Scotia, October 1978), 1.
11. Sister Mary Margaret Down (Edith Down), "The History of Catholic Education in British Columbia 1847–1900," in *Canadian Catholic Historical Association, Study Sessions* (1983), 569–590.
12. Sister M. Nepper, *The Heritage of the Sisters of Saint Joseph Lyons* (September 14, 1969, translated Toronto, February 11, 1973), 31.
13. Sister Mary Agnes, *The Congregation of the Sisters of St. Joseph: Le PuyΣLyon–St. Louis–Toronto* (Toronto: University of Toronto Press, 1950), 156.
14. Ibid., 158.
15. Ibid., 163.
16. Florence McNeil, "Memories—Grave and Gay," in *St. Helen's Jubilee Book 1912–1962*, p.14.

17. Dick Cotton, "St. Helen's School Celebrating Sixty Years of Tradition 1923–1983" (essay), 12.
18. Florence McNeil, "Memories—Grave and Gay," in *St. Helen's Jubilee Book 1912–1962*, p.14.
19. Elaine Colleran, "St. Helen's School Celebrating Sixty Years of Tradition 1923–1983" (essay), 13.
20. Dick Cotton "St. Helen's School Celebrating Sixty Years of Tradition 1923–1983" (essay), 12.
21. Steve Jackson, *The Catholic Parish of St. Mary's Ladysmith 1901–1988: Today and yesterday.*
22. *History of Missions in BC* (original account compiled by Sister Rooney for the years 1923–1971), 7.
23. *Golden Years 1923–73: Parish of Our Lady of Perpetual Help Vancouver, BC,* "Sisters and Parish" (taken from Tape One of the Edmonton Archives, made by Rev. John F. Coughlan), 38.
24. Sister Katherine Meagher, "Charities in the Diocese of Nelson" (paper from Sisters of Charity of St. Vincent de Paul of Halifax Archives, Halifax, Nova Scotia, 1995), 3.
25. Sister Barbara Schatz, "Burnaby Boys' Home" (paper from Sisters of Charity of the Immaculate Conception Archives, St. John, New Brunswick), 1.
26. *The Torch* (diocese newspaper, from Sisters of the Immaculate Heart of Mary Archives, Los Angeles, California, February, 1959).
27. "Magnificat" (from Sisters of the Immaculate Heart of Mary Archives, Los Angeles, California, October 1961), Vol. Six, No. 1.
28. Kay Cronin, "Kakawis nuns in BC's toughest mission" in *Our Sunday Visitor* (May 22, 1960), Vol. XLIX, No. 4.
29. Ibid.
30. *History of the School Sisters of Notre Dame in the Canadian Provinces* (Milwaukee, Wisconsin: Notre Dame Convent Press, 1943), 3.
31. Convent Chronicles, 1944 (School Sisters of Notre Dame Archives, Waterdown, Ontario).
32. Father Othmar Mussmacher, *Memories of Our Lady of Consolation School and Sacred Heart School, Ladner, British Columbia 1944–1992.*
33. Augustinian Chronicles (School Sisters of Notre Dame Archives, Waterdown, Ontario, 1944).
34. Sister Cajetan, "Ladner" (paper from School Sisters of Notre Dame Archives, Waterdown, Ontario).
35. Rumpel Ramily, *Memories of Our Lady of Consolation School and Sacred Heart School, Ladner, British Columbia 1944–1992,* p.47.
36. Maradee Olney, *Memories of Our Lady of Consolation School and Sacred Heart School, Ladner, British Columbia 1944–1992,* p.49.
37. Sister Louise Vanderploeg, *Memories of Our Lady of Consolation School and Sacred Heart School, Ladner, British Columbia 1944–1992,* p.22.
38. Convent Chronicles (School Sisters of Notre Dame Archives, Waterdown, Ontario, 1958).
39. Royal Columbian Hospital, Vancouver (1862) and St. Bartholomew's Hospital, Lytton (1870).
40. Rev. M.G. Doyle, *The Story of the Catholic Hospitals of Canada,* 33.
41. The Monthly Bulletin, "St. Paul's Hospital" (Catholic Information Centre Archives, Vancouver, BC, December 1917), 42.
42. Hortense Quesnelle, Précis of Chronicles, May 16, 1894, to June 30, 1978.
43. Harvey G. Agnew, *Canadian Hospitals 1920 to 1970: A dramatic half century* (University of Toronto Press), 141.
44. Gisele Villemure, *Who Is Délia Tétreault?: Mother Marie du Saint-Esprit 1865–1941,* (trans. Madeleine Delorme and Edita Telan, 1983), 7.
45. *Dreams of Soul Harvests Come True* (booklet printed in Canada, December 1954).
46. Délia Tétreault and the Canadian Church, (Letter written on September 4, 1916), 43.

47. One of the six sisters who left for China was Sister St. Alphonse-de-Liguorii, who later became Mother Mary of the Sacred Heart, foundress of the Missionary Sisters of Our Lady of the Angels.

48. Angela Lee, "From a Humble Beginning Mt. St. Joseph Blossoms into a First Class Hospital," in *Chinatown News* (March 3, 1993), 10.

49. Sister Noella Brisson, "Delving into the Missionary Sisters of the Immaculate Conception Roots in Vancouver" (Sisters of the Immaculate Conception, Vancouver), 1.

50. On June 2, 1928, Sister Marie-du-Sacré-Coeur (Frederica Giroux) left the Missionary Sisters of the Immaculate Conception to found the congregation of the Missionary Sisters of Christ the King.

51. The First Thirty Years of the Institute of the Missionary Sisters of the Immaculate Conception (letter from Sister Aimee-de-Jesus).

52. Allen Seager, "The Resource Economy," in *The Pacific Province*, edited by Hugh J.M. Johnston (Vancouver: Douglas & McIntyre, 1996), 211.

53. Ibid., 217.

54. Sister Noella Brisson, "Delving into the Missionary Sisters of the Immaculate Conception Roots in Vancouver" (Sisters of the Immaculate Conception, Vancouver), 2.

55. "St. Joseph's Oriental Hospital" (pamphlet, from Missionary Sisters of the Immaculate Conception Archives, Laval, Quebec), 5.

56. *Mount Saint Joseph: The little hospital that grew* (fiftieth/seventy-fifth anniversary booklet), 3.

57. Paul Yee, *Saltwater City* (Seattle: University of Washington Press, 1988).

58. Interview with Sister Theresa Fung by sister Huguette Turcotte, November 1995.

59. *Mount Saint Joseph: The little hospital that grew* (fiftieth/seventy-fifth anniversary booklet), 4.

60. "Catholic Health Association of British Columbia Anniversary Booklet, 1940–1990," (printed by the Little Printer Ltd.), 19.

61. "Catholic Health Association of British Columbia Anniversary Booklet, 1940–1990," (printed by the Little Printer Ltd.), 15.

62. Hortense Quesnelle, Précis of Chronicles, Providence Hospital Fort St. John, February1931 to April 29, 1976.

63. *Laus Deo! 1854–1954: Centennary of the Sisters of Charity of the Immaculate Conception* (Archives of the Sisters of Charity of the Immaculate Conception, St. John, New Brunswick).

64. St. Vincent's Hospital Vancouver, British Columbia, 1939–1989, p.12.

65. St. Vincent's Hospital Vancouver, British Columbia, 1939–1989, p.13.

66. St. Vincent's Hospital Vancouver, British Columbia, 1939–1989, p.13.

67. St. Vincent's Hospital Vancouver, British Columbia, 1939–1989.

68. *Laus Deo! 1854–1954: Centennary of the Sisters of Charity of the Immaculate Conception* (Archives of the Sisters of Charity of the Immaculate Conception, St. John, New Brunswick), 75.

69. Vera McIver, "The Society of the Love of Jesus" (paper from Diocese of Victoria Archivist), 5.

70. Ibid., 12.

CHAPTER 5

Growing Needs

Grey Sisters of the Immaculate Conception
Saint Marguerite d'Youville Founds the Grey Sisters in Montreal

ince their inception as a community of women religious in 1737, the Grey Sisters of the Immaculate Conception have modelled themselves after the exemplary spiritual life of their foundress, Saint Marguerite d'Youville (Marguerite Lejemmerais, 1701–1771). The proclamation of Marguerite d'Youville's sainthood on December 9, 1990, heralded her as the first Canadian-born person to receive such an honour. Her saintly life influenced the formation of five other religious congregations, all based on the foundation of her first congregation of Grey Nuns in Montreal, the Sisters of Charity of the General Hospital of Montreal.

Marguerite grew up in poverty. By the time she was twenty-eight, four of her infant children had died. She was

Saint Marguerite d'Youville 1701–1771. Archives Grey Sisters of the Immaculate Conception, Pembroke, Ont.

finally burdened with the death of her husband, who left her with two remaining sons and a very large debt. Marguerite opened a small store and dutifully paid the debts her husband had incurred while he was engaged in illicit fur and liquor trading. When Marguerite felt secure about her children being well cared for and educated, she began devoting herself to the sick and needy of Montreal.

In 1737 Marguerite and her companions began living together in Montreal, where, in a rented house, they accepted female boarders needing assistance. Their first boarder was a sixty-three-year-old blind woman. Marguerite's three companions, Miss Louise Thaumur Lasource, Miss Catherine Demers and Miss Catherine Cusson, became the first Grey Nuns when they secretly consecrated themselves to living communally.

Ten years later, in 1747, they took over the administration of the General Hospital of Montreal where "Mother d'Youville's resourcefulness and her talents as an executive and business woman were never more capably demonstrated."[1] In 1754 Marguerite opened a home for abandoned babies, the first of its kind in North America. The following year the women donned their religious habit and formally, as the first Grey Nuns, continued to devote themselves to a myriad of charitable works assisting the poor, needy, outcasts, sick, elderly and orphaned in Montreal.

For years, however, they were plagued with defaming accusations. The shadow of Marguerite's husband had followed them in the form of insinuations that they were carrying on his illicit businesses, and they were slanderously labelled as drunkards and prostitutes. In the streets they endured contemptuous and derisive shouts of "Les Soeurs Grises—The Grey Nuns." This jeering street call also was translated as "the tipsy nuns." The derogatory name-calling took on a new meaning over time, because as the sisters' devotion to their mission grew, so did the admiration of the people who witnessed their works of mercy. Mother Youville perpetuated their transcendence of the original insults by retaining the name "Grey Nuns" as a symbol of humility.[2]

Known as the Mother of Universal Charity,[3] Saint Marguerite d'Youville inspired Grey Nuns to carry her work on into the nineteenth, twentieth and twenty-first centuries. In 1840 four sisters left the Montreal community to start a new congregation of Grey Nuns at Saint Hyacinth. In 1845 four sisters left Montreal to establish the Ottawa foundation, calling themselves the Grey Nuns of the Cross.

From the Ottawa community, two autonomous English-speaking congregations emerged. The first was the Grey Nuns of Sacred Heart, established in Philadelphia, Pennsylvania, in 1921. The second was the Grey Sisters of the Immaculate Conception in Pembroke, Ontario, who were approved as a religious community in 1926 and were best known for their work in health care, education, geriatrics and social services. Four of the Pembroke Grey Sisters left their home to provide their services in British Columbia.

St. Vincent's Home and Shelter

The sisters had been asked to come to Vancouver by Archbishop Duke in 1931, the beginning of the Depression years. Four sisters arrived on September 11, 1931, and were directed to 853 Pender Street, where they managed Saint Vincent's Home and Shelter, located on the edge of skid row.

Saint Vincent's Home and Shelter was maintained as a residence for elderly and destitute men, and also offered food, clothing and shelter to transients who were trying to survive the Depression. The sisters received food donations that allowed them to provide hot meals to the needy men who formed long bread lines at their door. Even in the meagre Depression years, the sisters continued to be given the donations that furnished the home with beds, furniture and dishes.

The sisters' mission statement for the shelter read, "No man must be turned away if in need of food, clothing or shelter if it is at all possible to give accommodation."

Initially the sisters admitted fifteen elderly men. An average of 1,600 hot meals were served each month, and within the first three years, 71,650 meals had been prepared for residents and transients alike.

After the Depression subsided, the shelter service continued until 1969. Meals were still provided for male transients, who ate in the dining room with

Grey Sisters at St. Vincent's Home.
Archives Grey Sisters of the Immaculate Conception, Pembroke, Ont.

the regular residents. Apart from that, approximately 200 lunches were served at the door on a daily basis, again until 1969.

Saint Vincent's originally consisted of a wood building and a brick building, but adjacent buildings were purchased to expand the facility. In 1942 construction of a new wing provided accommodation for an additional fifty-one homeless men and space for a chapel, a dormitory and a dining room for transients.

Even with the additional buildings and expansions, the facility eventually became insufficient for the increasing demands of the community. The East Pender location became unsafe and too small to adequately serve the residents. At this time the welfare department began to assume some of the responsibilities previously met by the sisters. Under the changed circumstances the sisters decided to find a new location and slightly alter their ministry to care for both elderly men and women.

The sisters chose to construct their new building on a property at the corner of Thirty-third Avenue and Heather Street in Vancouver. They received assistance from the federal government, provincial government and private donors. On May 3, 1968, the sod was turned and on June 18, 1969, the Grey Sisters opened Youville Residence. The sisters named the facility in honor of Saint Marguerite Youville with the intention of memorializing her spirit of charity within the community.

The building accommodated 152 elderly men and women. The original residents attended to their own personal needs, but as provincial health-care programs changed, Youville Residence also changed. In January 1978 Youville Residence became a long-term care facility for residents who required more attention than previously planned. The sisters made the appropriate renovations to accommodate the new requirements and in 1981 added a sixth floor to Youville to provide living quarters for the sisters.

On December 9, 1990, the premier of British Columbia dedicated a commemorative stone on the grounds of Youville Residence to celebrate the canonization of Saint Marguerite Youville. She bequeathed her spiritual legacy to the generations of Grey Sisters, including those who work at Youville Residence today with a team of recreational therapists, nursing staff and volunteers to provide "care, compassion and respect for the dignity of the individual."[4]

Seminary in Ladner

Saint Marguerite d'Youville supported her two sons while they were preparing to become priests and through that time acquired a special concern for young men preparing for the priesthood. After the Grey Sisters took over the operation and management of the General Hospital in Montreal, they began to assist young men preparing for the priesthood. In 1761 the Grey Sisters managed a building near the hospital, where they provided young men with lodging and supported them during their preparations for religious life.

Their support for those entering the priesthood was reawakened in British Columbia when in September 1932 the Grey Nuns began working at the Junior Seminary of Christ the King in Ladner. The seminary had been established the previous year by the Benedictine monks of Mount Angel, Oregon, at Archbishop Duke's request. Mother Estella from the Grey Sisters' motherhouse in Ottawa sent Sister Saint Bernard and Sister Mary of the Rosary to accompany Sister Margaret Teresa, who was appointed superior of the mission.

The seminary, situated on 130 acres of prime farmland at the mouth of the Fraser River, had once been the old Jubilee Farm. The Archdiocese of Vancouver inherited the land upon the death of the wealthy Mrs. McNeeley, who had specifically requested that the house be used for a sisters' convent: "Archbishop Duke saw the need of a Junior Seminary and he built a wing for the Seminarians. The Sisters had their own apartment in the wing until a Convent was built later ... [It was] comprised of a Community room and Dormitory with three comfortable beds divided by a large space between. At the end of the room was a large wardrobe and extra space for trunks. There was also a private chapel and private dining room."[5]

The beautiful residence and grounds became an administration centre with offices, a reception room and a chapel. An additional building was constructed to provide space for two dormitories, dining and recreation halls, five classrooms, verandahs and a kitchen. The new building was connected to the old residence by a wing.

The first year, thirty boys registered for the seminary, and the sisters who worked in the kitchen seminary were so busy they "scarcely had time to breathe." The following year, their September records showed they had canned 137 1/2 gallons of jam, fruit and pickled butter beans. It is not surprising that two days later their annals read, "September 14—After early Mass we served breakfast to the Archbishop, five priests and thirty students. The Archbishop was well pleased, spoke kindly and promised to get us more help. We sisters have been so tired at night, we felt like crying. However, Divine Providence came quickly to our aid and we now have a non-Catholic man, who had spent the winter at St. Vincent's Shelter, come to work for us. He is wonderful—he can cook, wash dishes and do general house work."[6]

The next year they canned a total of 163 gallons of cherries, raspberries, strawberries, blackberries, rhubarb, plums, prunes, pears and pickled butter beans.

Although overworked, the sisters were blessed with a serene setting and the comfort of women religious visitors from throughout the lower mainland.

Sisters Day was held in October when the Sisters of Charity, the Sisters of Saint Ann and extern Sisters of the Precious Blood were entertained. Over Christmas holidays the Grey Sisters were able to visit their own community at Saint Vincent's Shelter in Vancouver. In the summer they went to Saint Edward's Seminary in Bothell, Washington, where they visited the Sisters of Saint Joseph from Montreal.

The sisters served for about seven years at the seminary in Ladner until they moved to Burnaby in 1939. The move coincided with the Benedictine monks' purchase of the Anderson house on Deer Lake in 1939. Four sisters were missioned to the culinary department at the seminary, but over the next ten years their numbers sometimes reached five and six sisters.

By 1946, however, the superior general of their community advised the monks that the sisters would withdraw their services. The lack of vocations made it too difficult to provide sisters for the seminary work. The superior general agreed the sisters could remain until replacements could be found, but three years later replacements still had not been found. The Grey Sisters finally withdrew their services on June 30, 1949. In 1951 the Benedictine Sisters of Saint Lioba from Frieburg, Germany, finally came to the rescue of the monks and stayed until 1968.

Grade school, downtown Vancouver. Archives Grey Sisters of the Immaculate Conception, Pembroke, Ont.

The Chinese Catholic Centre

Archbishop Duke requested the Grey Sisters of the Immaculate Conception, along with the Scarboro Foreign Mission Society of Toronto, to staff the Chinese Catholic Centre. The objective was to serve the spiritual and material well being of the large Chinese community in Vancouver. The Chinese Catholic mission was officially opened on December 3, 1933, the feast of Saint Francis Xavier, patron of the centre. It was staffed by one priest and three Grey Sisters, Sister Saint Oswald, Sister Mary Gertrude and Sister Anne Marie.

A house that was purchased at East Georgia and Princess streets operated as convent, church and

Chinese Catholic Centre 1934. Archives Grey Sisters of the Immaculate Conception, Pembroke, Ont.

Sister Saint Angela with child fingerpainting.
Archives Grey Sisters of the Immaculate Conception, Pembroke, Ont.

kindergarten. By 1934 a hall was rented across the street and upon renovation it accommodated the increased numbers of children attending the Chinese mission kindergarten. Soon a grade school was needed in conjunction with the kindergarten. The third floor of the Bank of Commerce building at Main and Pender streets was rented and renovated to accommodate the first fifty-five students who registered in September 1938. By this time the Grey Sisters staffing the Chinese mission numbered six, along with two priests.

By 1939 the kindergarten building was moved to the south side of Georgia Street and became the parish church. The property on the northwest corner of Georgia and Princess streets was purchased and a new small school was constructed. It consisted of three classrooms, a kindergarten, an auditorium and a kitchen. Apart from the academic program, the children also partook in athletics such as baseball, football, boxing and swimming, along with choir and drama.

An English-language school was opened at the centre in 1954 to meet the needs of an increasing number of Chinese immigrants. By 1958 the centre celebrated its silver jubilee, and in 1983 St. Francis Xavier Chinese Catholic School celebrated its golden jubilee with Sister Bernadette Kinsella, mother general of the Grey Sisters of the Immaculate Conception, present.

Over 160 Grey Sisters of the Immaculate Conception had lived and worked in British Columbia since their arrival in 1931. Their heartfelt contribution to the province is reflected today in Youville Residence and the Catholic school and parish of Saint Francis Xavier.

Sisters of Service
Sister Catherine Donnelly Founds a New Canadian Community of Women Religious

Catherine Donnelly (1884–1983) founded the Sisters of Service in Toronto, Ontario, on August 15, 1922. She founded the community with the specific intention of working in the outlying districts of the home mission field of Canada, particularly among new Canadians.

Catherine Donnelly was born in Alliston, Ontario. Her experience teaching in western Prairies schools motivated her involvement in religious instruction of the children of

Sister Catherine Donnelly 1884–1983.
Sisters of Service Archives, Toronto

Catholic immigrant settlers in Canada. She wished to establish "a community of religious who would live in isolated communities which had no priest or church and who would teach in public schools and live among the people of the local community."[7]

Upon her return to Toronto, Catherine searched for a religious community of women who would join her in ministering in western rural communities but was unable to find such a community. Undaunted, she approached the Redemptorist fathers in Toronto, who had worked in the West and were familiar with the problems she had encountered. Archbishop Neil McNeil, the archbishop of Toronto, agreed that a new religious community was needed to meet the needs of Canadian immigrants and those of rural Canada.

It was decided the new community of women religious would be "flexible, their habit inconspicuous, the members would teach, nurse the sick and help the most abandoned."[8] Their motto was "I have come to serve," and their Constitution stated, "The life of the Sisters of Service is one consecrated to the apostolate of Catholics most destitute of spiritual help, particularly among immigrants and their children dwelling in the outlying districts. They should always have before their eyes the specific work for which they were founded."[9]

Father George Daly came from Regina to Toronto in 1922 to assist the Sisters of Service in establishing their new community. The Sisters of Saint Joseph of Toronto sent Sister Mary Lidwina to be the first superior and novice mistress, supervising Catherine Donnelly and three companions, the first novices. When Catherine Donnelly completed her novitiate, she left with the first contingent of the new community to open a teaching mission in Camp Morton, Manitoba.

From the beginning the sisters devoted themselves to catechetical teaching and taught children in Toronto. To reach children in isolated areas by mail, they started a religious correspondence school in Edmonton in 1925. Energized by their faith and foundress, they continued west to start their first mission in British Columbia.

The Sisters of Service in Vancouver

On October 13, 1929, two Sisters of Service came to Vancouver to take over the Catholic Hostel of Saint Anthony, the first hostel in Vancouver for the care of immigrant women. The work had been initiated by the ladies' auxiliary of Our Lady of the Holy Rosary Pro-Cathedral Parish in Vancouver in 1928. The Franciscan Sisters of the Atonement had agreed to supervise the facility for one year, after which time the Franciscan sisters returned to their work with the Japanese mission in Vancouver, and the Sisters of Service took charge.

The Sisters of Service had been attending to the needs of immigrants almost since their inception as a religious community. The first sisters went to dockyards and train stations, where they met immigrants arriving in Canada, and they had successfully operated hostels for immigrant girls in Halifax, Montreal, Toronto, Winnipeg and Edmonton before expanding to Vancouver. In conjunction with government sponsorship and its provision of domestic employment for single girls, the Sisters of Service established "residential clubs" that were a safe home away from home for these girls.

Although the Catholic Women's League was paying the rent at Saint Anthony's Hostel, the girls found travel costs from this location to their places of employment too expensive. The hostel, located at 1290 Robson Street, was thus judged an unsuitable location for them, and Sister Gertrude Walsh and Sister Frances Church started soliciting donations to purchase a residence in a more suitable location.

Sister Frances Church, a talented musician and a famous singer in her day, unexpectedly received a donation of five thousand dollars while visiting a woman who heard her sing. This large donation went toward the purchase of the new residence on 1715 West Eleventh Avenue. In June 1930, eight girls who lived at Saint Anthony's Hostel helped the sisters relocate to Eleventh Avenue, which could accommodate twenty-five girls and four sisters.

Originally built for W.C. Hodgson of the Canadian Pacific Railroad in 1911, the new residence spanned two lots and included a spacious garden. The dining room and kitchen were located in the basement and looked out onto the garden, where the sisters later built a grotto. Recreation facilities included a sitting room and a recreation room with two pianos and a television. The sisters' rooms were on the main floor near the chapel, which had been added at the back of the house in 1957.

Sisters and 1935 Dodge in front of 11th Avenue residence. Sisters of Service Archives, Toronto

Within three years the girls started Saint Anthony's Girls Club with the motto, "Good deeds reap gladness." The young women raised money for special good works, one of which was the Ladner Seminary where the Grey Nuns were working. The orchestra that Sister Church helped them start continued to perform until 1972.

Although the sisters were mindful of their original focus on immigrants and tried to create a home away from home, the residence also provided a home for single young women whose families lived outside the city. The front page of the residence manual read:

The Duty of Welcoming Others

We cannot insist too much on the duty of welcoming others—a duty springing from human solidarity and Christian charity—which is incumbent both on the families and the cultural organizations of the host countries. Centres of welcome and hostels must be multiplied, especially for youth. This must be done first to protect them from loneliness, the feeling of abandonment and distress, which undermine all moral resistance. This is also necessary to protect them from the unhealthy situation in which they find themselves, forced as they are to compare the extreme poverty of their homeland with the luxury and waste which often surround them.[10]

As other facilities existed for young girls with serious problems,[11] the sisters did not accept seriously disturbed girls, pregnant girls, "incorrigibles" or those whose home was in the city. Their intention was to "safeguard youth" with an "emphasis on prevention rather than rehabilitation."[12] The young women who resided with the sisters were generally allowed to remain for two years, though exceptions were made in unusual cases. During the two years the sisters did what they could to provide a comfortable and secure environment for the young women. Within the last six months of each girl's stay, however, they focused on assisting her to live independently. A standard fee for room and board was set, but a sliding scale allowed girls enduring economic hardship to pay according to their financial capability.

At the residence the girls were given classes in cooking, sewing, home nursing, public speaking and various crafts, while after hours the sisters worked to help find them employment: "... but what was not visible to the eye were the hours spent studying foreign languages and passenger lists and the untold hours spent in the basement of girls' residences typing referrals. Anyone who has worked in a girls' residence knows why a haven in the cellar is necessary to find time for such work. A young Sister Kelly comes to mind as she typed into the night on one of the first electric typewriters, it had runaway tendencies. Somebody had discarded it and she was feeling like a millionaire with the machine."[13]

Once the young women found work, they were encouraged to find their own accommodation, which they often found with another girl they befriended at the residence.

Presentation by Mayor Thompson of Vancouver to group of Displaced Persons (Sister Furman in centre).
Sisters of Service Archives, Toronto

As years went by, Canadian girls working for the war effort took the place of immigrant girls. After the war the Canadian government issued a contract for displaced persons (DPs) to come to Canada as domestics. Many single girls from all over the world, including South America, Japan, South Vietnam, Taiwan and Peru, came into the care of the Sisters of Service, who helped them learn English and secure Canadian citizenship. Through integration programs sponsored by the Sisters of Service, the label of "DP" began to disappear and the name "hostel" was replaced with the Sisters of Service Girls' Residential Club.

In 1972, after housing over ten thousand women in forty-three years of operation, the Sisters of Service closed the residence. "There is not enough religious personnel to keep the residences in operation. Those joining the Order now want to go into teaching, nursing, religious education or social service fields rather than running the residence."[14] The sisters continued teaching and assisting in various social services until 1981, when they left the province after dedicating more than fifty years of service to British Columbians.

The sisters left a lasting memory with many impressionable young women, as one of the residents recalled: "I was and am a Protestant and before staying with the Sisters (SOS) I knew nothing about Catholics. The Sisters' unselfish lives of constant, patient service toward the girls here has impressed me tremendously with a faith that seems truly Christian ... My one-time cultural conservatism has been permanently altered for the better ... I shall never forget the warm, friendly way the Sisters greeted me nor their kindly, helpful interest in me throughout my stay at the house."[15]

Religious Instruction in the Interior

In 1928, the year before the Sisters of Service arrived at the hostel in Vancouver, their director, Father Daly, wrote to Reverend Casey in Vancouver to advise him of the intent of the Sisters of Service: "One feature of our connection with our prospective foundation in Vancouver, is our hope in time to make it a centre for Catechetical teachers for the interior of BC."[16]

In 1934 Father Daly wrote to the archbishop, "We are sending two Sisters this summer into the interior to work in Father A.L. McIntyre's scattered missions. I am sure you will be glad to hear also that from Edmonton our Sisters are instructing several hundreds of children by mail, in your diocese."

On May 6, 1934, the foundress of the community, Sister Catherine Donnelly, temporarily left her post in Regina, Saskatchewan, and arrived in Vancouver, where she met Sister Irene Faye. Together they drove their car to the Cariboo region and gave religious instruction at Big Bar, Springhouse, Quesnel, Meldrum Creek, Bradley Creek and Clinton. Many of their students were illiterate but the sisters taught them songs and prayers. The sisters also taught adults in the evenings, but in mid-July their summer excursion was cut short due to the

Sister Irene Faye in the Cariboo, 1934. Sisters of Service Archives, Toronto

From left: Sisters Pat Williams and Irene Faye, 1935.
Sisters of Service Archives, Toronto

extremely difficult road conditions: "In order to visit some of the families the sisters have to use an axe to remove the fallen trees from the road…one family was so isolated that the only way to go was on horseback…the people are so dreadfully poor…"[17]

Two years later these same two sisters returned to the Cariboo region, again by car. They did not take the van available to them as the roads were too difficult. Instead they slept in the car at night, removing the backs of the front seats so that both the sisters could stretch out. The sisters cooked over an open fire as they had done two years before. During this trip Sister Catherine Donnelly wrote, "As an addition to our car home we had a little tent. Canvas was brought and stretched over poles and a camp stove was placed in this shelter. In the morning one's eyes would open on the gigantic forest trees and the encircling mountains, with clouds of soft white mist hanging at various heights. To one's ears would come the twittering of many birds accompanied by the steady roar of the rapid river. We sometimes caught sight of the wild creatures in this hunter's paradise. It is a land of deer and moose, cougars, cariboo and black bears…We lived for a week at this place amid the luxuries that nature alone can provide."[18]

The sisters still lamented the road conditions in 1939 when one of them remarked that an inch is as good as a mile, especially at the edge of a cliff. The vast distances between stops in remote areas often meant extremely difficult travel. Driving to destinations such as Williams Lake, 150 Mile House, Big Bar, Alexandria and Quesnel meant motoring along roads that brought the sisters dangerously close to disaster, although their faith kept them high-spirited. On one of her summer trips in the Cariboo, Sister Catherine Donnelly wrote in her diary, "We are in the Cariboo mountain district of British Columbia. Though never far from the wild Fraser River, and sometimes so near the precipice that a little skid would hurl our car into the furious waters, we are never really in danger."[19]

The sisters, although missionaries themselves, were inspired by the generosity, self-sacrifice and courage of the people they met in the Cariboo. The people they encountered in the wilderness shared what little provisions they had with the sisters, sometimes offering them milk, butter, eggs and, if they had a garden, fresh produce.

They also received kind assistance when things did not go according to plan. One very wet muddy day, the sisters slid into a ditch. The nearest cabin dweller, an old feeble man, insisted on helping the sisters in the torrential mud and rain. After endless tries they finally left to find the nearest car to pull them out of their predicament. By the end of a long tiring day, they returned rain-soaked to find all their belongings had been moved from their car:

> How to get dry was worrying me ... If we could only have a warm fire and a little bit of shelter ... Mrs. Isnardy came running over from her house to tell us to go over to the little cabin. They had fixed it up for us and put a stove in it ... What a blessed relief! Thank the Lord for these kind people! Yes, the tiny cabin which had been a milk-house opened its little old crooked door to us and the glowing, hot stove with the fire showering through holes and cracks smiled and beckoned to us to come in out the the teaming rain. It was a never-to-be-forgotten sensation of joy and relief, and comfort! "Kind hearts are coronets." It was a royal welcome we received and that little log cabin with its mud floor and its crevices stuffed with moss, to me that night was perfect. I felt like a Queen in a palace and said so.[20]

Sister Faye reported on one of her trips to the interior when she spoke to the Catholic Women's League in Regina in 1937:

> Just to give you an idea of the immensity of the parish and the distances that have to be travelled it would be well to tell a little about the country itself. The territory is approximately three hundred miles square, very mountainous, with dense woods. It is the last great cow-country of the West—also the very famous district of gold mining ... The nearest neighbour might be five miles away or he might be twenty-five miles away. The people are very poor ... Not knowing whether we were human—the people at first were very reticent ... a good many children have never been to school ... In one of our summer classes were a girl and a boy, sixteen and eighteen year[s] of age, they could not spell their name ... The people very generously gave us a stove, tent, axe, and wood and saw that we were settled

comfortably...Our camp was right at the edge of the virgin forest...Immense trees, two hundred or more feet in length, towered above us, and only a few hundred feet from the river...The current was so swollen that ten feet of the bank was cut off in two days. Trees all lengths were falling into the stream—we would sit at our camp and hear them crash.[21]

Once they felt secure in having begun to accomplish their mission, the sisters reduced their visits to the Cariboo and began to visit other areas in the province. They also extended their services of teaching religion to places such as Powell River, Princeton, the lower mainland and Squamish. By 1945, at the end of war, three Sisters of Service went weekly to instruct children in various similar localities.

By the 1960s, at the request of a prison matron, the sisters had expanded their service to instruct, counsel and assist the women at Oakala Women's Prison. They also undertook work in Nelson and the surrounding area, which again required a good deal of travelling. There they trained teachers on how to instruct religious classes.

Sister Catherine Donnelly and her companions had dedicated themselves to religious instruction in remote and rural areas, and the Cariboo region certainly qualified: "Before I came here, I did not know that there existed in Canada a parish as large as this of the Cariboo and Fraser Plateau. The territory comprises thousands of square miles of mountains and valleys, much of which is heavily wooded...We are here at the request of the travelling Pastor of the Cariboo, who wished us to aid him in instructing the children in this vast field."[22]

Although the sisters reached hundreds of children through their correspondence school, they felt it was extremely important to make personal contact and readily left the modern luxuries of the city behind to brave the wilderness. Given the remoteness of the areas where they travelled and the added difficulties of the Depression years, this was no small task. The sisters endured inadequate sleeping conditions and held classes in vacated schoolrooms, abandoned cabins and even in their car. The Sisters of Service bore the badge of courage, spirit and adventure when they trekked energetically into the vast unknown territory of the Cariboo to spread the love of God.

Sisters Adorers of the Precious Blood
A Canadian Vision
Mother Catherine Aurelia (Caouette) founded the Congregation of the Sisters Adorers of the Precious Blood in Saint Hyacinthe, Quebec, on September 14,

Mother Catherine Aurelia. *Archives, Monastery of the Precious Blood, London*

1861. She was influenced by a powerful dream where she envisioned a procession of her daughters who would devote themselves to prayer, with a special dedication to the spirit of the Blessed Virgin Mary. When the contemplative community of Our Lady, Star of the Sea Monastery of the Precious Blood opened in Vancouver, Mother Catherine Aurelia's processional dream had already expanded to sixteen houses in Canada.

Although she founded her first community in Saint Hyacinthe, Quebec, she hoped the prayers of her companions would be felt throughout the world as monasteries were established across the globe. By the time the Star of the Sea Convent had been founded in Vancouver, monasteries inspired by her radiant spirit spanned the country from coast to coast. Three houses had been instituted in the United States and one each in Cuba, China and Rome.

Establishing Our Lady, Star of the Sea Monastery in Vancouver

> *The Sisters of the Precious Blood are a diocesan Congregation of Religious in simple vows and their cloister is called diocesan. By custom they enjoy the privilege of being called nuns, and their convent is known as a Monastery.*[23]

Mary Lyons (1889–1931), Mother Saint Catherine of Sienna, founded Our Lady Star of the Sea Monastery in Vancouver on August 15, 1930. At the time of the foundation Mother Saint Catherine was fifty-nine years old and had lived forty-one years of her life as a contemplative nun.

The Vancouver monastery, like all the Precious Blood monasteries, originated from the Toronto community and included choir, lay and touriere sisters.[24] In 1925 the Toronto community had sent sisters to establish Our Lady of the

Mother Saint Catherine of Sienna 1889–1931, Vancouver. Archives, Monastery of the Precious Blood, London

Blessed Sacrament Monastery in Edmonton, and from there two new autonomous houses emerged, one in Charlottetown on Prince Edward Island in 1929, and one in Vancouver the following year.

Although Mother Saint Catherine of Sienna had planned to open a monastery in Los Angeles, California, the bishop there did not feel he could accept the sisters. Archbishop Casey was eager to invite this group of contemplative nuns to his diocese in Vancouver. Mother Immaculate Heart, who had founded the Edmonton house, left with Mother Catherine on July 3, 1930, to look for accommodations in Vancouver.

Feeling the looming Depression, and the strained financial situation of the young city of 250,000 with its relatively small percentage of Catholics, Archbishop Duke did not believe they could support the financially dependent nuns. However, he welcomed them and assured them the support of the laity.

Mother Saint Catherine of Sienna, Sister Mary of the Five Wounds, Sister Catherine of Jesus and Sister Mary of Saint Gertrude arrived in Vancouver by train from Edmonton on August 14, 1930. They were met by friends and relatives and taken to Saint Paul's Hospital, where they stayed until their house on 1930 16th Avenue was ready:

The Sisters were situated in a "nice quiet residential district"... In the basement a corner was set apart for a kitchen near the furnace. The billiard room on the same floor was turned into a refectory. On the first floor, the small parlor was converted into a chapel and the dining room became the choir... On the second floor there were four bedrooms, one of which became Mother Catherine's bedroom and office... The largest of the four bedrooms became the community room. There were two verandahs,—one screened in,—also four fireplaces!... There was an orchard with plum, pear, apple and cherry trees in the back yard, plus a place to keep chickens. The wonderfully temperate climate fosters luxurious growth of plants, bushes and trees. "The scenery alone," wrote the Secretary, "is enough to make any heart that knows its creator throb with gratitude and joy."[25]

Financial Difficulties for the Cloistered Nuns

The sisters were able to pay only one year's rent at seventy-five dollars a month and were entirely dependent on the diocese for all their living expenses. The sisters received donations of all kinds, including candles, an organ, a washing machine, light bulbs, a rake and hose for the lawn, and countless more items, including a ton of coal. They kept chickens for meat and eggs and made use of their orchard by preserving everything they could for the winter.

When the sisters realized the house on Sixteenth Avenue was too small and they were advised that the benefits of property ownership would outweigh their rent expenditure, Mother Catherine began to look for a more suitable residence. She found a house in the elite Shaughnessy district but the price was too high. The Canadian Pacific Railroad Company, which owned much of the property in the area, reduced the original selling price of the house from twenty-two thousand dollars to fourteen thousand dollars. The sisters considered this a bargain price and purchased the house at 3651 Hudson Street, bringing their chickens with them. It was "a spacious dwelling of English-style architecture which had originally been built for a well-to-do family with numerous children. It had a fairly plain interior, no winding staircases or carved woodwork, as one might expect in such a stylish district as Shaughnessy Heights. There were several fireplaces, and no less than three porches ... once the Sisters' few possessions were inside, the place looked very bare and unfurnished. But there was certainly room for expansion. They were far from the ocean, but it could be glimpsed from an attic window. It was extremely quiet in this district, reserved for the wealthy."[26]

There was some irony in this exceptionally poor community of women living among the wealthy and elite of Vancouver. The sisters of course felt extremely rich in their spiritual life and judging from their tenacity and persistence in the face of privation, the contradiction seemed to balance in their favour. It did not, however, lessen the obvious material difficulties their life of prayer presented. They had relocated at the onset of the Depression, and the pinch of poverty was as keen as ever. They had so little furniture that they carried their chairs with them from one room to another. Basic necessities such as candles for celebrations and religious services were often nonexistent. They found old pieces of wax to melt for vigil lights and, when a new postulant arrived, would offer their own bed so the new religious would have a place to sleep, although there was little bedding. Laundry and kitchen soap were rare luxuries, and some days there was no meat, butter or salt, and at times not even a potato in the pantry.

The sisters survived the best they could on faith, love and charity from the outside community. While they committed themselves to a life devoted to prayer, earthly needs could not be ignored. By the end of March 1931, fifty baby chicks had arrived at the monastery and they made a brooder out of an old lampshade, an electric bulb and some burlap and straw. In August the sisters were busy reaping the benefits of their garden, canning pears, plums, peaches and blackberries. Four postulants were expected to arrive in September and the sisters requested materials from other Precious Blood monasteries to make them habits.

After just a year in Vancouver, Mother Catherine died, surrounded by her religious family. Her burial took place in Saint Peter's Cemetery in New Westminster and shortly after, Sister Mary Vincent was named in her place. Although only twenty-seven years old, Sister Mary Vincent excelled in her new responsibilities and years later commented, "Youth steps in where age doth fear to tread." At the end of 1934, the community became independent and the first general election was held. Mother Mary Vincent was elected as superior.

By this time the community had increased from four to seven members. To help sustain themselves they began making altar breads, which is the traditional work of cloistered nuns. To learn the trade they went to Portland, Oregon, where they gathered information about the process and the purchasing of equipment. The new enterprise contributed to their income, but the severity of the Depression began to take its toll.

The mortgage became a larger financial burden than the sisters could meet and they were compelled to request financial assistance from other monasteries. As well, they took the advice of Archbishop Duke and went on a begging tour. The sisters started the tour in San Francisco, where Sister Teresa of Mary, an American member of their community, knew the archbishop. Mother Mary Vincent left by train with Sister Teresa on February 10, 1934.

The United States was also in the grip of the Depression and the sisters did not fair as well as they expected. When the Canadian contingent reached their last stop at the Precious Blood Monastery in Brooklyn, New York, the community gave them five thousand dollars that had been designated for their own new monastery wing. The parish priest in New York assisted by collecting eight hundred dollars from his parishioners.

After nine months away the sisters headed home, bringing with them one of the touriere sisters from the Brooklyn monastery who was temporarily on loan to the Vancouver monastery. Their trip through the Panama Canal required a stop in Havana, Cuba, where two more Precious Blood sisters joined the entourage. Within hours the two had packed their bags and were travelling to Canada to help. During the voyage to Vancouver, the Spanish-English Dictionary was in constant use.

Some outstanding debts were paid from the collections of the begging tour but the mortgage and other ongoing bills kept the sisters in debt, as did repairs for leaky ceilings, deteriorating floors and much needed paint. The sisters decided to plant vegetables to help reduce grocery bills.

Life after the Great Depression

Although concerned with their financial situation, the sisters continued to focus on their spiritual life of prayer and allowed the serenity and contemplative nature of their lives to alleviate the seemingly insurmountable hardships they endured. They enriched their daily lives of prayer with religious sessions, conferences and retreats. Over the next few years they invited a number of visitors to share in their life, including sisters going to and from monasteries in China and Japan. By the end of 1934 twelve sisters resided at the monastery in Vancouver.

In March 1946 there were no touriere sisters, which meant that the cloistered choir nuns attended to the sacristy work. This prompted the cloistering of the sacristy: "This was done by placing the altar at the centre, as it originally had been, and making a lane at the back of the sanctuary leading to the sacristy, which was reached by cutting a door out of the stone wall. The sacristy was then divided into two, to provide an interior sacristy."[27]

In October 1947 the Precious Blood sisters received official notice from Rome granting the formation of a federation, with the intention to preserve the original spirit and customs of the community. The monasteries that until now had been autonomous became united under two separate federations, one English-speaking and the other French-speaking. Although the sisters hoped to be united with their French-speaking motherhouse in Saint Hyacinthe, Quebec, the English-speaking motherhouse in London, Ontario, became the centre of their new federation. It appears the church authorities thought it better to separate the French and English cultures: "The Sisters here have decided to accept the proposal; first, because it is the desire of the Holy See, and secondly, because we hope thereby to obtain the happy result of uniformity of customs, usages and fidelity to the primitive observance."[28]

Although the federation provided a renewed link between the distant cloistered communities, physical isolation was still a fact of enclosed life. Camaraderie did exist with other women religious in the area, particularly when the Sisters of the Cenacle came to Vancouver in 1947 and opened a retreat house only a block away. Over the next few years, apart from the added pleasure of new friendships, the sisters delighted in divesting themselves of virtually all debts.

The Nuns in the Modern World

The 1960s brought many changes to the modern world and although cloistered, the sisters responded. The first change, a new-style headdress, occurred in 1963. By 1966 their strict enclosure was mitigated by removal of the grilles in the chapel, which they then renovated. This same year the sisters received Holy Communion under "both species."[29] In 1970 Sister Lorraine was honoured with the task of making a hand-painted marriage certificate for the wedding of Pierre

Elliot Trudeau, the prime minister of Canada, to Margaret Sinclair of British Columbia. The community was now forty years old and the sisters were also getting older and fewer in number.

Although over twenty-seven candidates had entered the community since it opened in Vancouver, only ten remained to take the habit. As no new members were forthcoming and the older sisters were finding the house unsuitable, particularly the stairs, the sisters sold the Hudson Street property in 1978. On January 4, 1979, the five remaining sisters moved to 5780 Malvern Street in a secluded district in Burnaby. Four of them stayed there until September 17, 1983, when three of the sisters relocated to the Regina monastery and a fourth went to the Calgary monastery. The fifth sister had returned to London earlier.

Although the Sisters Adorers of the Precious Blood from the Star of the Sea Monastery had spent more than half a century in the lower mainland, their move to the Prairie provinces did not eliminate their presence in British Columbia.

The Monastery of Our Lady of Hope Begins in the Nelson Diocese
By the time the Precious Blood sisters in Vancouver had celebrated their thirty-second year in Vancouver, Bishop W. Emmett Doyle was officially welcoming a new community of Precious Blood sisters, also from the Edmonton monastery, to his diocese in Nelson. After his initial invitation in 1958, the sisters graciously accepted in 1962:

> ...In view of the need for a Congregation of Contemplative Religious within the Diocese of Nelson, whose principal purpose is a life of prayer and sacrifice dedicated first of all to personal holiness and perfection, and secondarily to intercession for the Clergy, Religious and Faithful of this Diocese that all may be perfected by holiness of life, vigorous faith and by exemplary virtue... I assign to this Religious House, the special works of making sacred and other ecclesiastical vestments, linens and altar breads; and of doing artwork, sewing and stenographic services as ordinary means of support to supplement the offerings of the faithful.[30]

The first ten sisters, led by their superior, Mother Mary of the Rosary, took up residence in Nelson on September 8, 1962, in what had previously been a nurses' residence at 60 High Street. Within the first month three postulants entered and a novitiate was established. By the following year, however, none had been accepted into the community and two of the professed sisters had chosen to leave. The remaining eight sisters stayed at this first temporary residence until

1964, when they moved into a private home on 810 Hendryx Street while a new monastery was to be built for them.

Although the sisters held the official sod-turning ceremony for the new monastery in 1963, it was not until 1970 that construction actually began on the building. They moved into their new monastery, located at 402 Richards Street, the following year and in 1987 celebrated their twenty-fifth anniversary in Nelson.

The sisters continued to live a life of prayer in Nelson until a painful decision to close the monastery was made due to lack of personnel. At the time the monastery was closed there were six sisters who made up the community, each of whom was assigned to one of the other eight Monasteries of the Precious Blood of the English-speaking generalate in Canada.

The decision to close the monastery was made on May 13, 1998, after which time a number of goodbyes began. One of the most moving and poignant came during the last annual retreat held at the Nelson monastery. On the last day of retreat a spiritual guide for the Precious Blood Sisters, Sister Donna MacIntyre, a sister of Saint Ann, who was also the retreat director, arranged for a prayer service at the Nelson cemetery.

Only one sister, Sister Marion Gaudin, had died in Nelson and was buried there. She had been a member of the community for over twenty years and was well known throughout the diocese. The sisters decided to leave her body rest in the peaceful tree-lined cemetery of Nelson where they bid their last farewells.

Each sister had taken a flower from their monastery garden to place on Sister Marion's grave and shared their memories of her during the touching service. In the annals of July 1998, the community recorded that they struggled amid smiles and tears to sing their traditional community hymn, "Glory to Thee, Blood of Our Saviour," thus completing the little ceremony.

After thirty-six years of service in Nelson the monastery was closed on September 25, 1998, thus ending the prayerful services of almost one hundred Precious Blood Sisters in British Columbia.

Missionary Sisters of Our Lady of the Angels
Mother Mary of the Sacred Heart Becomes a Missionary Sister in China
Mother Mary of the Sacred Heart (Florina Gervais, 1888–1979) founded the Missionary Sisters of Our Lady of the Angels in 1919 with her young companion from China, Mother Mary Gabriel (Chan Tsi Kwan, 1899–1974) as co-foundress. This missionary society's work involved the formation of religious, catechists and lay apostles for teaching religion. They also carried out charitable work in the social, medical and educational fields.

In 1906 at the age of eighteen, Miss Florina Gervais joined the Missionary Sisters of the Immaculate Conception, receiving the name Sister Saint-

Mother Mary of the Sacred Heart 1888–1979 and co-foundress Mother Mary Gabriel 1899–1974.
Courtesy of the Missionary Sisters of Our Lady of the Angels

Alphonse-de-Liguori. Within four years she was on her way to Canton, China, as part of the community's first foreign mission.[31] There, Sister Saint-Alphonse-de-Liguori met a young Chinese woman by the name of Chan Tsi Kwan, to whom she taught French and catechism.

The mother general called Sister Saint-Alphonse-de-Liguori back to Canada in 1914. Sister Saint-Alphonse-de-Liguori had previously written to the mother general at the end of her temporary vows, stating that she was not disposed to pronounce her perpetual vows with the Immaculate Conception congregation. Consequently, she left the congregation of the Immaculate Conception. As she wanted to pursue her desire to consecrate her life to Christ, on July 11, 1915, she officially received the name of Soeur Marie du Sacre-Coeur (Mother Mary of the Sacred Heart) from Bishop Paul Larocque.

Her experience with the Chinese led her back to China in 1915, where she reconnected with her previous student, Chan Tsi Kwan, who resolved to follow Mother Mary of the Sacred Heart. Together they left for the Spanish Dominican mission at Chouan Chow Fou in China, where they studied language and attempted to work in the formation of the lay apostles (Vierges Chinoises). Unsuccessful, they decided to return to Canada but lacked the funds required for the trip. In an attempt to secure money they decided to purchase a lottery ticket. To help their chances of winning, they held a novena[32] for the cause. On the last day of their novena they won the lottery and left for Canada soon thereafter.

A Canadian Foundation

The two sisters arrived in Canada in 1918 and the next year, with the approval of the bishop of Sherbrooke, Paul Larocque, they founded the Missionary Sisters of Our Lady of the Angels in Lennoxville, Quebec. Mother Mary of the

Sacred Heart gathered courage for her mission from the apostolic letter Pope Benedict XV had written, speaking of the need for lay missionaries. Mother Mary's effort was specifically encouraged by bishops in China, where the two sisters hoped to return. Bishop Larocque of Sherbrooke also supported these new religious and on September 7, 1922, approved the canonical erection of their new community. The following day, eight sisters made their first profession and five of the sisters received the nomination for their first mission in KweiYang in China.

Their work in China included hospital work in Canton and eventually a noviatiate in Macau (1928) and a catechetical centre for women. They also opened orphanages, a crèche[33] and a leprosarium in China. Mother Mary of the Sacred Heart returned to China in 1928 and went back to Canada in 1930. She left again for China in 1936 and stayed until December 1938, when she arrived back in Lennoxville a few days before Christmas.

The Sisters Begin a New Chinese Mission in Victoria

It was impossible to continue to send missionaries to China during the Sino-Japanese war, and it was during this time that Bishop Cody asked the Missionary Sisters of Our Lady of Angels to establish a Chinese mission in his diocese in Victoria. By the time these sisters arrived in Victoria, their devotion to working among the Chinese had already resulted in twelve missions, a few in eastern Canada and the others in China. Victoria became their thirteenth mission.

Loretto Hall, Guest House, Victoria. Courtesy of the Missionary Sisters of Our Lady of the Angels

The sisters' work in Victoria began on December 15, 1939, when they opened a boarding house for young ladies and a guest house called Loretto Hall. Mother Mary of the Sacred Heart arrived in Victoria with Sister Marguerite-Marie (Lucie Vachon) and Sister Saint-Rita (Alice Renaud) to establish the mission and stayed with them for seven months.

This house, located on 309 Belleville Street, was the former old Pendray house and was known for its beautiful topiary gardens. The property provided a perfect setting and accommodation for laywomen who came to tour Victoria. The rooms varied in price and meals were served, as was afternoon tea, which became quite popular. Many of the young sisters who worked in Loretto Hall had the opportunity to improve their knowledge of the English language through courses and immersion. For thirty years this operation subsidized the Chinese mission in Victoria, which had begun at the request of Bishop John Cody.

The Chinese mission began with the opening of a Chinese kindergarten, known as the Holy Angels Mission, on January 22, 1941. It was located on 866 North Park Street, near the Chinese district. The property, which had been difficult to secure, allowed room for expansion of the mission. With the assistance of the Missionary Circle of the Little Flower, a group interested in the Chinese mission, the kindergarten school was established and operated until July 31, 1963.

The building itself was in disrepair and the sisters began fixing it up with help from Reverend Father Matte, who was called from his mission in China. They started by fumigating the place, then painted it inside and out, installed new plumbing and rejuvenated the garden. When the property was ready for occupancy, the children, who had been taught in the interim at Loretto Hall, began classes. Apart from regular classes, the sisters taught religion, music and art, and also visited Chinese patients in the hospitals.

One year after the mission started, the co-foundress, Mother Mary Gabriel, came to participate in it and Loretto Hall, staying until October 1964.

The Japanese in British Columbia During the War Years

Shortly after the bombing of Pearl Harbor on December 7, 1941, the Canadian government issued an order in council to evacuate some twenty-two thousand Japanese Canadians who were living on the Pacific Coast. They were considered a national security threat and were not allowed to live within one hundred miles of the coast. Those who were Canadian citizens went either to the interior of British Columbia or to sugar-beet farms in Alberta. The Japanese who did not hold Canadian citizenship were sent to Toronto.

The Japanese Canadians sent to the interior of British Columbia went to isolated and abandoned mining ghost towns. Numbering approximately eight thousand, they were packed "without too much care" into dilapidated houses in places such as Slocan City, Bay Farm, Popoff, Lemon Creek, New Denver, Sandon and Kaslo. Japanese Canadians already living in the interior were expected to report regularly to the local police. Some communities in the interior "did not welcome the idea of having Japanese come to live among them."[34]

The evacuation of Japanese from the Pacific Coast was supported by the Royal Canadian Mounted Police and carried out by the British Columbia Security Commission, established specifically for this purpose. First a curfew was imposed on all Japanese living in Vancouver and Lulu Island. All other Japanese living outside the city were brought to Vancouver and taken to Hastings Park. Finally, all were forced to leave behind their homes, their businesses and their possessions to go to the interior.

When they arrived, the government denied provision for high schools and Japanese students were left without access to a high-school education. The physical and social conditions were severely inadequate and a number of missionary groups were asked to participate in improving this extremely difficult wartime situation.

The Missionary Sisters Assist the Japanese in New Denver

The Missionary Sisters of Our Lady of the Angels were petitioned to help the Diocese of Nelson with the Japanese. With the bishop's permission three sisters left Sherbrooke, Quebec, for the interior of British Columbia. They arrived in

Sisters of Our Lady of the Angels with Japanese at first Holy Communion, New Denver.
Courtesy of the Missionary Sisters of Our Lady of the Angels

Sister Saint Gemma teaches cooking to Japanese women.
Courtesy of the Missionary Sisters of Our Lady of the Angels

New Denver on April 24, 1943, and were welcomed by the parish priest, Father Clement Lepine. Sister Saint Marc (Aldea Lavigne) had been appointed superior and Sister Saint Raphael (Rita Casavant) and Sister Saint Gemma (Maleleine Guertin) were designated teachers. Sister Saint Gemma had been given the additional task of cooking.

New Denver, as described by Sister Saint Raphael, was "a 'lovely Ghost Town place' with a nice lake with a glacier in front ... [where they] ... used to visit often the Sanatorium for tuberculosis ... with Father Clement, a former Japan missionary who spoke to them in Japanese."

The sisters had planned to open a kindergarten but the United Church, upon hearing of their mission, "hurried to open one" first. A delegation of Japanese parents then approached the sisters to open a high school for their children. The sisters accepted and before the end of the month they opened Notre Dame High School for Japanese students, where they taught until June of that year. In September two more sisters from their community arrived, Sister Saint Camille de Lellis and Sister Saint Rita (Alice Renaud), who was named principal.

The sisters taught classical, general and commercial courses at the high school and private classes in French, music and religion. They obtained permission from the government to allow students of "junior matriculation" to take the official exams from the province and thus continue with their education if desired. To their delight, all the students in New Denver passed their classes.

Sister Saint Gemma taught "domestic art courses" after hours for some of the Japanese women. The sisters also oversaw the formation of various clubs, including baseball, home economics and a choir: "Our pupils, Buddhists and Shintoists formed the choir and played the organ."[35]

A drama club was also formed and it "attracted the people from all around, [e]specially the 'white people.' As the local doctor said: 'It was as good as in Vancouver.' The presence of the 'white people' was quite special, since they were members of the United Church."[36]

Although the majority of the sisters' Japanese students were Buddhists and Shintoists, there were also eighteen Japanese Catholics in the community at New Denver. The sisters taught them catechism and prepared them for the sacraments of baptism, Holy Communion and confirmation.

After the war the sisters prepared to close Notre Dame High School and ended classes there in June 1947. During the community's four-year mission in New Denver, Sister Saint Marc remained superior and Sister Saint Rita kept her position as principal. Sister Saint Gemma also remained as teacher for those four years. Five other teachers assisted at various times over the four years.

In 1947 Bishop Martin Johnson of the Diocese of Nelson had asked the Missionary Sisters of Our Lady of Angels to stay and take over the sanatorium from the lay personnel who operated it. In May, however, their superior general wrote to inform the bishop that due to lack of personnel they could not accept the mission. Before the end of June he responded with gratitude for the work they had already done for the Japanese. Sister Saint Raphael recalled, "We did all we could to make their situation in the camp more acceptable...the pupils always were grateful and many of them are still writing to us..."

Asian countries began to open up to foreign missionaries after the Second World War, and the Missionary Sisters of Our Lady of Angels were sent to various foreign missions. They eventually established more missions in Japan, Macau, Hong Kong, Peru, Brazil, Tahiti, Tanzania, the Democratic Republic of Congo (Zaire), the United States, Rwanda, Chile and the Philippines.

Franciscan Sisters of the Atonement
An Anglican Sister Founds a New
Catholic Community of Women Religious
Mother Lurana of Graymoor (Lurana Mary White, 1870–1935), foundress of the Franciscan Sisters of the Atonement, began her religious career as an Anglican sister. She became a novice with the Episcopal Sisters of the Holy Child Jesus in Albany, New York, in 1894. Three years later she wrote to

Reverend Lewis Wattson, an Episcopalian priest, expressing her desire to "enter a religious community whose members publicly professed the vow of poverty and lived according to the Franciscan spirit."[37]

Father Wattson wrote back telling her of his desire to found a religious community called the Society of the Atonement, "dedicated to Christian unity and mission."[38] After exchanging numerous letters, they met and made a "covenant with each other and God" to found the Society of the Atonement. In 1898 under the auspices of the Anglican Church, they founded the Society of the Atonement in Graymoor, New York, which included a community of religious for men and a community of religious for women.

Mother Lurana of Graymoor 1870–1935. Archives Franciscan Sisters of the Atonement, New York

From the outset they worked toward the corporate reunion of the Anglican community with the Roman Catholic community, beginning with the publication of a monthly magazine called *The Lamp*. By 1907 Mother Lurana initiated a meeting with the archbishop of New York to discuss the community being received into the Catholic Church. Although individual converts had been welcomed into the Church, the entrance of an entire religious community of another faith was unprecedented.[39] Two years later, in 1909, the Roman Catholic Church accepted both the friars and the sisters of the Atonement into their faith.

By 1935, the small community of the Franciscan Sisters of the Atonement increased their ranks, spreading outside the United States into Italy, England, Ireland, Japan, Brazil and Canada. They established their first Canadian foundation in the Diocese of Edmonton, Alberta, on October 5, 1926. One week later they established their second Canadian foundation in Vancouver, British Columbia.

Sister Mary Stella O'Melia Assists the Japanese in East Vancouver

The first four Franciscan Sisters of the Atonement arrived in British Columbia in 1926 to begin their work at the Catholic Japanese mission on East Cordova

Street. The mission had originated more than a dozen years before with the work of Sister Mary Stella O'Melia. With the help of a number of religious men and women, she taught English and religion to Japanese students in east Vancouver. Sister Mary Stella O'Melia eventually learned to speak Japanese and, as demonstrated by her many years of service, became devoted to the cause of the Japanese mission in Vancouver.

Kathleen F. O'Melia (Sister Mary Stella O'Melia) began this work as a lay member of the Anglican faith. She came to Vancouver from England in 1902 and at the age of thirty-three began her new life in Canada, living and working at Saint Luke's Home on Cordova Street. This private hospital for the elderly was associated with Saint James' Anglican Church, Sister O'Melia's church.

Sister Mary Stella O'Melia, foundress of the Japanese Mission in Vancouver with Sister Clare and Father Bedard. Archives Franciscan Sisters of the Atonement, New York

Soon after her arrival in Vancouver, Sister Mary Stella was overcome by a spiritual desire to introduce Christianity to the Japanese. She opened a small school for the Japanese on Pender Street, then moved it to Hastings Street and finally to East Cordova Street. Finding herself drawn to Catholicism, Sister Mary Stella went to New Westminster, where the Catholic Oblate fathers gave her a teaching position at Saint Louis' College. Shortly after, in September 1912, she converted to Catholicism. Archbishop McNeil asked her to come back to Vancouver and resume her work among the Japanese, this time as a Catholic. In

1916, remaining a layperson but taking a private vow of perpetual chastity, she became professed in the Third Order Secular of Saint Francis.

At the request of the Franciscan friars, three other tertiary (Third Order) sisters came to assist Sister Mary Stella, but the work was still too demanding. They realized a religious community would be required to continue the expanding apostolate among the Japanese. It was suggested to Sister Mary Stella that she form her own community of women religious or become a member of an existing community that would be willing to continue the work she had started.

Sister Mary Stella wrote in her biography, "if the first plan was to be the solution, might not the work be held back, and opportunities and even souls lost through the insufficiency of means and workers during the long period which it would take to build up a new community? If, on the other hand, the second was the solution, where was the Franciscan Community—for Franciscan I felt it must be—which would come to take up the work?"[40]

The Franciscan Sisters Arrive in Vancouver

Sister Mary Stella had been introduced to the Franciscan Sisters of the Atonement of Graymoor through reading *The Lamp* magazine. Their similar histories of conversion from Anglicanism to Catholicism must have struck a cord with Sister Mary Stella. She requested their help and they responded favourably.

While the Franciscan Sisters of the Atonement were preparing to take over the mission in Vancouver, Sister Mary Stella had decided to join their community. In May 1926 she left Vancouver to enter the novitiate in Graymoor, New York. In the interim, one of the tertiary sisters, Sister Francis from Quebec, continued the mission until the Franciscan Sisters of the Atonement arrived in mid-October.

Sister Monica Garrigan, Sister Paula Dougherty, Sister DeChantal Caylor and Sister Margaret Mary Jacobellis were the first sisters of the Atonement to come to Vancouver. They taught English to the Japanese students and gave them catechetical instruction, which was interpreted for the students by a Japanese dentist, Dr. Nomura.

Mother Lurana, the foundress of the community, arrived in Vancouver by train in 1927. She and Sister Monica, the superior of the Vancouver mission, began to look for a new location for the convent and school as the building was deteriorating to the point of becoming a health hazard. For $16,500 they purchased a property in the Japanese business district.

The property had two houses that were replaced by a hall to make room for the expanding mission activities, which included catechism classes, English instruction for the Japanese and Italians, and the distribution of food and clothing to the poor. Altar boy classes, Children of Mary meetings, a meal program expansion and a day nursery and kindergarten were also added.

Sister Mary Stella, known to the Japanese as O'Melia San, returned from Graymoor in 1928 as a professed Franciscan Sister of the Atonement. She went on to dedicate her life to the Japanese mission and died in 1939. Sister Antoinette McDonough, who began at the Vancouver mission in 1930, remembered the inspiration of Sister Mary Stella: "She encouraged and inspired us with her great love and zeal for the Japanese people. Sister visited the sick in their homes and hospitals, she taught Religion and English, went begging, acted as interpreter and any other work that needed doing. Nothing was too much for her. I was fortunate to be her companion almost daily on her visits to wherever duty called, and so my first year in Vancouver passed very quickly and I hope not without catching some of Sister Mary Stella's charism."[41]

The year of Sister Mary Stella's death was also the beginning of World War II.

When the Japanese left Vancouver during the war, other families came and occupied their homes. These new residents took up work in the shipyards, ammunition factory and other areas where war work was available. The few sisters who remained in Vancouver opened a kindergarten and daycare for these families. After the war the need for the day nursery remained, as noted in this article in the *Candle* (1948):

> ...Now that the war is over there is still a great need for this work especially in this congested area, as the housing situation is very bad. Whole families are living in one or two rooms with no facilities whatsoever for their children to play outdoors. Very few landlords will receive tenants with small children, and then only on condition that the children will not be in the building during the day. If the parents fail to co-operate in this respect they find themselves walking the streets in search of another place. Knowing that they will have a hard time to find one, they try to follow the landlord's wishes. The Day Nursery solves the problem...During recess time when the children are playing in the yard, grown-ups passing by love to stop and watch them and marvel at how well they all agree, since almost every nation is represented among them: Chinese, Japanese, Dutch, Icelanders, Swedes, Italians, Ukrainians, Germans, English, Danish, etc...[42]

The expansion of the mission to include food distribution for the poor resulted in a food line that from the beginning of the Depression into the 1950s served upwards of three hundred unemployed men a day. By the 1990s as many as one thousand people were fed every day until help from government agencies reduced the number to seven hundred a day. This program continues to this day through the help of volunteers and donations from various companies and parishioners from across the lower mainland.

Serving the Japanese in Steveston

In 1931 Archbishop Duke asked the sisters to open a mission at Steveston, a fishing village on Lulu Island. Eighty percent of the two thousand residents in Steveston were Japanese people engaged in either the fishing or gardening industry.

Sister Antoinette began the mission by knocking on doors to advise the Japanese women that they were prepared to open a daycare centre for their children. She was accompanied on her rounds by Sister Mary Stella, who could speak Japanese. The sisters offered to take care of the Japanese children who had been going with their mothers while they worked in the fields or canneries. The first registrant was the relative of a Steveston resident who knew of the sisters' work in Vancouver and was convinced of their "wonderful care of children." Although hesitant, the Japanese mothers eventually brought their children to the sisters, who also offered English classes to those Japanese women who wished to learn the language. By early December a group of women were registered for English classes.

A convent had been purchased for the sisters and Archbishop Duke celebrated its opening with Mass on May 7, 1931. The increasing numbers of registrants for daycare and kindergarten required more space, and by 1935 a larger two-storey building had been constructed across the street from the original convent: "This new Convent contained a large chapel, which was used for Church, the entire second floor with a sacristy room and a bathroom. The first floor front section of the house, one room was for the Nursery and one for the Kindergarten, both large rooms. The back section of the house, downstairs, were the living quarters of the Sisters."[43]

Archbishop Duke officially opened the new convent mission on January 13, 1935, when he blessed it in the presence of more than three hundred guests.

The Sisters Move with the Japanese to Greenwood

The British Columbia Security Commission opened a processing centre for the evacuation of the Japanese people at Steveston, using the day nursery and kindergarten as the place of registration. The processing team consisted of a doctor, clerks, immigration officers and the Royal Canadian Mounted Police, who "invited" the Japanese to register for the move to Greenwood.

The friars of the Atonement had come to Steveston in 1932 to work with the sisters and in 1938 Father Alphonsus Hoban came to join them. At the request of the Steveston residents, who wished to remain as a community, and the sisters and friars organized their move to Greenwood. They asked the bishop of Nelson to help them find a place to accommodate a large number of Japanese people. Father Alphonsus Hoban recalled a meeting he and a fellow friar, Father Benedict Quigley, had with the Mayor of Greenwood: "The Friars then went to Greenwood and explained to Mayor MacArthur what they had in mind. Surprisingly, he was well disposed to the idea and arranged to call a town meeting. A good number of people who attended opposed the idea, absolutely, and said so. But MacArthur spoke strongly in favor of the move, and assured his people that there would be nothing to fear because the RCMP would be in complete control. The vote was taken and the people agreed to allow us to bring our Japanese to Greenwood."[44]

The sisters spoke with the Japanese in Steveston, describing "the location of Greenwood and the general conditions they could expect living there as evacuees."[45] The majority of Japanese at Steveston registered for the move to Greenwood. The Japanese living in Vancouver were also invited to register for the move to Greenwood and some did, but many held out in the hope of not having to move at all.

Sister Eugenia Koppes and Sister Jerome Kelliher, along with Father Benedict Quigley, went to Greenwood ahead of everyone else so that they could be there to welcome the Japanese on their arrival. Beginning on April 26, 1942, the evacuation continued daily until some seventeen hundred people were relocated. Three of the sisters from Vancouver, Sister Mary Angela Waters, Sister Mary Danielle Hussey and Sister Regina Koelzer, travelled in the same coach as the evacuees and tried to be of service to the mothers. Sister Antoinette McDonough and Sister Dorothea Ferguson remained in Steveston until the last trainload was ready to depart: "It was a very sad day for all of us...Each person was given a dollar to purchase their meals, but they were not permitted to leave the coach to purchase anything. It was a very difficult trip for the mothers with babies and young children. There were no facilities even to heat the babies' bottles."[46]

The sisters moved constantly between cars as the Japanese were not allowed to move freely on the train. They endured this for seventeen hours until they reached Greenwood. An unexpected difficulty arose when many of the Japanese men were sent to the interior to work on the unfinished Trans-Canada Highway. They were escorted by the Royal Canadian Mounted Police to road camps and worked there until September, when they were reunited with their families in the interior. The remaining Japanese lived in "summer cabins or abandoned warehouses, which were divided into cubicles which served as family dwellings."[47]

April 1942: Sisters Jerome Kelliher and Eugenia Koppe assisting the Japanese during their evacuation to Greenwood. Archives Franciscan Sisters of the Atonement, New York

The Sisters Open Sacred Heart School for the Japanese in Greenwood

Seven hundred Japanese children arrived in Greenwood. They were "not permitted or accepted into the Public School System. So it was up to us…after many ups and downs, Sacred Heart School opened for children from Kindergarten through two years of commercial High School…During that time there were many conversions among the adults as well as the children."[48]

The government gave the sisters a vacated two-storey wooden fire-house for the school: "Lumber was brought in and partitions put up to create classrooms. Sister Mary Samuela David and Sister Rosita Perpetua came to join us, and with seven Sisters, two Friars, and Mary Nakamachi, a lay woman, we prepared to open our school. By September, we were able to provide daily grammar and high school classes, evening Business courses and piano lessons; and the Sisters also opened a kindergarten in the basement of a different building."[49]

When school started in September, everything went very smoothly, as if Sacred Heart School had been in operation for some time. The sisters followed the provincial curriculum, teaching Christians and non-Christians alike. There was some adjustment in academic planning as the children had not completed their previous school year due to the traumatic uprooting of their lives.

Sister Jerome Kelliher and grade 5 and 6 students at Sacred Heart School, Greenwood.
Archives Franciscan Sisters of the Atonement, New York

The sisters persevered and their diligence and commitment to the education of the Japanese children was reflected in the advancement of their students. The children at the school took prizes in poster competitions for their extraordinary artwork. At the end of June in 1944, the first graduation of an all-Japanese class in the province was held. By 1949 a graduate of the school had become the first Japanese Canadian to work in the post office and another was the first Japanese Canadian to be employed by the Bell Telephone Company in Montreal. Another student began publishing a community newspaper.[50]

In 1946, after the end of the war, a few families chose to remain in Greenwood, but most left for eastern Canada, the West Coast or Japan. This dispersion from Greenwood brought the Japanese mission to an end, twenty years after the first Graymoor sisters arrived in Vancouver. Sister Regina Koelzer recalled life at Greenwood:

> ... cold, very cold; living in poverty; having very little, sometimes not knowing where the next meal would come from ... The Sisters in the school, working two shifts, meeting deadlines—examinations, Provincial tests and inspections, working late nights. But with it all

there was a happiness, a joy, as each day passed; just doing, never counting the cost, excelling with very little, enjoying the smallest of events...Each year the Japanese people from the East return to Vancouver and stop in to visit the Convent on Cordova Street, they always recall with fondest memories their experiences at Greenwood...'carefree and good, yet with challenging opportunities'...Among the Japanese people of Greenwood there was no bitterness. As one mother expressed it:"It was war time." But they could trust the Sisters, who would not let anything happen to them.[51]

The Japanese Catholics were absorbed into various parishes in their new communities. There was never again any parish specifically for Japanese people. In Vancouver, Sister Mary Pius Demers had formed a club for the young Japanese who had already settled on the coast. It was named the Maria Stella Club, honouring Sister Mary Stella O'Melia, the woman who had devoted her life to assisting the Japanese in British Columbia.

Additional Missions by the Franciscan Sisters of the Atonement, 1940s to the Present

In June 1943, three sisters came directly from Graymoor, New York, to handle the catechetical and social work in the Saint Francis of Assisi Parish at Revelstoke. Their mission continued into the 1990s. Three sisters staffed a new mission in Michel-Natal, a coal-mining town located in the Crows Nest Pass.

Sister Paul Eugene Faryna playing "London Bridge" with kindergarten children.
Archives Franciscan Sisters of the Atonement, New York

The sisters there taught catechism and kindergarten in addition to music. They remained until 1976.

In 1949 four sisters took charge of a new convent in Cranbrook and began various parochial duties, including kindergarten classes, religious instruction, parishioner and hospital visits, and the organization of sodalities and other clubs. Due to the scarcity of new vocations to their religious community, the sisters in Cranbrook withdrew in 1987.

During World War II when the Japanese were relocated, the mission at Steveston closed, but after the war, the archbishop asked the sisters to reopen it. By 1950 the student population was largely non-Japanese. The sisters opened a kindergarten and started teaching religion classes. The number of children increased each year and clubs were organized for their benefit, including a sodality and junior and senior choirs.

By the late 1960s vocations in religious communities waned and the shortage of sisters resulted in the closing of the Steveston convent in 1968. Sisters from Vancouver came to continue religious instruction for the children.

The sisters went on to new missions in Castlegar and Golden in the 1960s, and then in the 1970s and 1980s, on to Nakusp, Parksville, Victoria and White Rock.

Their work continues in Vancouver where it began, and in 1996 the Franciscan Sisters of the Atonement celebrated their seventieth anniversary in British Columbia. The sisters uphold the spirit of their foundress, ministering to the poor at the Cordova Street convent and addressing the needs of the community wherever they can.

Sisters of the Assumption of the Blessed Virgin Mary
A New Community of Women Religious Founded in Quebec

The four foundresses of the Congregation of the Sisters of the Assumption of the Blessed Virgin Mary adopted their religious habits and names on August 17, 1855. Mère de l'Assomption, Mère de Jésus, Mère Sainte-Marie and Mère Saint-Joseph chose to dedicate their lives to the Christian education of youth with a special concern for the poor. Exactly one year later Bishop Cooke of Trois-Rivieres promulgated the canonical erection of this new community of women religious in the town of Saint-Gregoire, Quebec. In 1872 the young community of religious moved their novitiate and motherhouse a few miles away, to Nicolet.

In 1891 four sisters left from Quebec on their first mission to educate Cree children on the prairies. In the same year four sisters left for New England to educate Franco-American children whose parents wished them to retain their ethnic and religious traditions while residents of the United States. The increased need for teachers resulted in the addition of a teachers' college to their motherhouse, the first of four such colleges built in Quebec by the Sisters of the Assumption.

By 1934 the sisters expanded their teaching mission to Japan, and within a decade a group left Quebec for the interior of British Columbia to help with the education of the Japanese during World War II.

The Sisters Arrive in the Slocan Valley to Teach Japanese Students

In 1943 the Franciscan Fathers of the Atonement set up Slocan City as the centre for a number of Japanese missions in the interior. Bishop Johnson of Nelson asked the Sisters of the Assumption to help in the Slocan Valley. Although the superior general was reluctant to send sisters, when she learned that a knowledge of Japanese was not required, she allowed four sisters to leave for the British Columbia interior. On February 21, 1943, the appointed superior of the group, Sister Marie-du-Crucifix, left the motherhouse in Nicolet, Quebec, with one newly professed sister. With two other sisters they picked up in Calgary, they arrived in Nelson on March 11.

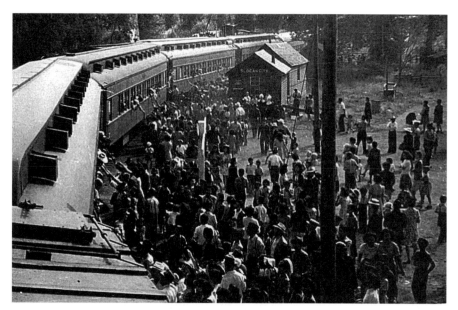

Japanese at Slocan City station. *Sisters of Assumption, Edmonton*

Until their house in Slocan City was ready, the sisters lodged with Mrs. Bennish, an elderly Polish woman. The Japanese high-school students wasted no time in asking the sisters for help with their correspondence courses. Indeed, the sisters were in such demand that every room in their convent had been, in the sisters' words, "invaded."

By summer the sisters had been given permission to use the church as a school. Although there were no books or desks, the church accommodated fifty students. At least twenty were still using the convent as a makeshift school.

The summer holidays were bustling with activity as the church was transformed and enlarged to accommodate the ever-increasing number of high-school students. In September 1943 the Slocan Catholic High School was established by the Sisters of the Assumption of the Blessed Virgin Mary: "The nave was separated into two parts by cardboard sliding doors that were painted so as to be used for blackboards. The sacristy became a classroom and behind it was added an annex that could hold a fourth classroom. In this manner, one hundred and eight students distributed into the four years of High School, would be accommodated. The Fathers who lived in the vestry found refuge in the former jail-house."[52]

Teaching reinforcements quickly followed with the arrival of Sister Saint-Zenon and Sister Saint-Eugene-de-Milan in September. Sister Saint-Jean-Chrysostome was scheduled to arrive from Japan in February 1944.

As the church had now been converted to a school, parish services were held in the convent chapel. The convent itself was enlarged through an additional storey built above the kitchen to accommodate more students and sister teachers. The sisters used their convent parlor as a study hall, a refectory and at times as a bedroom for the many visitors who frequented the missionary centre. After the additional storey to the convent had been built in 1943, an annex of two more classrooms and an office was built in the summer of 1944 in an effort to make room for the more than 150 students expected.

Chemistry class. Sisters of Assumption, Edmonton

Because the government did not contribute to funding for parochial high-school students, initially facilities and supplies were lacking. Donations, including money and books, came from Quebec or from the New England states. Some donations came from people the sisters had befriended and who were sympathetic to the situation. In addition, the bishop of Nelson and the apostolic delegate in Ottawa also donated money to purchase gifts for the Japanese people to express the charitable attitude of the church toward them.

The sisters had been impressed by the study habits of the Japanese students and their keen interest in school. On behalf of the students, Sister Marie-du-Crucifix travelled to Victoria to ask that graduating Japanese students be permitted to receive official grade-twelve diplomas. Much to the surprise of the sisters the request was granted before the end of the 1944 school year. In characteristic fashion, on June 24, 1944, the Japanese students received their diplomas on graduation day, followed by their traditional custom of Japanese tea.

Two new teacher-missionaries, Sister Sainte-Clarie-de-Remini and Sister Francoise-de-Saint-Joseph, left the motherhouse in Nicolet and arrived on September 9, 1944. They were joined by a Japanese Catholic lay teacher from Greenwood, who taught with them until the war ended and the Japanese families began to leave the area. Many students remained to complete their academic year of 1946.

Students at Slocan, 1946. Sisters of Assumption, Edmonton

Between 1943 and 1946, the sisters taught 250 students at Slocan Catholic High School, many of whom graduated from the school. When the Slocan mission ended in 1946, the Sisters of the Assumption of the Blessed Virgin Mary were summoned to teach in other parts of the world, including the poorer parts of Brazil, the African bush (Burundi and the Ivory Coast), South America and Japan.

Fifty years later the Japanese of the Slocan Valley remembered their former teachers in a special gathering. A fifty-year reunion of the closing of the Slocan Catholic High School was held in Toronto in August 1996. The crowd of 180 former students, teachers, family and friends attending the two-day event attested to the importance of this part of their lives. Although many who attended were residents of Toronto, people also came from other parts of Canada and from across the United States, from California to Florida. Two of the sisters who had taught at the school and who had been invited to this gathering "were presented with a gift as a memento of the reunion and as a small token of the students' appreciation and gratitude."[53]

Missionary Sisters of Christ the King
Mother Frederica Giroux Follows Her Heart

In 1928, twenty years after entering religious life as a Missionary Sister of the Immaculate Conception, Mother Mary of the Sacred Heart (Frederica Giroux, 1888–1968) founded the Missionary Sisters of Christ the King.

As the seventeenth sister to make her profession with the Missionary Sisters of the Immaculate Conception, Mother Frederica Giroux had worked closely with the foundress, Mother Marie du Saint-Esprit, who was devoted to the Immaculate Mother. As the foundress, Mother Marie du Saint-Esprit endeavoured to instil this same spirit in the hearts of her community of sisters. Mother Frederica Giroux (at the time called Sister Mary of the Sacred Heart), however, found she had a deep personal devotion to the Sacred Heart, an innermost calling that was "Christocentric." Mother Giroux recalled, "She had tried to

Mother Frederica Giroux 1888–1968.
Missionary Sisters of Christ the King, Quebec

spread the practice of reciting the Little Office of the Sacred Heart among the young Sisters of the Immaculate Conception. It was already the sign of branching off, for the spiritual evolution of the Superior General of the Immaculate

Conception was directed, rather, toward a devotion to the Blessed Virgin based on the writings of Grignion de Montfort."[54]

Mother Giroux worked faithfully with the Missionary Sisters of the Immaculate Conception and in 1921 was sent to found the community's first mission in British Columbia. Although appointed as superior of the group, Mother Giroux and her three companion sisters were recalled from the mission two years after starting it because of difficulties they were experiencing while getting established.[55]

Although still a sister of the Missionary Sisters of the Immaculate Conception, Mother Giroux realized her calling to start a new religious community. In 1928, with the help of a few priests and bishops, she founded the Missionary Sisters of Christ the King in Gaspé, Quebec. Since that time the community has flourished, with missions in Japan, Democratic Republic of Congo (Zaire), Haiti, Ivory Coast, South Korea, Chad and Canada.

The Japanese Mission in Kaslo and Sandon

Four years after their establishment as a religious community the Missionary Sisters of Christ the King left for their first foreign mission to Japan. The outbreak of World War II followed and ties with their motherhouse were quickly severed. Sending additional missionary sisters to Japan was, of course, no longer possible. During this difficult time in Japan the Missionary Sisters of Christ the King were frequently visited by the military police, although they had not been

Sisters of Christ the King with Sandon high school students, 1944.
Missionary Sisters of Christ the King, Quebec

confined to concentration camps like many other foreigners: "We were polite, obeyed regulations, took part in the activities of the district...One of the aspirants used to go out to seek provisions. Dexterity and the grace of Heaven joined together assured them their freedom. They not only managed to survive, but also found means to help the interned seminarians and priests."[56]

The sisters' connection to the Japanese people took root in Canada when in 1943 Bishop Johnson of Nelson invited the Missionary Sisters of Christ the King to his diocese. They went to Kaslo and then Sandon to help Japanese who had been evacuated from the Pacific Coast and who were living in camps in the interior.

Sister Saint Bernard, Sister Saint Stanislaus and Sister Saint Peter were chosen for the mission. Accompanied by Mother Giroux, they travelled for five days by train from the motherhouse in Gaspé, Quebec, to British Columbia. They received a warm welcome from the bishop and the sisters of Saint Joseph's Academy, who introduced them to the British Columbia teaching program. Mother Giroux stayed with the three missionary sisters for three months (April to June of 1943) but the mission was looked upon as ineffectual: "Unfortunately, they asked for us a year too late for the Japanese have had time to set up classes for themselves and their little Japanese teachers, well trained in the public schools, seem to teach as well as we could, with the exception of religion. They are helped by Protestants and this makes our apostolate difficult."[57]

There were about one thousand Japanese in Kaslo, none of whom were Catholic. Given that the Protestants had already established classes from kindergarten to high school and the school year was already more than half over, the sisters set up a recreation centre for after school hours and during this time offered piano lessons. While in Kaslo the sisters also visited the sick in the local hospital.

In August the president of the parents' committee from Sandon approached the sisters in Kaslo to ask if they would teach their children in the high school, "which had been left without an organized teaching staff."[58] The sisters had come to Kaslo with the understanding that they would teach primary school and hesitated when asked to prepare for a secondary school program. By September, however, they were on their way to Sandon.

Sandon High School classes were held on the upper floor of the railway station and the sisters acquired the nickname of "CPR Sisters": "We were now three full-time Sister-teachers to four classes of grade nine and ten students. We also monitored a group of students of grade eleven and twelve who studied by correspondence. Except for half a dozen of old timers, we were the only non-Japanese residents among nine hundred 'Nissei' (second generation of Japanese in Canada); a very sympathetic population who greeted us with much kindness."[59]

Of this time in Sandon, Sister Noella Bourgeois wrote, "The sisters were there as volunteers. The only funding they received was $500.00 given to them by the Apostolic Nuncio. They had to buy books and supplies and on one occasion received them through The Red Cross from War Relief Services -National Catholic Welfare Conference, New York."[60]

By September 1944 the Canadian government had transferred the Japanese population in Sandon to other camps in British Columbia and other provinces. Some Japanese were sent to Montreal and one of the sisters from Sandon returned east to assist them there. The sisters opened a Japanese centre in Montreal that operated as a hostel for young women. This provided some continuity for those who had been together in the interior. With no Japanese left in Sandon, the sisters closed the mission.

During their one-and-a-half-year stay in Sandon there had been a few converts to Catholicism, notably one Japanese girl from New Denver who joined their religious community. Although a short mission, it was a gratifying experience for the sisters as they developed some long-lasting relationships with the students.

New Missions after the War

Archbishop Duke of Vancouver asked the remaining Missionary Sisters of Christ the King in Sandon to work in the Native mission of Anaham. The sisters had visited their first Native reservation during Mother Giroux's three-month stay in the West in 1943 and accepted Archbishop Duke's invitation to Anaham, British Columbia. There they taught and nursed the First Nations people in 1944 and also directed a new community of Native women religious founded by Archbishop Duke.

Archbishop Duke believed that a Native community of women religious was needed to provide teaching, health care and social work services to the Native people living on reserves. Sister Mary Saint Paul directed the young women who joined the Novitiate of the Sisters of Mary Immaculate. Although their numbers increased to the point where Archbishop Duke had a spacious convent built for both communities on the Anaham Reserve, it was found generally that the Native women did not readily adapt to the convent lifestyle, and the community was discontinued in 1950.

Apart from attending to the religious formation of the young Native community, the Missionary Sisters of Christ the King also taught on the reserve and provided health care. Two sisters began teaching in the community hall, where a wall had been erected to make space for two classrooms. Four years later the Department of Indian Affairs built a school, and attached to this was a small hospital and dispensary. Sister Mary Saint Paul, the superior and director of the Native novitiate, was also a nurse. Attending to the health-care needs of the

Native people also meant leaving Anaham to minister to patients in the surrounding area.

A good deal of stamina was required for this ministry as much travel was involved, often over very rough terrain and in difficult weather conditions. Sister Therese Bernard, a nursing sister at Anaham, was remembered to have taken the Jeep (the first motorized vehicle in the area) on a twenty-four-hour round trip through a foot of snow to bring a sick Native woman to the nursing station at Anaham. The ordeal entailed travelling the frozen "road" across Konni Lake. Her adventure was one of endless displays of endurance and courage, not unlike the adventures many of the sisters faced at the Native missions, where they lived in extreme poverty.

Sister Therese takes sick baby across makeshift ferry, circa 1952. Missionary Sisters of Christ the King, Quebec

In 1994 the Native people, in a great celebration, expressed their gratitude to the Missionary Sisters of Christ the King for providing fifty years of service to the Chilcotin people.

In 1956 the sisters accepted a mission at Anahim Lake: "We simply had to accept a new Indian mission, some 150 miles from Anaham to avoid the disaster of seeing a Protestant hospital being set up in an entirely Catholic Reserve. God will simply have to provide (October 23, 1955)."[61]

Two sisters taught at the Upper Dean River Indian Day School and one sister acted as nurse to provide health care to the people in the area. The Native people built two log buildings, each twenty by fourteen feet, which served as dormitories for their children. The sisters worked there until the mid-1980s.

Two years after the Anahim Lake mission was started the sisters arrived in the Pemberton Valley, in Mount Currie, where they began to teach at the Indian Day School. They stayed there for over thirty years and also served in Chemainus, Chehalis, Church House and Iskut.

The sisters still work at the Anaham and Mount Currie missions, where they reach out to Native people living in the neighbouring reservations. They no longer minister to the sick under the conditions experienced by the first mis-

Sister Nurse with Native people, circa 1950.
Missionary Sisters of Christ the King, Quebec

sionary sisters but have adapted their ministry to the changing needs of the time. Today their concern and care extend to new forms of pastoral involvement among people trying to promote their physical and spiritual well-being.

In 1969 four Missionary Sisters of Christ the King were invited by Archbishop Duke to take over the administration of Holy Rosary Residence, a home for Catholic senior women in Vancouver's West End. The residence had been built just three years previously, in 1966, to accommodate forty-nine women.

Holy Rosary Residence was founded in 1962 by Archbishop Duke and Mother Elizabeth Chiorando, a Sister of Charity of the Holy Rosary.[62] Next door to the residence, the Sisters of Charity of the Holy Rosary had a convent that originally housed seven seniors until the facility was ready for occupancy. As Mother Elizabeth neared retirement, the Missionary Sisters of Christ the King, who benefited from Mother Elizabeth's experience, took over the facility.

In 1972 the Missionary Sisters of Christ the King purchased the residence and, in honour of its founder, renamed it Duke Residence. As the needs of the aging residents changed, the sisters turned the facility into a health-care operation, which necessitated hiring a nurse and other staff, including a dietitian. Over the years they served women of diverse ethnic and religious backgrounds, with full-time nursing care, doctors' visits, exercise therapy, religious services, music and entertainment. The forty-nine-bed institution finally closed its doors in 1995.

From 1977 to 1985 some Missionary Sisters of Christ the King also taught in the Archdiocese of Vancouver at Saint Paul's Elementary School in Richmond, and at Saint Jude's Elementary School from 1978 to 1995. Although no longer teaching in those parishes, they still serve in Saint Jude's parish, participating in pastoral and catechetical activities.

CHAPTER FIVE NOTES

1. Marie Cecilia Lefevre and Barbara Applegate, *A Woman of Vision: Marguerite d'Youville 1770–1771* (1982).
2. Ibid.
3. The name was given to her by Pope John XXIII on her beatification in 1959.
4. *Catholic Health Association of British Columbia Anniversary Booklet 1940–1990* (The Little Printer Ltd.), 23.
5. Sister Margaret Teresa, *Recollections of Our Mission in Ladner, BC* (Sept. 16, 1933).
6. Ibid.
7. Sisters of Service Archives, Toronto, Ontario.
8. Sisters of Service Archives, Toronto, Ontario, section 1, page 1.
9. *Rules and Constitutions of the Sisters of Service* (Toronto, 1934), 8.
10. "The Duty of Welcoming Others" (from the front page of the residence manual, Sisters of Service Archives, Toronto, Ontario), Appendix, Section II.
11. Other communities of women religious in Vancouver were already providing those types of services to girls in difficult situations, namely the Religious of the Good Shepherd and the Sisters of Charity of the Immaculate Conception.
12. "The Duty of Welcoming Others" (from the front page of the residence manual, Sisters of Service Archives, Toronto, Ontario), Appendix, Section II, p. 2.
13. Sister Lita Camozzi, 1985 (Diocese of Nelson Archives).
14. Sister Isabel Ellis quoted in the *Vancouver Province*, May 18, 1972.
15. Rosemary Kent-Barber, *Impressions of Vancouver Club* (booklet, July 1960), 6.
16. Sister Leona Trautman, (Sisters of Service Archives, Toronto, Ontario), Section III, p. 1.
17. "Along the Cariboo Trail: Dedicated to the Sisters of Service" (from unidentified newspaper article, Sisters of Service Archives, Toronto, Ontario).
18. Sister Catherine Donnelly, "The Shepherd of the Cariboo in Canada: Today on priest has parish with seventy-five missions" (Sisters of Service Archives, Toronto, Ontario).
19. Ibid.
20. Sister Catherine Donnelly, Diary Notes, May 30, 1934, p.7.
21. Talk given by Sister Faye to the Catholic Womens' League in Regina, 1937 (typewritten), 2-3.
22. Sister Catherine Donnelly "The Shepherd of the Cariboo in Canada: Today on priest has parish with seventy-five missions" (Sisters of Service Archives, Toronto, Ontario).
23. *Community History Sisters Adorers of the Precious Blood—Monastery of "Our Lady of Hope" in the Diocese of Nelson, British Columbia* (letter from Bishop W.E. Doyle to community of Precious Blood in Nelson, Sept. 8, 1962), 16.
24. See "Chapter Two, Religious of the Good Shepherd" for clarification of these terms.
25. *History of the Vancouver Foundation of the Sisters Adorers of the Precious Blood*, p.7.
26. Ibid., 18.
27. Ibid.,.45.
28. Ibid., 49.
29. Holy Communion consists of hosts and wine.
30. *Community History Sisters Adorers of the Precious Blood—Monastery of "Our Lady of Hope" in the Diocese of Nelson, British Columbia* (letter from Bishop W.E. Doyle to community of Precious Blood in Nelson, Sept. 8, 1962), 17-18.
31. See "Chapter Four, Missionary Sisters of the Immaculate Conception."
32. A novena is a devotion that continues nine consecutive days of recitation of specific prayers.
33. This refers to a home for abandoned children.

34. Father Alphonsus Hoban, "The Society of the Atonement as a Missionary Society: The Western Canadian Experience" in *Heritage Bulletin* (May 1984), Vol. I, No. 6, p.7.

35. Sister St. Raphael (Rita Casavant), "Report on the New Denver Mission" (Missionary Sisters of Our Lady of the Angels Archives, Lennoxville, Quebec).

36. Ibid.

37. Franciscan Friars and Sisters of the Atonement Centennial 1898–1998 (booklet, Sisters of the Atonement Archives, Graymoor, New York), 5.

38. Ibid., 6.

39. Ibid., 14.

40. Sister Mary Stella O'Melia, Biography, (Sisters of the Atonement Archives, Graymoor, New York), 27.

41. Sister Antoinette McDonough, "The Society of the Atonement as a Missionary Society: The Western Canadian Experience" in *Heritage Bulletin* (May 1984), Vol. I, No. 6, p.14.

42. "Happenings in Vancouver with the Evacuation of the Japanese in 1942," article in *Candle* magazine (1948),16.

43. "A Gathering of History from our Missions in British Columbia" (Archives of the Franciscan Sisters of the Atonement, Graymoor, Garrison, New York, 1998).

44. Father Alphonsus Hoban, "The Society of the Atonement as a Missionary Society: The Western Canadian Experience" in *Heritage Bulletin* (May 1984), Vol. I, No. 6, p.7.

45. Ibid.

46. Sister Antoinette McDonough, "The Society of the Atonement as a Missionary Society: The Western Canadian Experience" in *Heritage Bulletin* (May 1984), Vol. I, No. 6, p.15.

47. "A Gathering of History from our Missions in British Columbia" (Archives of the Franciscan Sisters of the Atonement, Graymoor, Garrison, New York, 1998), 26.

48. Sister Antoinette McDonough, "The Society of the Atonement as a Missionary Society: The Western Canadian Experience" in *Heritage Bulletin* (May 1984), Vol. I, No. 6, p.15.

49. Father Alphonsus Hoban, "The Society of the Atonement as a Missionary Society: The Western Canadian Experience" in *Heritage Bulletin* (May 1984), Vol. I, No. 6, p.8.

50. Marcia Harris from the Canadian Messenger of the Sacred Heart, February, 1949.

51. Sister Regina Koelzer, "The Society of the Atonement as a Missionary Society: The Western Canadian Experience" in *Heritage Bulletin* (May 1984), Vol. I, No. 6, p.13.

52. Slocan City (1943–1946), 91.

53. September Issue Newsletter, August 2-3, 1996, (the Japanese Cultural Centre, Toronto, Ontario).

54. Simone Poissant, *Mother Frederica Giroux* (Montreal, Quebec, 1985) 36.

55. See "Chapter Four, Missionary Sisters of the Immaculate Conception."

56. Simone Poissant, *Mother Frederica Giroux* (Montreal, Quebec, 1985), 105.

57. Ibid., 109.

58. *The Missionary Sisters of Christ the King in the Diocese of Nelson, BC, 1943–44* (written for Diocese of Nelson Archives 1986 Golden Jubilee), 2.

59. Ibid., 60.

60. Excerpt of letter from Sister Noella Bourgeois to Miss Nishiguchi, July 10, 1992.

61. Simone Poissant, *Mother Frederica Giroux* (Montreal, Quebec, 1985) 111.

62. Community founded by Archbishop Duke in 1949, dissolved in 1954, reorganized in 1956 and ended when the last surviving member died (Catholic Information Centre Archives).

PART III

Contemporary Times

1946 to the Present

CHAPTER SIX

Changing Habits
The Changing Social Climate of British Columbia

atholic sisters began providing social services to British Columbians when the first sisters set foot on the shores of Victoria in 1858. Since those early years the tales of adventure and stories of hardship of countless Catholic women religious continued to bring education, health care and numerous forms of social assistance to people of all faiths throughout the vast region of British Columbia. Apart from contributing to a rich spiritual legacy in British Columbia, these selfless women helped to create a vital social net for all those who fell through what little mesh existed.

Following the Depression years and the Second World War, a public attitude of social equality began to emerge in contemporary Canadian society. It became manifest in federal government aid programs such as unemployment insurance (1940) and family allowance (1945), and also emerged in provincial assistance programs such as the British Columbia Hospital Insurance Service (1949). Economic aid from governments helped to alleviate discrepancies between the wealthy and underprivileged in an attempt to provide a minimal standard of living for every person.

The Catholic sisters had founded and operated numerous charitable institutions throughout British Columbia by the time a social welfare system was finally initiated in British Columbia. Some of their charitable institutions could now benefit from government assistance programs. Other facilities such as parochial schools still depended largely on the involvement of Catholic sisters for their continued operation and did not benefit from provincial assistance until the late 1970s.

Following the Second World War the provincial government also attempted to eliminate social inequalities. Between 1874 and 1931 the Japanese, Chinese, Native people, East Indians, Mennonites and Doukhobors had been disenfranchised. Between 1947 and 1952 the provincial government granted these groups voting privileges. In 1947 the immigration policy also changed, repealing the Chinese exclusion act of 1923 and allowing Chinese Canadians to bring their families to Canada. In 1951 the federal Indian Act was re-examined and resulted in the integration of Native children into provincial "white" schools. Indian agents were replaced by band councils in a move toward First Nations autonomy. By 1969 the Official Languages Act formerly recognized an important aspect of French-Canadian identity.

French-speaking Catholic women religious made up the vast majority of sisters who came to British Columbia in the nineteenth century. As members of a religious and ethnic minority they experienced various hardships and, like all women in the province, endured political disempowerment until they were allowed to vote in 1917. Despite these circumstances, Catholic sisters remained focused on ministering to those in need and continued to render charitable services to the disenfranchised and underprivileged.

As early as the mid-nineteenth century the Sisters of Saint Ann taught First Nations children and African-Americans. At the turn of the twentieth century the Religious of the Good Shepherd ministered to orphans and outcasts. In the early 1920s the Missionary Sisters of the Immaculate Conception assisted the elderly and poor Chinese immigrants, and by the late 1920s the Sisters of the Atonement had begun to help the Japanese. By the 1930s the Sisters of Service were caring for young immigrant women while the Grey Sisters of the Immaculate Conception were caring for elderly destitute men. In the 1940s four communities of women religious came to the aid of the Japanese sent to evacuation camps—the Missionary Sisters of Christ the King, the Sisters of the Atonement, the Missionary Sisters of Our Lady of the Angels and the Sisters of the Assumption of the Blessed Virgin Mary.

The Changing Religious Climate

The period after the Second World War resulted in not only social and economic change, but also change in religious life. In an endeavour to respond to the modern world, the seat of religious government in Rome started the move toward adaptation to contemporary life. The seeds of revolutionary change were sown in 1950 when the Vatican department responsible for the Sacred Congregation for Religious convened its First General Assembly of Religious in 1950.[1] In 1965 Vatican II decreed the "Adaptation and Renewal of Religious Life" and thus initiated the framework for structural change that would profoundly affect the lives of women religious in the modern world: "The adaptation and renewal of the religious life includes both the constant return to the sources of all Christian life and to the original spirit of the institutes and their adaptation to the changed conditions of our time."[2]

The Vatican message focused on living life as exemplified in the Gospel teachings, being faithful to the original spirit of the founder of the institute and promoting the education of religious members to adjust to the needs of the Church and modern society.

As requested by Rome, a general chapter was held to interpret the directive for change. Each community of women religious implemented reform appropriate to their circumstances. Apparently Rome anticipated only minor changes, but the resultant change was of an order of magnitude far beyond expectations. Although the issues involving adaptation were many and complex, the most visible reality to the outside world was reflected in the change of habit.

It was during this period that a number of congregations of Catholic women religious arrived in British Columbia. The communities discussed in this chapter represent some of the congregations that came to British Columbia between 1945 and 1958, the centennial of the arrival of the Sisters of Saint Ann's to British Columbia. One of the first of these communities was the Congregation of Our Lady of the Cenacle, which came from the United States.

The Congregation of Our Lady of the Cenacle
Saint Therese Couderc Inspires the Religious of the Cenacle

The Sisters of the Congregation of Our Lady of the Cenacle were empowered by the spiritual leadership of their foundress, Mother Therese Couderc (Marie Victoire Couderc 1805–1885). At the time of their founding in France in 1826, the community was called the Sisters of Saint Regis, a name associated with the shrine of Saint John Regis in La Louvesc, France. Thousands of people visited this shrine every year. The sisters responded to the needs of the visiting pilgrims by opening their first Cenacle, a shelter and place of spiritual retreat for women on pilgrimage.

Their response to this worthy need scattered the seeds that flowered into the retreat ministry of the

Marie Victoire Couderc 1805–1885.
Religious of the Cenacle, Vancouver

241

Cenacle. The name, the Congregation of Our Lady of the Retreat in the Cenacle, was suggested by a French Jesuit in 1846 who based the work of retreat in the mystery of the Cenacle: "Scripturally, it was in the "coenaculum"—the dining room (that upper room) where Jesus, joined by his friends in the last supper, left a legacy of love and service. After the Ascension,[3] in this upper room (Cenacle), Mary, the apostles and the holy women awaited, in prayer, the coming of the Holy Spirit on the first Pentecost."[4]

Mary in the Cenacle and waiting in prayer for the coming of the Holy Spirit is the model for the Religious of the Cenacle, personally and in their ministry. Inspired by her exemplary figure, the sisters enabled women on pilgrimage to further their spiritual growth. The success of their retreats encouraged them to continue their spiritual ministry to women pilgrims and enhanced the growth of their religious community.

Although Mother Therese Couderc was appointed superior general, she held this position for just a short time. She continued to actively participate in the ministry of retreats after she was replaced, inspiring her companions and those she encountered with a spiritual energy and humility that prevailed long after her death. Mother Therese was canonized in 1970. Her words remain with the Sisters of Our Lady of the Cenacle to this day: "I have but one desire: that God be glorified and that he may be especially glorified by our little congregation."[5]

Not long after Mother Therese Couderc's death, and after fifteen convents were established in France, Italy and England, the religious community of the Cenacle boldly set out for the United States to begin their first mission in New York. They arrived in North America in 1892, but it was not until 1947 that these women religious set foot on Canadian soil. At that time two houses were opened, one in Toronto, Ontario, and the other in Vancouver, British Columbia.

The Beginning of the Cenacle in Vancouver

In 1941 Archbishop Duke asked the Congregation of Our Lady of the Cenacle to open a retreat house in his Vancouver diocese. Because of difficulties during the war years, the sisters were unable to accept his invitation. Six years later Mother Ida Barlow, provincial superior of the Cenacle of the Midwest, contacted the archbishop to determine if their services were still needed. The day the archbishop received their letter he also received a letter of acceptance from the Sisters of Christ the King, whom he had asked to begin retreat work in the Diocese of Vancouver. As retreats were the special work of the Cenacle, the archbishop relieved the Sisters of Christ the King of their obligation and wrote to the Sisters of the Cenacle asking, "How soon can you come?"[6]

In an effort to locate a site for their new mission, on February 2, 1947, Reverend Mother Ida Barlow and her companion, Mother Quinlan, boarded the train in Milwaukee, Wisconsin, and headed for Vancouver. Heavy snowfall extended their trip and they arrived fifteen hours later than expected. When the weary sisters arrived, the Sisters of Providence, who "were kindness itself," accommodated them at Saint Paul's Hospital. The travellers stayed for only one week and could not find a property large enough to satisfy the needs of their new mission. The sisters returned to Vancouver that summer, when their real estate agent had arranged for them to view a number of houses.

The sisters decided that if on this trip they found nothing suitable, they would abandon all hope of opening a Cenacle retreat house in Vancouver. On their last day of searching, with resignation and heavy hearts, the sisters were driving through Shaughnessy Heights, an elite neighbourhood of Vancouver. Mother Ida Barlow pointed to a house, commenting, "There is the kind of house I would like. It is large and has plenty of ground."[7] Although the house was not advertised for sale, the real estate agent stopped and inquired. The last load of furniture had just been removed and the house was to go on the market the next day. Their search had ended.

The sisters received word from their motherhouse in France enabling them to purchase the stately 1910 mansion, originally built for the A.E. Tulk family and with a long history of distinguished residents. The architect of the house was the acclaimed Samuel MacLure and among its well-known residents was Lieutenant Governor Fordham-Johnson. Now the Sisters of the Cenacle would be added to that distinctive list of residents.

On August 11, 1947, Reverend Mother Ida Barlow, Sister Quinlan and Miss Maristella Trainor left Milwaukee, Wisconsin, and boarded a morning train for their new residence in Vancouver. On the train they said their prayers together and then had meditation. They ate lunch at noon in their seats but in the evening ate supper in the train's dining car. On the second day they delighted in the spectacular scenery of Montana, recording in their travel journal, "... the canyons, the mountains, the deep ravines, the trestles, the rivers and the streams are all stupendous and kept our thoughts in God and his attributes."[8]

To the delight of the sisters, the train made an unscheduled stop at Saint Regis, the namesake of the beloved shrine where their community originated. In Saint Regis they met one priest who waxed eloquent of Saint Regis himself and another who was reading the life of their foundress, Saint Therese Couderc, with whom he was deeply impressed. They continued by train to Seattle. In their journal they recorded, "... we piled into two taxis with our ten suitcases and a big box with 'Our Lady's' statue and ... our electrolux."[9]

From Seattle they journeyed by boat to Vancouver: "As we turned into Vancouver harbour we stood in silent awe and bewilderment at the immensity of it all , the majesty of the towering mountains on three sides, the beauty of the panorama...The city spread out on three sides with a backdrop of tall snow-capped mountains. It was a sight worthy of the long trip."[10]

When the sisters arrived in Vancouver, their beautiful new convent seemed immense, as they had no furnishings. They spent their first night sleeping on cots with bedding provided by the Sisters of Providence from Saint Paul's Hospital. The following day they received an invitation from the Sisters of the Precious Blood to join them in the celebration of Mass—thus beginning many years of friendship with their neighbours who lived just around the corner.

The Sisters Prepare Their House for Retreats

Before the retreat apostolate in Vancouver could begin, the sisters had to prepare the house and grounds for retreatants. They organized painters, carpenters and other tradespeople to renovate the house and garden. They hired a man to steam clean the brickwork around the house and a gardener to tidy the grounds. Slowly they began to acquire furniture for all the rooms, including the dining room and library, for which they received books from the United States.

Neighbours, friends and other religious brought the sisters flowers, fruit, vegetables, preserves, linen, furniture and many other useful items for their new convent retreat house. "Rosemary" began to take shape.[11]

The house was blessed on the feast of the Guardian Angels by Archbishop Duke when he celebrated the first Mass in their chapel. Up until this time the sisters arose every morning at 6:30 to celebrate Mass at the nearby Convent of the Precious Blood or they went to the parish church. When the archbishop arrived they took the opportunity to ask him to assign a chaplain and soon after, Father Francis Hill was appointed, allowing Mass to be said every day in their new retreat house chapel.

A number of nearby religious communities had already come to visit the sisters and affirmed interest in spiritual renewal for themselves and for those to whom they ministered. Among the first to visit the Sisters of the Cenacle were the Sisters of Saint Ann, who lived only a short distance away and taught at Little Flower Academy. They were interested in offering retreats for the girls at the academy. The Sisters of Saint Joseph of Toronto from Saint Patrick's School in Vancouver also visited the Cenacle, as did the Sisters of Charity of the Immaculate Conception from Saint Vincent's Hospital. The Sisters of Service requested a private retreat for one of their sisters, and the Sisters of Providence called soon after to request a private retreat for one of their postulants.

By mid-October the archbishop approved the Cenacles Sisters' plan to extend luncheon invitations to pastors and directors of diocesan organizations in the area. Thirty visiting religious clergy arrived to enjoy the hospitality of the sisters and view the new retreat house: "There was great interest and amazement at the beauty of the house and how well and comfortably all had been planned and arranged. All were certain that people would be anxious to come for retreats once they saw the physical beauty of the house and then would remain to enjoy the spiritual beauty of the house. The archbishop was like a proud father...and when he visited the chaplain's apartment he jokingly said to Father Hill, 'How are you ever going to keep the vow of poverty in this palatial place?'"[12]

To expand their potential group of retreatants, the sisters also sent letters and distributed pamphlets inviting parishioners to make a general retreat. In November they held an open house that allowed guests to visit the renovated house and garden, which the sisters had transformed into a serene and contemplative place for spiritual retreats. Although the sisters offered general retreats, they preferred directed retreats specific to the needs of individuals or the groups they were accommodating.

The sisters also held an open house for women religious of the Archdiocese of Vancouver. Thirteen convents in the area received invitations. While many attended, their cloistered neighbours, the Sisters of the Precious Blood, declined, as did the Religious of the Sacred Heart and the Good Shepherd Sisters due to their rule of enclosure.

A streetcar strike limited the opportunity for many of the sisters to attend. Fortunately the Grey Nuns from Saint Vincent's Shelter and the Missionary Sisters of the Immaculate Conception from the Chinese Mission sought private transportation, allowing them to take advantage of the first-time visit. Approximately forty sisters attended the open house and all were very impressed with the beautiful facility. They assured the Sisters of the Cenacle that they would spread the news of the new retreat site.

Spiritual Retreats in Vancouver

Imbued with spiritual strength originating from the legacy of the Cenacle, the sisters focused on the formation of faith. Their retreat ministry included individual spiritual direction, group discussions, days of prayer, seminars and ecumenical retreats: "We find God present in the ordinary experiences of life, and we try to help others to seek God there. We accompany women and men on their journey of faith as they grow in awareness of God's presence in their lives. They may be single or married, religious or priests, beginners on their journey or seasoned travellers. Gradually they come to find God present in their normal struggles of human growth and development..."[13]

Although the sisters offered spiritual retreats to both men and women, in the early years they focused on spiritual renewal for women because the Augustinian fathers in Ladner provided retreats for men.

Cenacle Sisters in the garden. Religious of the Cenacle, Vancouver

The sisters welcomed women of all ages, individuals and groups, including postulants, religious, schoolgirls, young working women, nurses, teachers, sodalities and many others. The Cenacle sisters also started guilds with members that came every month for a time of spiritual enrichment. The guilds were comprised of women with similar needs and interests—Married Women Guild, Business and Professional Women Guild, Young Business Women Guild, High School Guild and Ecumenical Guild.

Although the retreats varied in form and audience, they all shared one characteristic—the participants all wished to extend their stay. Thousands of women benefited from their experience at the Cenacle and departed from Rosemary with a sense of personal spiritual development. The Cenacle sisters provided this opportunity. As one retreatant remarked, "…from the time I first had contact with the Cenacle sisters, the thing that has struck me about them is their hospitality. Creating a welcoming space demands putting aside what normally fills that space—ourselves and our own needs—in order to let others in. Real hospitality requires a kind of dying that's largely unseen, but which yields an open space in which life can grow."[14]

Another commented, "It's difficult to separate the meanings the word 'Cenacle' has for me. It's a place to grow, to heal, to commit, but it also means 'our sisters'—the life-givers, the listeners, the sharers of God's space."[15]

Catechetical Work

An important feature of the Cenacle ministry was the catechetical apostolate. Each week the sisters taught preschoolers and grades one through eight, preparing them for the sacraments. They also welcomed high-school students and adults who came for instruction and spiritual help. Sessions for the formation of teachers of religion were offered regularly and were held in Vancouver and in Victoria and Prince George. Sisters Adelfinger and Grasso contributed much to the advancement of the catechetical movement in Vancouver by giving courses at the Cenacle Retreat House and various parishes throughout Vancouver. They taught teaching methods and provided the theological background for catechetics taught to the children.

Catechetics with the children. Religious of the Cenacle, Vancouver

The Sisters Change with the Times

Although the sisters found it initially difficult to interest the Catholic community in retreats, their success eventually necessitated further development of their property. To accommodate visiting chaplains and retreat masters they redesigned the "Shakespearean villa," which had been previously used as a stable and gardeners potting shed. They placed statues throughout the large garden and constructed an arbor walk around the lawn to encourage use of the grounds. The immense trees on the property contributed to the contemplative ambiance as well as to the community's enjoyment at seasonal events like walnut shelling time.

The garden also became the site of strawberry teas, which later became garden parties that included booths, pony rides for the children, raffles of all kinds and a special fashion show feature. At the day's events over one hundred guests

Retreats in the modern world. Religious of the Cenacle, Vancouver

were served supper, followed by an auction in the evening. Over the years numerous volunteers assisted in the organization of the teas and garden parties with the money raised being used to maintain the retreat house and grounds. Later "appeal letters" replaced the need for fundraising through garden and tea parties.

The 1960s and 1970s were a time of expansion and growth for the Cenacle ministry in Vancouver. As people in British Columbia joined the trend of testing the limits of convention, including alternative spirituality, the Catholic Church also contemplated their place in the modern world. In the spirit of Vatican II and the changing times, the Cenacle sisters welcomed not only Catholics but a number of other Christian groups, Jewish persons and even transcendental meditation groups.

As did all women religious, the Cenacle sisters found empowerment in the words of their foundress: "I had, a few days ago, an insight which consoled me very much. It was during my thanksgiving, when I was making a few reflections upon the goodness of God ... I was extremely touched by these reflections when I saw written as in letters of gold this word 'Goodness,' which I repeated for a long time with indescribable sweetness. I beheld it, I saw written upon all creatures, animate and inanimate ... they all bore the name of goodness ... I understood then that ... we may meet it in everything and everywhere."[16]

For fifty years the sisters had welcomed thousands of women and men into the Cenacle Retreat House on Selkirk Street. The retreatants had come from the diocese, the lower mainland of British Columbia and the Pacific Northwest of the United States.[17] By the early 1990s, however, the house needed major repairs and renovations to conform to the city's building code. Even with renovation it was no longer suitable for the retreat ministry and in March 1994 the sisters announced their decision to sell the house and look for a smaller residence where they could continue their ministry in new ways.

After almost three years on the market, the house was sold in July 1996. The Grey Sisters welcomed the four Cenacle sisters to live in the top floor of Youville Residence while they looked for a new home. The Cenacle sisters lived there for two years while continuing their ministry as best they could.

In September 1998 they moved to their new residence on 5989 MacKenzie Street in the Kerrisdale area of Vancouver. There they continue their ministry of spiritual direction, prayer card office and small groups for morning or evening prayer. They also take their ministry outside the house, giving retreats in parishes, other retreat centres, CWL (Catholic Women's League) groups and home retreats.

> The Cenacle remains ever young
> For it radiates that which never grows old
> And because it rests on the essential realities
> It will never go out of style.[18]

Sisters of Providence of Saint Vincent de Paul
A Legacy of French Saints Inspires the Formation of an English-Speaking Community

Sister Philomene, the superior general of the French-speaking community of Sisters of Providence in Montreal, agreed to send some of her community's sisters to Kingston, Ontario, to lay the foundation for an English-speaking community there. They served at the request of Bishop E.J. Horan of Kingston, who applauded their accomplishments and wished to see similar work among the poor in his diocese. On December 13, 1861, four Sisters of Providence from Montreal arrived in Kingston. Under the guidance of their appointed superior, Mother Mary Blessed

Catherine McKinley, Mother Mary Edward.
Archives, Sisters of Providence of St. Vincent de Paul

Sacrament, they founded a new community of English-speaking Sisters of Providence.

For the next five years these four sisters initiated eight new candidates into religious life. They made home visits to the sick, cared for orphans, worked in the prisons and solicited funding to ensure those they cared for were adequately clothed and fed. When the eight candidates had been trained, the four French-speaking sisters returned to Montreal. The Kingston convent was called the House of Providence and the congregation, the Sisters of Charity of the House of Providence.

The first of the four candidates to profess her religious vows was Mother Mary Edward (Catherine McKinley), who became the general superior of the new community. In 1866 the group gained official status as an independent community of women religious, eventually becoming known as the Sisters of Providence of Saint Vincent de Paul. Mother Mary Edward was a wise and compassionate leader who carried forth a vision that saw the new establishment grow and flourish.

The English-speaking community embraced the spirit of the Canadian-founded Sisters of Providence begun by Mother Emilie Gamelin in 1843. And like their French-speaking counterparts, they also embraced the spiritual heritage of Saint Vincent de Paul and Saint Louise de Marillac. Their general superior, Mother Mary Edward, exemplified this spiritual tradition by guiding the new community for eighteen years. She endured "the hardships of pioneering...[and] the exhausting collecting tours...So much attention has been given to Mother Mary Edward's executive ability and success in financing projects that her love and consideration for the needy may have been overlooked. But letters show that the material progress was not uppermost in her thoughts."[19]

The mission statement of the new congregation reflected the same spiritual devotion of their seventeenth century predecessors and expressed commitment to the virtues of humility, simplicity and charity: "Impelled by the compassionate love of Jesus and Mary, we seek to empower others, especially the poor and oppressed, to achieve a quality of life in keeping with their human dignity. We strive to be prophetic leaders in our Church and in society through the promotion of structures and relationships of equality and mutuality and through attitudes and actions for justice and peace. Strengthened by prayer, we are bonded in unity and love through our corporate mission."[20]

In 1952, just a few years after opening their first mission in Vancouver, the community incorporated the name of Saint Vincent de Paul into their title and became the Sisters of Providence of Saint Vincent de Paul.

The Sisters Open Holy Family Hospital in Vancouver

In the mid-1940s the city of Vancouver responded to the increased health-care needs of its expanding population by asking the archbishop of Vancouver to find sisters to establish another hospital in the city. In the autumn of 1946 Archbishop Duke invited Mother Mary Anselm (Egan), the superior general of the Sisters of Providence of Saint Vincent de Paul, and her assistant, Mother Mary Zita (Welsh), to make a visit to Vancouver while on tour of their western missions. During their visit the archbishop asked them to inspect a property that he thought might be suitable for a hospital for chronically ill and aged women, and he asked them to start this health-care mission in Vancouver.

In January 1947, with the approval of Archbishop O'Sullivan of Kingston, the sisters wired their accep-

Early Sisters at Holy Family Hospital.
Archives, Sisters of Providence of St. Vincent de Paul

tance to the archbishop of Vancouver. The three-acre property at 7801 Argyle Drive in Vancouver was purchased for $9,800 and became the site of Holy Family Hospital.

Sister Mary Dolorosa (Bekar) was appointed superior and arrived in Vancouver with Sister Mary Catherine (Dooley), Sister Mary Ita (Coleman) and Sister Mary Alacoque (Scott) on April 29, 1947. They focused on the immediate task of renovating the empty two-storey house on the property into a hospital, although their long-range plan was to build a 250-bed hospital and convalescent home.

The sisters converted the English-style cottage into a fifteen-bed facility and by October 12, elderly women were comfortably accommodated in Holy Family Hospital. Shortly thereafter, the two-storey hospital reached its capacity of fifteen. These patients were unable to pay for their health care and the nominal sum the sisters received for their care from the Social Service Department of Vancouver was insufficient to meet costs. The sisters helped to pay the bills by selling flowers that grew on the property.

Holy Family Hospital, Vancouver. Archives, Sisters of Providence of St. Vincent de Paul

Land for construction of a new fifty-two-bed hospital was procured by purchasing an additional lot adjoining the Argyle Drive property, which increased the sisters' site from three to five-and-one-half acres. Approval for hospital construction was delayed, however, until city hall could appease Fraserview neighbours concerned with the hospital's potential for obstructing their view.

On March 21, 1954, Archbishop Duke and the Honorable Eric Martin, the minister of health and welfare, officially opened the new hospital. A few years after its opening, the *Vancouver Province* newspaper reported: "Holy Family is a hospital for chronic cases, but most of its patients are elderly. It can accommodate fifty-two patients, all women. Last year it was able to discharge back to normal life sixty-six patients. It was able to do this because it assumes and acts as though old people were intended to live and function, and not just lie in bed or sit in a chair awaiting death. I talked to almost every patient in the place, and I could feel the hope that was in them. The love there was almost visible; the practical help most certainly was."[21]

After the new hospital opened, the sisters transformed the original Holy Family Hospital into a boarding home called Marian Villa. The main floor accommodated six women and the upper floor served as the sisters' quarters, their first bedrooms since they arrived seven years prior. Up until this time, to accommodate the elderly patients the sisters had been sleeping under the stairways of the first Holy Family Hospital.

In 1961 the hospital was recognized as a rehabilitation hospital and the sisters began planning for an expansion. The opening of the new addition took place on June 20, 1976.

From the earliest days of their mission, the sisters sought help from one of four original patron saints, Saint Elizabeth of Hungary, the patroness of aged and infirm women. It appears her spirit became part of the work of the sisters. Holy Family Hospital became recognized as a geriatric rehabilitation centre for the province of British Columbia and is a fully functioning care facility for the elderly today.

Sisters of Saint Joseph of Hamilton
The Sisters of Saint Joseph Expand from Toronto to Hamilton

The first community of the Sisters of Saint Joseph originated in LePuy, France, in 1650 when the sisters opened a hospital for orphans and homeless women. They disbanded during the French Revolution and were re-established in 1816 by Mother Saint John Fontbonne at Lyons, France. Twenty years later, in 1836, the congregation expanded to North America, where the sisters established a foundation in Carondelet, Missouri. From there a group of sisters were appointed in 1851 to the community's first mission in Canada.

The sisters had been in Toronto for only one year when Vicar General Gordon invited them to assist with orphan children in the Hamilton area, rekindling the spirit of their predecessors' mission. Three sisters left the Toronto house for the new mission in Hamilton under the guidance of Sister Martha Von Bunning, their superior.

The sisters began working with Hamilton's orphans and within two years they found themselves in the midst of cholera and typhus epidemics, caring for the sick and dying and preparing the dead for burial. Although the sisters were in constant contact with the victims, they maintained their health. None contracted the virulent diseases.

The Sisters of Saint Joseph established a novitiate in their motherhouse at Saint Joseph's Convent in the Diocese of Hamilton in 1856. The following year, they decided to build a larger motherhouse to accommodate the increasing number of entrants. It was established on Park Street in Hamilton.

By the turn of the century the sisters had established a number of branch houses throughout Hamilton. In addition to taking a key role in starting the separate school system in Hamilton, the sisters opened an orphanage, two hospitals and two houses of providence.

The Sisters Open a New School at Fort St. James Indian Reserve

Almost one hundred years after arriving in Canada, this Hamilton-based religious community made its way to the West to begin a mission at Fort St. James Indian Reserve in British Columbia. Sister M. Kentigern Brady, the superior of the community, was accompanied by a nursing sister, Sister M. Pauline Monoghan, and two teaching sisters, Sister Francis Xavier Ruth and Sister Eulalia Marie Robinson. They arrived in September 1950 and opened a school that had an initial enrolment of forty-five students.

Apart from regular classes the sisters taught catechism and offered classes that prepared students for the sacraments of Holy Communion and confirmation. The sisters organized an informal program of extracurricular activities for the young single girls. It included singing and dancing lessons, which the sisters thought to be successful in reducing what they referred to as the natural shyness of the girls.

Sister Pauline, who came to provide nursing services, accomplished a great deal in the six years she worked in Fort St. James. She visited the Native women on a number of surrounding reserves and assisted them in childbirths. To celebrate in

Sister Pauline Monaghan in the baby clinic, 1952. Archives of the Sisters of St. Joseph of Hamilton

the joy of parenting, Sister Pauline organized baby contests and distributed gifts to all the parents. She set up a small dispensary in the school and accompanied patients to Prince George when they required hospital services. She also opened a small clinic on the reserve to serve people both on and off the reserve. Sister Pauline also initiated a homemakers club where, she taught women how to make quilts.

The four founding sisters contributed a total of twenty-one years of service to the mission. Many sisters in their community continued with the spirit of their initial work, providing nursing and educational services for the Native people at the mission. In July 1969, the sisters left the reserve.

The Sisters at Fort Saint John, Dawson Creek, Chetwynd and Terrace

Three Sisters of Saint Joseph of Hamilton arrived in Ft. Saint John on September 3, 1954. Five days later, they registered eighty students for school. Sister M. Saint Brigid Hayes acted as both superior of the convent and principal of the school. Sister M. Helena Kroeplin taught at the school along with Sister M. Michaeleen Callaghan, who taught music lessons after school and on Saturdays.

These sisters' extracurricular activities for the students included concerts and music festivals. They also taught catechism classes and prepared the children for the sacraments of Holy Communion and confirmation. In addition they participated actively in parish work and ministered to Native people on the surrounding reserves. The sisters operated the mission at Fort St. John for thirty-four years, finally closing it in 1988.

In 1976 Sister Margaret Kane and Sister Anne Karges arrived in Dawson Creek and opened Notre Dame School. Both taught at the elementary school, where Sister Margaret was principal. Outside of formal teaching activities, the sisters coordinated a religion program for teenagers of the parish, and the high-school youth groups that developed from the program were very successful. The sisters also visited the sick, prepared children for the sacraments and held retreats for teenagers, single women and married couples. When classes were out for the summer, the sisters taught catechism to the Native people at Kelly Lake. This mission continued until 1982, when the sisters left for other missions.

From 1977 to 1981 Sister Gemma Kernick acted as pastoral assistant in Chetwynd, where she taught catechism to Catholic children attending public school.

By 1988 the Sisters of Saint Joseph of Hamilton had closed all of their missions in the West. At that same time Sister Anne McLoughlin arrived in Terrace to direct Saint Joseph's Centre of Spiritual Growth. Sister Anne McLoughlin was instrumental in starting the companions' program, which allowed parishioners to learn more about the spiritual charism of the sisters and become more involved in the sisters' communal prayer life. Sister Anne McLoughlin directed retreats and workshops and opened her home to those who needed time alone. She continued her work until 1992, when she was the last Sister of Saint Joseph of Hamilton to leave the province.

Sisters of Holy Cross
Brothers and Sisters Form a Family of the Holy Cross in Canada

Leodacie Gascoin, Mother Mary of the Seven Dolors 1818–1900. Archives of the Sisters of St. Joseph of Hamilton

In 1837 Basil Moreau founded the Congregation of Holy Cross in Le Mans, France. Connected with this congregation of male religious were a group of women religious called the Congregation of the Marianites of Holy Cross. They originated in 1841 and under the direction of their founder, Basil Moreau, the early Marianites provided domestic services for the priests and brothers. As time went on the sisters moved away from domestic service and began to devote themselves to education and the care of the sick. The religious family of Holy Cross adhered to the spiritual values of the early community: "...there is a spirituality proper to the religious family of Holy Cross...the spirit of unity and confraternity...[22] We strive for a congregational sense that encompasses not only our local communities and our respective provinces, but all our sisters throughout the world. Our spirit of unity likewise extends to all the members of the family of Holy Cross and to our brothers and sisters in the Church. The strength that results from such unity enables us to accomplish together our common mission of love and service."[23]

Mother Mary of the Seven Dolors (Leodacie Gascoin, 1818–1900) directed the first Marianites of Holy Cross. She continued the formation of her companions in religious life until 1847, when she left France to establish a new congregation in Canada. She was appointed superior of the Sisters of Holy Cross at Saint Laurent near Montreal, and by 1883 this Canadian congregation had become autonomous under the name Sisters of Holy Cross, with provincialates in 1902 in Edmonton, Ottawa, Montreal and the New England states.

The Sisters Arrive in Moricetown to Teach the First Nations Children

Bishop Anthony Jordan, the Prince Rupert vicariate, first asked the Sisters of Holy Cross to work at the Babine Lake Reservation in 1952. Due to lack of available sisters, they could not go. Additional requests for sisters in British Columbia came again in 1953 and 1954. Monseigneur Antoniutt, the apostolic delegate to Canada, pleaded with Mother Mary of Saint Rose, the superior general, to send sisters to help the Native children in British Columbia. By 1956 Reverend Fergus O'Grady,

The first four Sisters of the Holy Cross, Moricetown reservation, 1956. Archives of the Sisters of St. Joseph of Hamilton

who had succeeded Bishop Jordan as the vicariate, had again asked the sisters to come to Moricetown. This request was met with a positive reply.

The first day of school. Left: Sister M. Andrew of Jesus (Swaile). Right: Sister M. Miriam Hilda (Curran). Archives of the Sisters of St. Joseph of Hamilton

In 1956 Sister Andrew Apostle, Sister Thomas Becket, Sister Andrew of Jesus and Sister Miriam Hilda left their motherhouse in Ottawa, Ontario, and boarded the train for Jasper, Alberta. From there they drove by car to Moricetown. On the way they stopped at LeJac Residential School to visit the Sisters of the Child Jesus.

Like so many pioneers before them, they found their proposed quarters at the reservation uninhabitable. The Sisters of Saint Ann, who operated a hospital in Smithers, warmly welcomed the new missionaries and housed them until their residence was ready for occupancy. During the two weeks it took to prepare their new home, one of the townspeople drove the sisters twenty-five miles every day to the reservation in Moricetown.

The four sisters moved into a two-bedroom house attached to the school. Its electricity came from a generator that rarely worked. Although the bathroom was equipped with fixtures, "there was no water. It had to be hauled by the barrel from the river for use both in the school and in the house."[24] The physical conditions made life difficult enough but to add to their troubles, in an attempt to keep the sisters away, the previous teachers had circulated a petition. Unaware of this situation, the sisters befriended the people and they in turn responded warmly toward the sisters.

Once settled in Moricetown the sisters operated the reservation school, where approximately sixty-five children were registered. Sister Miriam Hilda taught with Sister Mary Andrew of Jesus, who was appointed principal. Few of the young children could speak or understand English and their parents did not allow them to speak it at home. This made communication and teaching difficult, as did the children's sporadic attendance.

While the two sisters taught, Sister Mary Andrew Apostle organized a church choir and found a number of enthusiastic singers. She also organized the Moricetown Club House, where she educated women about "budgeting, health and cleanliness." Health and cleanliness were particular sources of concern, given the only access to water in the village was a single tap. While the three sisters assisted the Native people, Sister Thomas Becket took charge of the sisters' household, preparing meals and also attending to the upkeep of the chapel.

The Sisters Move to Smithers, Lake Cowichan and Maillardville

In 1959 the sisters moved into the town of Smithers to teach at the parish school of Saint Joseph's. The Native children of Moricetown took a bus every day into Smithers to learn beside white children in an integrated school, a phenomena of the early fifties that attempted to integrate Native children into the Canadian mainstream. Preschool children, however, remained at Moricetown. For twenty years Sister Bertha Cruikshank drove every day from her home in Smithers to the reservation to teach the younger children. In 1983 the sisters withdrew from their mission due to lack of personnel.

In August 1967 Reverend John Callaley requested three Sisters of Holy Cross to teach catechism and do some social work in the parish of Saint Louis de Montfort in Lake Cowichan on Vancouver Island. In August 1968 Sister Margaret Fleming, Sister Jean Goulet and Sister Eveline Swaile arrived in the parish to begin work.

Weekly catechism classes for elementary and high-school children began in September for the small lumber towns of the area—Lake Cowichan, Youbou,

From left: Sisters J. Goulet, M. Fleming and E. Swaile arrive in Lake Cowichan, 1968.
Archives of the Sisters of St. Joseph of Hamilton

Honeymoon Bay and Cayacuse. Once a month, travelling along logging roads, the three sisters crossed the island to conduct classes in Port Renfrew. Classes for both adults and adolescents were well attended and in a short time a church choir also began in Lake Cowichan.

Eight sisters worked in the area for fifteen years. Toward the end of those years the number of priests in the area began to dwindle and the sisters then became involved in assisting the parishioners in coordinating the activities of the parish.

In all, twenty-nine Sisters of the Holy Cross served the missions in British Columbia. The last of the twenty-nine sisters taught at Our Lady of Fatima School in the French-speaking community of Maillardville. In 1968, at the request of Father Guy Michaud, three Sisters of Holy Cross came from Alberta to teach at Our Lady of Fatima School. Sister Therese Michaud was named principal of the elementary school and arrived on August 22 with teachers Sister Alice Desfosses and Sister Suzanne Baron, who also came to teach at the school. They lived in a house overlooking the Fraser River with a magnificent view of Mount Baker. Their garden, typical of West Coast gardens, provided them with ample fruit from apple, plum and pear trees, and with numerous flowers. The sisters moved three times until, in 1975, the parishioners built a home for them at 351 Walker Street.

Sister Alice taught grade one until 1974, when the sisters set up a kindergarten and then a preschool. Three years later she began teaching catechism classes to grades four, five, six and seven students:"The superintendent of public schools asked if he could send some of his teachers to observe Sister Alice's teaching as she was an inspiration to them."[25]

A qualified chef, having graduated from Northern Alberta Institute of Technology, Sister Alice also gave lessons in gourmet cooking to the public and to the women of the parish.

Sister Suzanne began teaching grade one but went on to teach the older children art classes. She excelled in painting and working with clay. Sister Suzanne recognized the need to preserve their children's French-Canadian language and in 1970 she started a choir called Chante Clair. She encouraged eighteen young children to sing in their native language. Sister Suzanne moved back to Montreal and in 1971 a laywoman, Evelyn Christie, took over the direction of the children's choir. Taking inspiration from Sister Suzanne's work, Evelyn subsequently founded an adult choir called Les Echos du Pacifique.

Leaving behind their inspiring and innovative service, the sisters departed from Maillardville in 1977.

Sisters of Mercy
Mother Mary Catherine McAuley Begins Her Work of Charity

Mother Mary Catherine McAuley (Catherine McAuley, 1778–1841) filled her life with works of charity and concern for the poor in her native country of Ireland. At the age of forty-four she inherited a fortune from her adoptive parents and became a wealthy woman. Catherine used her inheritance to help the poor to help themselves and her influence survived long after she died: "She was a woman for all times who, with the genius of love, was sensitive to the inadequacies of her society and who created structures to meet contemporary problems of social misery,

The Venerable Catherine McAuley 1778–1841.
Irish Sisters of Mercy in British Columbia

social injustice and religious intolerance ... she showed her readiness to renounce wealth, comfort, offers of marriage and social position and to accept instead cold, hunger and want."[26]

Five years after Catherine acquired her inheritance she constructed a building on Baggot Street in Dublin, Ireland. The building specifications provided for "schoolrooms, dormitories for working girls, an oratory and living-quarters for herself and for the associates she hoped to attract to her enterprise."[27] This House of Mercy on Baggot Street opened in 1827 and became the first convent of the Sisters of Mercy: "I never intended founding a religious congregation. All I wanted was to help the poor because that seemed to be what God was asking of me."[28]

As the foundress of the Sisters of Mercy, Mother Mary Catherine McAuley focused on educating the poor, especially women. During her life she suffered a good deal of criticism, at first for her adherence to the Catholic faith and later for the "impropriety of a woman encroaching on such masculine prerogatives as business, finance, philanthropy and religious foundations."[29]

Mother Mary Catherine McAuley made no apology for putting her ideas and skills to work to help those in need. Indeed, she influenced many women to join in relief work. She and her companions became known as the walking nuns and eventually grew to be one of the largest congregations of women religious in the English-speaking world. Although Mother Mary Catherine McAuley initiated her work in Ireland, a century-and-a-half later, twenty-two thousand Sisters of Mercy worldwide were emulating her practical and spiritual ideals.

The first Sisters of Mercy who came to Canada arrived in Newfoundland in 1842. Inspired by the centuries-old spirit of their pioneer sisters, they carried out the good works of Catherine McAuley. The first Sisters of Mercy, however, to arrive in British Columbia did so over a century later, in 1957.

The Irish Sisters Come to the Diocese of Prince George

Mother Alphonsus, Sister Gonzaga, Sister Peter, Sister Clare and Sister Anthony answered the request of Bishop O'Grady, who had gone to Ireland to recruit the sisters and frontier apostles for the building and staffing of the Catholic schools of his diocese.

The sadness of leaving behind family, friends and their religious community in Ireland was soon replaced with the excitement and anticipation of beginning a new mission in a foreign country. Unlike their counterparts a century earlier, who endured the perils and hardships of long journeys across the ocean and expansive unexplored territory, the modern pioneer sisters began their adventure with a space-age flight across the Atlantic.

The sisters marvelled at the luxury of travelling by air. Their hosts on KLM airline contributed to the sisters' enjoyment by inviting them to view the mountains from inside the cockpit with the pilots. In their travel journal the sisters describe the novelty of being served their meal on the plane:

> ...we also got a little packet of "Life-savers" each. They are sweets something like Fruito. We are coming down gradually now the end of our journey by air, Deo Gratias! May he give us all the grace and strength we need to start to-day our new work for Him. We are facing it with smiling Irish eyes and very willing spirits, so here on "wings" of Faith and Hope, we wish each other all the best, and send our love back to dear old IRELAND! The Captain got a message just now to say that there will be TV camera men below waiting to "shoot us"! We must remain 'till last getting off the plane. Did you ever hear the like?![30]

The Irish Sisters of Mercy arrive at Vancouver Airport, 1957.
Irish Sisters of Mercy in British Columbia

Upon their arrival in Vancouver on August 28, 1957, the Sisters of Mercy "gazed in wonderment at the millions of coloured electric light advertisements twinkling from beginning to end of every street. The cost of these ads, must be tremendous. The city is huge. In one of the parks we saw a flood-lit fountain, the water reaching up about twenty feet. The colours changed every second. The streets are very straight and wide. The whole city seemed to be on fire with these electric advertisements."[31]

The Sisters of the Child Jesus of North Vancouver met the Sisters of Mercy at the airport and provided overnight hospitality. The sisters went on to Fort St. James the next day, stopping en route north to visit the Sisters of Providence in Vanderhoof. One of their final travel-journal entries mentions the difficulty of writing in a car travelling on bad roads, concluding "this is real bush country."

When the sisters reached their destination they found their convent was not yet complete. The Sisters of Saint Joseph of Hamilton, who had been in Fort St. James for seven years, offered them accommodation. When they finally moved into their own convent, they found themselves stoking its sawdust stove and painting plywood walls.

Once settled, the sisters began adjusting to new ways of living quite unlike those of their native Ireland: "Just imagine, moving a big school-room on a truck! Whole houses are moved from one place to another by the same method in these parts."[32]

One year after the sisters began teaching at the integrated school in Fort St. James, three more Sisters of Mercy from Ireland arrived in British Columbia. They were to teach in the integrated school in Vanderhoof, which also served children from the Stoney Creek Reserve. Sister Paul, Sister Dominic and Sister Emmanuel departed from Ireland on the *Saxonia* on July 31 and continued by train to Vanderhoof. There they taught in Saint Joseph's School, which had just been built. They also became quickly involved with the local people in every aspect of their lives.

In 1960, two years after the opening of the new school in Vanderhoof, a new parish, Saint Mary's, and a new school were established in Prince George. Three sisters, Sister Mercy, Sister Stanislaus and Sister Regina, arrived from Ireland to teach in the school. In 1988, at the request of the archbishop of Vancouver, the sisters moved south, opening a house in Richmond and in Burnaby. There they were engaged in full-time pastoral work.

Over the past four decades, more than forty Sisters of Mercy have lived and worked in British Columbia. Some came for short periods of time, others came for long periods of time, while some of the original groups returned to Ireland. Their teaching ministry included going to remote Native villages to help missionary priests instruct children in religion and prepare them for the

Sacraments. Later their ministry expanded to involvement in pastoral work, including Eucharistic ministry to seniors, the sick and shut-ins; hospital visitations; bible study programs; renewal programs; prayer groups and grief counselling.

Sisters of Charity of Saint Louis
A Countess Becomes a Woman Religious

Countess Marie Louise Elizabeth Mole, Mother St. Louis 1763–1825. Provincial Archives Sisters of Charity of St. Louis, Edmonton

Immediately after hearing of her husband's execution at the guillotine in1794, Countess Marie-Louise Elizabeth Mole (Mother Saint Louis, 1763–1825) consecrated her life to God. During their married life, the count and countess had been known for their generous assistance to the poor and the countess would continue that generosity as a widow and religious. The grief-stricken wife and mother consoled her children upon their father's death. She would take action on her vow to dedicate herself to God only after her children were adults, turning her attention to ensure their care before that. As Mother Saint Louis recounts in a letter to one of her children: "The priest who announced to me your father's death, witnessed at that very moment, the sacrifice I made to God of my liberty so cruelly recovered. The accomplishment of this sacrifice was only delayed to enable me to fulfil my duties towards you, presiding at your education and establishment."[33]

Within a decade Mother Saint Louis had drawn up the constitutions for a new congregation of women religious called the Sisters of Charity of Saint Louis. The name of the congregation memorialized Saint Louis IX, a French king well known for his charity toward the poor. Now as a religious and foundress, the countess assumed this name as her own.

In an effort to alleviate some of the suffering caused by the Revolution, the sisters' first mission in Vannes, France, provided destitute orphan girls with free room and board, employment, education and means to support themselves in the future. Mother Saint Louis reported on her work to the minister of cult and worship (church affairs) in 1816: "In my house, I receive one hundred girls who are provided with everything both in illness and in health. My purpose has been to teach them the principles of religion . . . also to accustom them to read, write, and keep accounts . . . I have established workshops for lace-making and cotton-spinning . . . The success of this undertaking has far exceeded my hopes"[34]

Her success at Vannes prompted a request for a similar house in Auray in 1807. In 1816 she initiated the foundation of another house at Plechatel, again furthering her objective to educate poor girls. Mother Saint Louis established yet another house in Saint Gildas de Rhuys in 1824, the year before she died. The Sisters of Charity of Saint Louis continued with her work, establishing houses across France and in 1898, in England.

Mother Saint Louis was direct in urging others to continue her work: "It is not enough for a soul to be consumed by divine love . . . it is also necessary that this love be translated into action"[35]

Coincident with the anti-clerical laws of France and the developmental needs of North America, the Sisters of Charity of Saint Louis began their first education mission in Canada in 1902. From there, they expanded south into the eastern and western United States. By 1913 they had travelled west across the Prairies to establish the first Catholic school in Medicine Hat, Alberta. In that same year they answered a request for teachers in Moose Jaw, Saskatchewan. The sisters established missions in Haiti in 1945 and in Madagascar in 1956. In 1958 they would arrive in British Columbia.

The Sisters Come to Burnaby

Between 1951 and 1961, the population of greater Vancouver had almost doubled and Archbishop Duke of Vancouver decided a new Catholic school in Burnaby was warranted to meet the growing need. Construction of a number of new residential subdivisions in Burnaby spurred him to purchase property at Tenth and Holmes streets, on the boundary between Burnaby and New Westminster. The land was bought from the BC Electric Company and the corporation of Burnaby.

Construction started in May 1958, and five months later a new school and rectory were complete. To the delight of the parish, 123 students registered at Saint Michael's School, which opened on September 8, 1958.

The Sisters of Charity of Saint Louis accepted the invitation to teach at the new elementary school and selected three sisters for the mission on the Pacific

The 1958 "Pioneer Sisters," from left: Sisters Rose of the Child Jesus, Jane Frances and Sister Carmella de Jesus, Holy Cross, Moricetown. Provincial Archives Sisters of Charity of St. Louis, Edmonton

coast. Sister Jane Frances, who held a bachelor of education degree, was named the school's first principal. Sister Carmella de Jesus served as homemaker. Sister Jane Frances taught grades five and six, while Sister Rose of the Child Jesus, taught grade one. Two lay teachers completed the staff to teach grades two, three and four. Eventually a convent and Saint Michael's Church were built on the four-acre property.

In 1965 the Sisters of Charity of Saint Louis built Marian High School for girls, underwriting the $275,000 cost of the new six-room structure with their teacher salaries. The sisters taught university entrance courses and general programs of commerce and community service. The plan for the high school accommodated expansion to six more classrooms, plus full facilities for home economics, science and commerce.

The Sisters of Charity of Saint Louis remained on the teaching staff at Saint Michael's school until 1977. In 1978 they sold Marian High School to the Archdiocese of Vancouver, although they continued to teach there until June 1985.

Apart from teaching, the sisters were involved in pastoral care at Saint Mary's Hospital in New Westminster, as well as catechetics, counselling, elderly care, and prison and parish ministry. By 1995 the sisters were no longer working in the Burnaby or New Westminster area, but one sister was employed at the Vancouver School of Theology.

In 1986 two sisters joined a mobile team for Native ministry in the Okanagan Valley, serving Native groups at Westbank, Penticton, Oliver and Keremeos. Four other sisters extended their team's services of pastoral care and parish ministry to Oliver and Penticton. Their ministry in the Okanagan continues and has expanded to Abbotsford, where one sister has assumed the role of chaplain in the Matsqui prison.

Since their arrival in 1958, a total of thrity-seven Sisters of Charity of Saint Louis have provided services for British Columbia residents. In 1994 the sisters told the *Western Catholic Reporter*:

> Wherever the Congregation has expanded, education among the disadvantaged has been a priority. However, as needs in our society change, so too do the forms of education in which we are involved ... Since Second Vatican Council, many sisters became involved in parish ministry, retreat centres and Catholic leadership formation centres for adults ... Although the sisters no longer stand out with a distinctive habit we believe and hope that our life of dedication ... as expressed through works of mercy and justice will bring others to ... experience the love of God ... There have been changes, shifts and upheavals in religious life ... If religious life is to continue to be a vital force, we know dramatic changes must occur ... We struggle ... to read the signs of the times so that we might make a generous and faithful response ... We believe in the value of communal life, a life that may have diverse and expanded forms of expression. We believe in authority and leadership that encompasses a feminine consciousness, perspective and style ... In this fast-moving world we are not merely victims of change; we wish to facilitate change that is beneficial and transformative ... Like other congregations, we know that we can die because new forms of religious community life are needed. We can resist that change or willingly undergo the deaths that lead to a totally new life ... A new paradigm for religious life is struggling to be born ...[36]

The Sisters of Charity of Saint Louis eloquently expressed the profound changes that began about the time of their arrival in British Columbia and which continue today.

Entry into the Modern World
A Change of Habit
More than twenty congregations of Catholic women religious arrived in British Columbia between 1959 and 2000. Like their predecessors, these women blazed trails, but the modern world challenged them with new frontiers and a demand to keep pace with contemporary society.

This direction had been initiated in the early 1950s by Pope Pius XII, who was concerned about the decreasing numbers of religious vocations in Europe and cited restrictions and archaic customs of religious communities as the causes. The outmoded customs and traditions of religious communities were brought into question. These concerns and questions resulted in Vatican II directing religious communities in 1965 to "adapt and renew" religious life in accordance with the modern world.

Although interpretations of the changes varied among communities of religious, one of the most personal yet public and visible expressions of women religious was about to change: "In pre-Vatican II days, we were almost completely culturally different from our contemporaries. We wore dress that could in no way be confused with secular clothes."[37]

The habit of women religious traditionally consisted of a long loose robe belted at the waist with rosary beads. On their heads they wore a coif and veil. Variations of this basic theme denoted membership in a particular community. The habit signified commitment to a spiritual and communal way of life.

Wearing the habit originally embodied the notion of being "dead to the world" and was a response to the calling. Wearing the habit designated entry into religious life and commitment to the vows of poverty, chastity and obedience. It meant leading a life separate from secular society, notably in terms of distinct spiritual virtues. Although religious communities had undergone relatively little change in appearance for decades, and in some cases centuries, a radical transformation was about to take place.

The documents Vatican II put forth in 1965 initiated a tumultuous time of change; they seemed to unravel the base of spiritual virtuosity for women religious. First, they emphasized that all members of the Church had received the same call to Christian life by virtue of their baptism, and second, they stated that the Church was to be in solidarity with the world.[38] These tenets seemed to suggest that women religious were equal with the Christian laity, contradicting or at least mitigating the previous perspective that women religious could come closer to attaining spiritual excellence upon entering religious life. The documents seemed to undermine a previous premise by asking religious to adapt to and become more a part of the world, rather than remain separate from it. This brought the question of dress to the fore.

In celebration of their centennial in 1954 the Sisters of Charity of the Immaculate Conception provided some insight into their perception of the "holy habit": "The modern world sometimes wonders at the anachronism of a medieval religious habit at the desk of administration, in the science laboratory or at the wheel of a car; but the habit is the symbol of the abiding need for dedication, discipline and self-control ... It is all a part of the story of the mustard seed, the living organism that is the Church, destined to grow and spread its branches, ever adjusting itself to the changing environment while guarding the unchanging spirit of Christ."[39]

Although most communities of women religious changed their habits by the late 1960s, they did so with varying degrees of acceptance. Sister Mary Rose McVarish recalled the first day of wearing the new habit in public:"The Feast of Pentecost was a memorable day this year as we all appeared with the first change of the habit—the collar. All accept the change in a spirit of obedience but it was with some reluctance that the old was replaced by the new. Now all are quite contented with the renovation."[40]

Reactions by the laity were mixed. The first day of wearing the habit in one institution caused such a stir that the sisters went throughout the facility modelling their new dress so that work could continue and the commotion in the ranks of the laity would be calmed.

Suzanne Kidd had been a student at Saint Helen's School from 1960 to 1967. She returned as a teacher ten years later and had this to say about the changes she saw in the Sisters of Charity of Saint Vincent de Paul of Halifax:"They were out of the long black habit, coif and veil and the children could see that they did indeed have legs, and under their veils they had hair like everybody else. Surely we must have known it too, only there was such an aura of mystery and awe about the sisters that we didn't often credit them with human characteristics."[41]

Transforming Residence and Ministry

> Periodically throughout their history, Roman Catholic religious orders have undergone significant periods of growth and decline, often triggered by political or economic changes in secular society.[42]

The declining numbers of women religious in British Columbia were part of a trend that swept North America after Vatican II. The political, social and economic developments of the modern world, as well as the Church's response to it, created a new set of circumstances for women religious that resulted in their decreased numbers.

The Sisters of Charity of Saint Vincent de Paul of Halifax cited declining numbers when recalling the history of their ministries in their western province: "Numerically, the high water mark for the province came in 1965 with a total of 150 sisters. Then the numbers began to dwindle, slowly at first but rapidly after the General Chapter of 1968. Under the new missioning policy of the congregation which took into account the preferences of the sisters, more transferred from West to East than vice versa. There were no longer sisters available to fill the many teaching positions for which the congregation had once taken some responsibility."[43]

While some women religious chose to leave their communities during this time of turmoil, those who remained adapted their lives to the modern world and shaped the direction of their community.

The initial withdrawal of members from communities coupled with the lack of new entrants resulted in a demographic change. Toward the later part of the twentieth century an elderly population of women religious became more noticeable, with very few new replacements. Religious life appeared to come full circle for women religious in British Columbia.

When the first religious communities came to British Columbia, they arrived in small groups of three or four. They often found accommodation in a small house, which they converted into a convent. The convent frequently incorporated a school, hospital, orphanage or other social institution until a new facility could be built. The sisters either remained in the institution with a separate living accommodation for themselves, or they occupied a convent in close proximity to the institution they operated. Variations of this developmental pattern typified many active congregations of women religious throughout British Columbia.

Toward the end of the twentieth century, however, large convents were past their prime and underpopulated. Women religious began to search for new accommodations more suitable to their reduced numbers. They once again began to live in small groups in single family residences, or sometimes by themselves in apartments. These changes paralleled a change of ministry.

The trend after the mid-1970s was toward individual apostolates. Individual members of communities of women religious began to take control of their own destiny by looking for employment that both met the needs of the surrounding community and matched their own particular skills and interests. Their ministries began to diversify, becoming less concentrated in education and health care, although still related to various aspects of these traditional fields.

The ministries of these self-directed women religious included parish and diocesan work, as chaplains and tutors in federal and provincial institutions, as spiritual directors, and as facilitators of encounter groups and other self-directed social-service activities. Like so many of the sisters who struggled to adjust to the post Vatican II era, the Sisters of Mercy reported changes in their religious lives:

> … There will also be a move from the convent back to the community. The plan is for groups of four and five sisters to move into 'ordinary houses in ordinary places,' closer to the people who need them. And there will be a shift away from their traditional spheres of influence. 'Whereas in the past we were very much associated with institutional

ministries like schools and hospitals, in the future we hope to minister to people in the community'. Though still very concerned about education and health care, [the sisters] feel the need to change with the times...Now we have to look and see where else we might be needed. But we are not doing this to further our own preservation. It's really about more effective deployment of resources for the help of others...In preparation for this, many sisters have completed counselling training in specialist areas including Aids, addictions, feminism and ecology. This work will complement the traditional missionary work abroad undertaken by the sisters...[44]

Spiritual Influences

> ...The seeds of the future lie in the past and in the present...a sense of collective memory is basic to both our identity and to the realization of our dreams...It is basic to our dreams by turning them into directions.[45]

Women mystics throughout history found strength through their profound spiritual experiences, which endowed them with authority to speak, teach and influence people.[46] The individual efforts of these powerful women were played out in various ways over the centuries, but each created a legacy for the future. Saint Scholastica, who inspired the Order of Benedictine Sisters, and Saint Clare, who founded the Order of Saint Clare, were followed by Saint Marguerite Bourgeoys, who organized the Congregation of Notre Dame in Montreal, and Saint Marguerite d'Youville, who founded the Grey Sisters of the Immaculate Conception. These four women are just a few examples of the many sisters who have inspired countless women to enter into the spiritual realm of religious life.

Although non-religious factors influenced membership in communities of Catholic women religious, piety and spirituality were the primary factors for entering religious life in the nineteenth century.[47] Many women were inspired by mystics who founded communities of women religious. These inspirational role models provided the opportunity for contemporary women to succeed in their ideals by becoming members of a particular community centuries later. Each community of religious lives the "charism," a particular spiritual focus or identity developed by the community's founder.

The charism of the community was handed down through its members through oral tradition, personal letters, writings and example, enabling the foundress' ideals and spirit to be kept alive and new members to continue her tradition. The memory of the foundress was not merely nostalgic, but rather a collective living memory that provided the community its future direction. "I saw my sisters listening attentively to stories of 'the olden days', the heritage of the past, and I realized that they drew their vitality from our family history."[48]

Although a distinct charism did not appear to take on the same importance in congregations founded in the nineteenth century,[49] preserving the memories of the mystics, charismatic leaders and women who embraced their ideals is still of the utmost importance today for women religious and for society as a whole.

Reclaiming Women's History

> The long and slow advance of women intellectuals toward group consciousness and toward a liberating analysis of their situation proceeded in a spasmodic, uneven, and often repetitive manner. Marginalized from the male tradition and largely deprived of knowledge of a female tradition... women's creations sank soundlessly into the sea, leaving barely a ripple and succeeding generations of women were left to cover the same ground others had already covered before them.[50]

Only recently has society begun seriously to address the role of women in history. As Gerda Lerner pointed out in the late 1970s, "The first challenge of Women's History to traditional history, is the assertion that women *have* a history."[51]

Catholic women religious, particularly, have been given little recognition for their involvement in and contributions to society. Ruth Compton Brouwer notes that "the historical study of women and religion needs to pay more attention to matters of theology and personal spirituality. It also needs to broaden its range to include women who are not middle-class Protestants."[52] Even the Catholic Church devotes little space to the roles and contributions of Catholic women religious in its historical accounts.

Women religious richly deserve recognition for their place in history. The wealth of information found in the historical accounts of women religious can contribute to the appreciation of both the individual and communal identity of women religious and the broader social context of their lives. Acknowledgement of women's history allows memories of the past to provide a source of direction for the future. The mystics and charismatic leaders of the orders can provide role models for future generations of women.

Recounting the past is a powerfully important notion in understanding the spiritual origins of communal life, the contextual development of women religious and their impact on society. It is just as important for society today to acknowledge the historical contributions of women religious as it is for sisters to document their work in contemporary society. The integrity of their accomplishments should be recognized with pride.

Contemporary women religious vary in their interest and motivation to chronicle and acknowledge their history. Many communities, particularly the older communities, have established archives and are striving toward maintaining standards of excellence in these facilities. Preserving and compiling written documentation is the first step in acknowledging women's history and in providing a frame of reference for the future.

Reclaiming Women's History through Historic Preservation

Some of the most valuable artifacts of Catholic women religious cannot be preserved in the archives. These are the numerous institutions built throughout the province of British Columbia beginning in the mid-nineteenth century. These icons of the past represent the works of love, compassion and mercy of Catholic women religious who have significantly contributed to British Columbia.

Since women religious have discarded their habits, society cannot recognize their work in the same way it did before Vatican II. Before Vatican II, the sisters were recognized by their anachronistic habit. They presented themselves and their work as part of a living legacy. The witness of the habit publicly acknowledged, on a daily basis, their spiritual commitment and their connection to the past.

Even the nineteenth-century sisters heralded a habit similar to those communities founded much earlier. George C. Stewart remarked that in Antebellum America, "[r]eports circulated widely during epidemics about sisters in habits nursing and entering infected homes when no one else would. Even lukewarm Catholics swelled with pride on seeing sisters going about their business. The "witness of the habit" had a profound impact."[53]

Worldwide, the sisters long preserved their history and heightened society's awareness of their work by preserving their habit. The determined and loving women religious of British Columbia brought part of a centuries-old spiritual legacy to the West. Their manifestations of that legacy are strongly represented in the economic, social and cultural history of British Columbia, and also in its visible environment.

The private lives of women religious were made public through the construction of the facilities in which they carried out their charitable services. Their buildings are powerful witness to their courageous spirit and communal strengths.

Recently, "reclaiming women's history through historic preservation"[54] has been identified as an important and powerful tool in the public awareness of women's history. The declining numbers and seeming disappearance of women religious from contemporary society, combined with the pressures of development, make urgent the need for action on the preservation of the historic structures built by British Columbia's women religious. The stately and venerable edifices founded by the sisters are priceless examples of the work of women religious whose contributions to British Columbia should not be forgotten.

CHAPTER SIX NOTES

1. Patricia Wittberg, *The Rise and Fall of Catholic Religious Orders: A social movement perspective* (Albany: State University of New York Press, 1994), 210.
2. Second Vatican Council Decree on the adaptation and renewal of the religious life, October 28, 1965 (National Catholic Welfare Conference, 1312 Massachusetts Avenue, NW, Washington, DC), 3.
3. Christ's ascension into heaven.
4. Sisters of the Cenacle pamphlet, Vancouver, BC.
5. St. Therese Courderc.
6. Chronicles of the Congregation of Our Lady of the Cenacle, 1947–1949, Vancouver, BC.
7. House Journal of Our Lady of the Cenacle, Vancouver, BC, 1947–1949.
8. Ibid.
9. Ibid.
10. Ibid.
11. The former owner of the house, Mr. A.E. Tulk, named the house "Rosemary" after his daughter.
12. House Journal of Our Lady of the Cenacle, Vancouver, BC, 1947–1949 Oct. 23, 1947.
13. Sister Margaret Mayk and Sister Barbara Regan, *The Congregation of Our Lady of the Cenacle* (Rochester, NY: St. Vincent Press), 6.
14. Ibid., 17 (quote by Roberta McInerney, retreatant).
15. Ibid., 8 (quote by Sharon Johnton, retreatant).
16. *Women of the Cenacle* (Convent of Our Lady of the Cenacle, Milwaukee, Wisconsin, 1952), 52–53.
17. Until 1957 the sisters had offered retreats to a number of women who came from the Pacific Northwest of the United States. But when the Visitation Retreat House opened in the Seattle-Tacoma area, the sisters considered it unethical to recruit women from south of the border. They redirected their efforts to increasing the involvement of parishes and other groups.
18. Sisters of the Cenacle pamphlet, Vancouver, BC.
19. Sisters of Providence of St. Vincent de Paul Spiritual Heritage, September 1992, pp.27–28.
20. Mission Statement of Sisters of Providence of St. Vincent de Paul, Archives, Kingston, Ontario.
21. *The Sisters of Providence of St. Vincent de Paul* (Palm Publishers, 1961), 125.
22. The Religious Family of the Holy Cross (pamphlet/brochure) 1987, p.34.
23. Constitutions of the Marianites of Holy Cross, 1983.
24. Sister Mary Andrew of Jesus (Eveline Swaile), (notes on the history of the sisters at Moricetown, November, 1998).
25. Sister Therese Michaud, 1996, Sisters of the Holy Cross, p.2.
26. Sister M. Angela Bolster, *Catherine McAuley in her own words* (Wexford: John English and Co. Ltd., 1978), 18.

27. Ibid., 22.
28. Ibild., 24–25.
29. Ibid., 29.
30. Sister of Mercy Journal notes, 1957, Vancouver, BC, p.7.
31. Ibid., 4.
32. A Special Report with the *Irish Times*, May 18, 1994.
33. *Our Source—Our History Sisters of Charity of St. Louis Handbook* (Provincial Archives, Calgary, Alberta), p.17.
34. Ibid., 43–44.
35. Ibid,. 139.
36. "A religious order describes its call" in *Western Catholic Reporter*(February 7, 1994), 21.
37. Patricia Wittberg, *The Rise and Fall of Catholic Religious Orders: A social movement perspective* (Albany: State University of New York Press, 1994), 252.
38. Ibid., 214.
39. *Laus Deo! 1854–1954 Centennary of the Sisters of Charity of the Immaculate Conception* (Archives of the Sisters of Charity of the Immaculate Conception, Saint John, New Brunswick), 71–72.
40. Sister Mary Rose McVarish, author of article titled "History" (Vol II from Archives of the Sisters of Charity of St. Vincent de Paul of Halifax, Halifax, Nova Scotia).
41. Suzanne Kidd (Bowering) St. Helen's School Celebrating Sixty Years of Tradition 1923–1983, p.21.
42. Patricia Wittberg, *The Rise and Fall of Catholic Religious Orders: A social movement perspective* (Albany: State University of New York Press, 1994), 40.
43. Sister Marilla Silver, "Ministry in the Western Province 1923–1978 (paper prepared for Congregational Ministry Weekend, October 1978, Long Island, New York, from Sisters of Charity of St. Vincent de Paul of Halifax Archives, Halifax, Nova Scotia), p.3a.
44. A Special Report with the *Irish Times* May 18, 1994.
45. Sister Jane Klimisch, *Women Gathering: The story of the Benedictine Federation of St. Gertrude* (Toronto: Peregrina Publising Co., 1993), 7.
46. Gerda Lerner, *The Creation of Feminist Consciousness* (New York: Oxford University Press, 1993), 88.
47. George C. Stewart Jr., *Marvels of Charity: History of American Sisters and Nuns* (Huntington, Indiana: Our Sunday Visitor Publishing Division, 1994), 176.
48. Landmarks in the History of the Canadian Church 1987 from the Congregation of the Sisters of the Assumption of the Blessed Virgin, Nicolet, Canada.
49. Patricia Wittberg, *The Rise and Fall of Catholic Religious Orders: A social movement perspective* (Albany: State University of New York Press, 1994), 48.
50. Gerda Lerner, *The Creation of Feminist Consciousness* (New York: Oxford University Press, 1993), 220.
51. Gerda Lerner, *The Majority Finds its Past: Placing women in history* (Oxford: Oxford University Press, 1979), 169.
52. Ruth Compton Brouwer, "Transcending the 'unacknowledged quarantine': Putting Religion into English-Canadian Women's History," in *Journal of Canadian Studies* (1992), Vol. 27, No. 3, p.47.
53. George C. Stewart Jr., *Marvels of Charity: History of American Sisters and Nuns* (Huntington, Indiana: Our Sunday Visitor Publishing Division, 1994), 178.
54. First annual RCWHTHP conference (Reclaiming Women's History Through Historic Preservation), held in 1992 at Bryn Mawr College, Pennsylvania.

About the Author:

Deborah Rink's interest in women, history and the socio-spatial development of women has led to a decade of research, writing and lectures on Catholic women religious. Her thesis "Convents as Planned Communities" was the spark which ignited this seminal study. Deborah Rink was born and grew up in Saskatchewan, where she received a B.Sc. in Agriculture from the University of Saskatchewan. In 1990 she completed master's degrees in landscape architecture and urban planning at the University of Oregon. Deborah resides in Vancouver with her husband and daughter.